All information contained in this book and associated digital files (skp, dwg) are for educational purposes only.

All rights reserved. No part of this publication may be reproduced, distributed, stored in a retrieval system or transmitted in any form or by any means, including photocopying, recording, or other electronic or mechanical methods, without the prior written permission from the author.

The book is an informative guide and resource only. It is not intended in any way to be a substitute for the advice of a fully qualified professional who will apply their skill, knowledge and experience to the specific projects on which they are engaged.

It is the responsibility of the users of this guide to carry out their own due diligence when working up construction details, and to seek advice from fully qualified professionals.

Under no circumstances should any of the contents of the book be used as construction drawings or otherwise form the basis upon which any construction is built. Drawings must always be prepared, checked and verified by a fully qualified architect or associated professional having regard to the specific construction to which they relate.

The content of the book is based on the research, training and professional experience of the author and is true and complete to the best of their knowledge. Whilst to the best of the author's knowledge the content reflects current Building Regulation requirements within the United Kingdom as at the date of publication, it is the reader, architect, contractor or project manager's overall responsibility to ensure compliance and to seek approval from the appropriate Building Control Officers (or equivalent/alternative certifiers in jurisdictions other than the United Kingdom). No warranty is given or should be implied as to the accuracy of the information in the book for any specific application.

While every effort has been made to check the accuracy and quality of the information given in the book, the author does not accept any responsibility for the subsequent use of this information, for any errors or omissions that it may contain, or for any misunderstandings or adverse effects or consequences arising from it use.

It should be noted that only one of many permutations of thermal insulation type and positioning is shown in each example. Insulation requirements, performance, positioning, installation all vary according to manufacturer.

Materials and textures used in the 2D and 3D details have been selected for clarity of information – the materials or textures are not always an accurate representation of the colour of the element or product used in reality, and not all materials and textures are available everywhere.

For full terms of use please visit www.firstinarchitecture.co.uk/about/terms-of-use/

Copyright © 2022 by Emma Walshaw
ISBN: 978-1-7395952-2-7
First In Architecture

Emma Walshaw asserts the moral right to be identified as the author of this work.

Acknowledgements
A massive thank you to Aida Rodriguez-Vega for her contributions to the book.
Thank you to Johnathon Clous for his ongoing involvement in the UAD series and Richard Bollands of Home Extension Plans for his contributions to the book.

Contents

INTRODUCTION	4
BEFORE YOU START	5
ASSESS THE BUILDING	5
EXISTING BUILDING	6
ROOF TYPE	6
PARTY WALLS	7
CHIMNEYS	8
LOAD BEARING WALLS	8
FOUNDATIONS	8
PLANNING & PERMITTED DEVELOPMENT	9
PERMITTED DEVELOPMENT RIGHTS	9
NEW STRUCTURE	11
FLOORS	11
ROOF STRUCTURE	12
DORMERS AND ROOF EXTENSIONS	12
THERMAL PERFORMANCE	15
STAIRS	17
WINDOWS AND DOORS	18
MATERIALS, CHOICES AND LIMITATIONS	20
BUILDING REGULATIONS	22
FIRE SAFETY	22
BUILDING REGULATIONS NOTES	23
CONSTRUCTION DETAILS	24
GENERAL LOFT DETAILS	30
FRONT DORMER WINDOW DETAILS	50
REAR DORMER EXTENSION DETAILS	64
ZINC STANDING SEAM DETAILS	82
FACETED ZINC DORMER DETAILS	106
VELUX DETAILS	130
RESOURCES	138

INTRODUCTION

Understanding Loft Conversions is the fifth book in the UK "Understanding Architectural Details" series. Readers of the first four books have often requested a publication on extensions, retrofits and conversions. This is the first of those.

Understanding Loft Conversions, like the previous books, aims to simplify construction details and provide clear drawings and diagrams to demonstrate the building assembly. The book touches on assessing the existing building, planning and permitted development, along with building regulations. We look at how the new structure is implemented, different types of dormer options, windows and materials.

The real body of the book however, is the detail section. Here we demonstrate a selection of details in both 2D and 3D format to help guide and explain the different factors of a loft conversion.

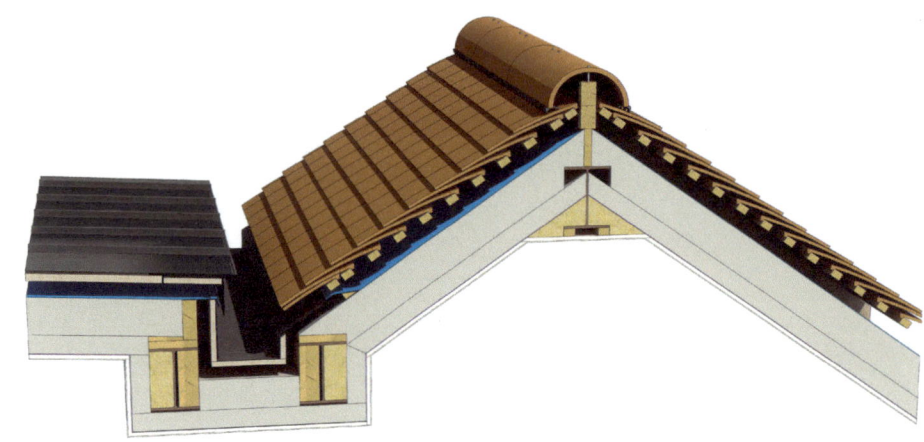

The book covers standard loft conversion details, front dormer window details and rear dormer extension details. The details also include some more contemporary constructions looking at zinc standing seam details and connections.

I hope that the book provides a good starting point for any architect, student, contractor or self builder looking to gain a better understanding of loft conversions, or find interesting details to consider for their next project.

Of course, the book does not claim to be a complete guide, or to include detailed building regulation, planning or design guidance, but rather an overview of the construction details for loft conversions.

I hope you find the book useful.

Emma Walshaw
First In Architecture

BEFORE YOU START

Assess the building

Prior to carrying out a loft conversion project, an assessment should be made on the existing building to assess the feasibility of creating a room or rooms in the loft space. This assessment will include looking at the existing structure, structural integrity, the roof space, head height, condition of the building, possible planning restrictions, and much more.

It is always recommended to engage professionals at the earliest point possible. An architect can guide you through the whole process from conception, planning, following the works, certifying work and post construction. They can also assist in appointing the professional team, design the best solution for you and your budget, maximising the loft space and ultimately the property. Architects can also survey the property to better understand the existing situation. Alternatively someone can be appointed to complete a measured survey of the house.

If the proposal requires any structural work, it will be necessary to appoint a structural engineer. They will propose a structural solution and calculations for the builder and building control.

A party wall surveyor may be required to advise and complete a party wall award. Within the Resources section on page 138, you can find a link to approved party wall inspectors.

Unless you are completing the works yourself, a contractor or builder will also be required. There are plenty of contractors who specialise in only loft conversions. If the loft works are being combined with general renovations or a ground floor extension, most residential building contractors will be able to carry out the work. An architect can help you in the process of finding and tendering for a contractor, making sure the price reflects the works required as well as inspecting the works during the build.

An architect or contractor can conduct an assessment of the property and assess the feasibility of it. It is also worth looking at the street the building is located and see if anyone else has converted the loft; this is usually a good sign that it can be possible, what types of loft extensions have been approved and what volume the council or permitted development rights allow. However, this is not always a guarantee.

The following sections go into further detail on some of the key features of loft conversions.

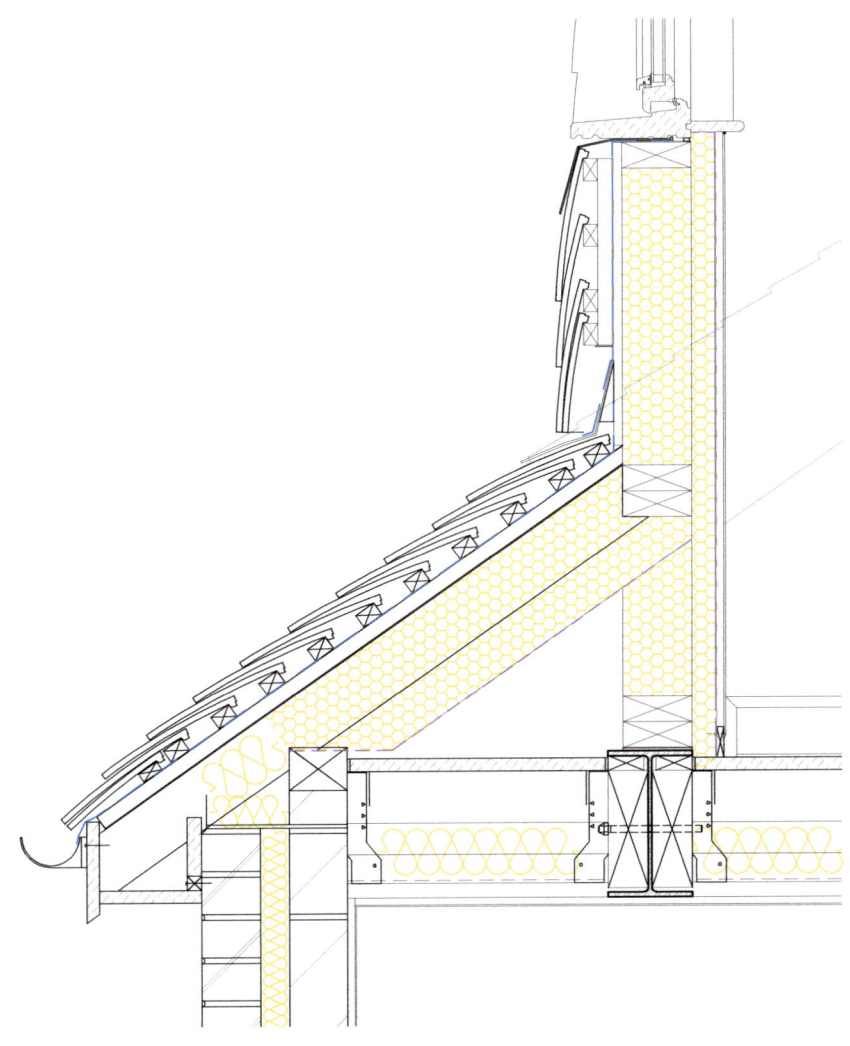

EXISTING BUILDING

It is necessary to carry out a survey of the existing building to assess the feasibility of the building for conversion. An on-site survey can quickly identify issues that will require further consideration or create potential high costs. Small inspection holes can also be a useful tool prior to construction to further understand the existing structure and services which are not visible. Unlike other areas of a house, existing lofts tend to have visible structure which make this process a little easier.

Some of the main areas of the existing building that need to be assessed are explored in the following pages [this list is not exhaustive, and requirements depend on existing building and location].

Roof Type

There are three main pitched roof types.
- Traditional cut timber roof
- TDA trussed roof
- Trussed rafter roof

Plus:
- Room in roof (RIR) truss
- Butterfly roof
- Lean-to roof

Traditional cut timber roof
This type of roof is most common in houses built before 1950, and consists of rafters and purlins spanning between load bearing walls. There are many variations of this type of roof depending on the pitch, size, distance between load bearing walls, age, and so on. This roof type tends to be the easiest to convert, generally having good headroom and an unobstructed loft space.

A structural engineer should advise on the existing structure of the roof and how to accommodate the proposed conversion.

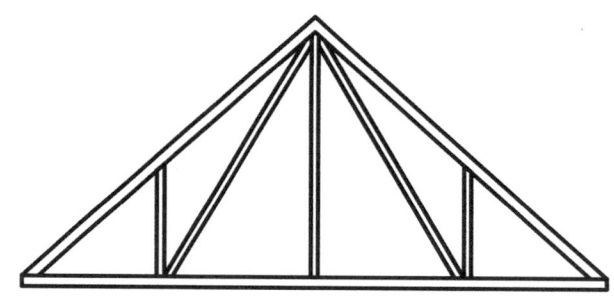

TDA trussed roof
Properties built after the Second World War often employed the TDA trussed roof, which uses less materials than the traditional cut timber roof, as at the time construction materials were in short supply. The trusses are spaced quite widely apart at about 1.8m, so you may only see two or three of these trusses within the roof space. These types of roof are considered more difficult to convert. It is advisable to obtain input from a structural engineer.

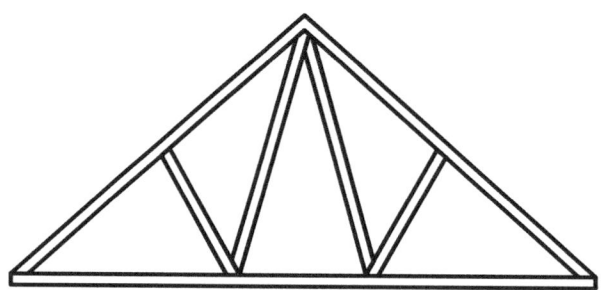

Trussed rafter roof
The trussed rafter roof was developed around the late 1960's, so many houses built since the 1970's are likely to have a trussed rafter roof. These are factory manufactured trusses, delivered to site ready to install. They can span good distances and use less material than the traditional timber roof. This type of roof is difficult to convert as it is not possible to cut areas of the truss to make space without the use of structural steel or timber reinforcement, or without compromising the integrity of the roof. The trussed rafter roof also tends to have a fairly shallow pitch with limited headroom which was fashionable at the time.

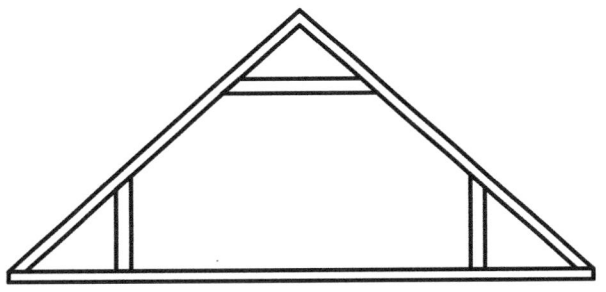

Room in Roof (RIR) Truss

RIR trusses are complete units that have the central area free, specifically to allow for a usable space in the roof. These trusses can be used in a trussed rafter roof conversion by replacing the existing roof trusses. These RIR trusses are now used more often in new build roof construction to allow owners to convert the loft space more easily in the future.

Butterfly roof

Also called 'inverted pitch roof', 'butterfly roof', 'v-shaped roof' and even 'London Roof', this is a surprisingly common type of roof. However, it is usually hidden behind a front brick parapet wall and is therefore not visible from the street. It may seem like a complicated roof structure to work with, but as the existing roof sits within two gable walls and the front parapet wall, most of the new roof structure and loft extension will also sit within these three walls and therefore have a solid footing.

Lean-to roof

This type of roof is normally found on existing addition at the rear of a property, known as outriggers. They are a single, sloping roof, usually attached to a taller wall.

Roof Condition

After establishing the type of roof at the property, it is important to note the condition of the roof. Will the existing roof require any work to ensure it is waterproof? Is there any sign of leakage or water damage? Will any tiles need replacing?

Roof Information

Assessing the roof space during the survey is an important task. Some other key areas include:

- Measure the space of the attic, taking as many dimensions as possible.
- Note the pitch of the roof and the general roof layout.
- Note any party or gable walls and the type of construction they appear to be.
- Are there water storage and header tanks? Note the location and dimensions.
- Note any pipework, ducts, flues and chimneys.
- Check for any wiring or electrical fittings.
- Note the direction of existing joists, roof and structure.
- Take photographs of the loft space.

Party Walls

If the proposed conversion is in a terraced or semi detached property, the party wall will need to be assessed. Depending on the age of the property, the party wall may be single skin brickwork, double layer brickwork, single skin blockwork, cavity wall, or maybe not even exist at all! Structural steel is often supported off party walls so it is important to establish whether the wall is suitable for this, and whether the neighbouring properties are already supporting their own steelwork off the party wall. It is likely the party wall will require upgrading to comply with fire regulations.

For this, you may require a party wall surveyor to advise and complete a party wall award. See Resources on page 138 for links to approved party wall inspectors.

Chimneys

It is worth noting that chimney breasts are not permitted to be used to support new steelwork, which can sometimes cause difficulties as they often run up the party wall.

Make sure chimneys are located and dimensioned on your plans so that they can be considered when positioning structure and any roof windows. If you are planning on removing any part of the chimney, it must be adequately supported below. It is also worth noting that planning permission may be required if you intend to demolish the whole chimney, including the external stack as this does not usually fall under permitted development rights. If the building is located in a conservation area or, if the building is listed, the chimney will probably have to remain externally and be supported structurally below.

It is worth checking the general condition of any existing chimneys as they tend to be more exposed to the elements than walls, leading to water ingress from joints and old flashing. It is also a good opportunity during the works to re-point any mortar and carry out any other maintenance.

If you are planning to use a chimney flue, a full flue survey should be carried out to make sure the flue is safe to use and does not expel smoke or other gases. A survey may have been undertaken prior to the purchase of the house.

Load Bearing Walls

All existing load bearing walls must be able to support the additional load proposed by the loft conversion. The walls must be able to transmit the load to the foundations safely. It is important to establish the construction of the existing load bearing walls and review any existing lintels and their bearings. Any defects must be identified and replaced.

Foundations

The existing foundations must be able to transmit the additional loading proposed by the new conversion to the ground without excessive movement. To inspect the foundations, a trial hole or pit may be required to see the footings below ground level, this can seem a little invasive but allows for a greater amount of accuracy when assuming the design of the existing foundations in lieu of the existing as built drawings. Some things to consider when looking at the foundations include:

- Type of foundation
- Depth of foundation
- Any evidence of subsidence
- Any evidence of heave, or frost damage
- Any mature and large trees within the vicinity of the foundations that are cause for concern
- Any information regarding the local water table, and any existing water courses.

In the event that the foundations require upgrading to accommodate the additional loading, an engineer must be engaged to design and execute the work.

Other things to consider during the survey:

- Are the internal walls load bearing? If so which ones.
- What is the headroom in the existing loft?
- Where are the existing stairs and landing located?
- Where do you anticipate the new stairs being located, being mindful of headroom.
- Where are the existing services located?
- Is there a water tank that needs to be relocated?
- How will the fire regulations be satisfied?
- Is the ground floor open plan or is there a protected corridor from the top of the house to the front door?

PLANNING & PERMITTED DEVELOPMENT

Once the project is deemed feasible, the appropriate planning consent will need to be obtained from the local authority. Some loft conversions can be built under permitted development rights and will not require planning consent, while others, perhaps in a conservation area or a listed building, will need planning consent. Check with your local authority, the online Planning Portal, www.planningportal.co.uk or speak with a professional for further guidance on the planning process. Some owners may also be required to seek permission from their freeholders.

Permitted Development Rights

As mentioned above, some loft conversions can be built under permitted development rights. The details of which as can be found in "the enlargement of a dwellinghouse consisting of an addition or alteration to its roof" as detailed in Schedule 2, Part 1, Class B of the The Town and Country Planning (General Permitted Development) (England) Order 2015. Some of the points from this document are outlined below:

Converting the loft of a house is considered to be permitted development (not requiring planning permission) subject to the following limits and conditions:

The current house:
- Is not a building containing one or more flats, or a flat contained within such a building.
- Has not already had additional storeys added to it under permitted development rights.
- Was not changed to be used as a house (from a previous non-residential use) under permitted development rights.
- Was not built as a 'New Dwellinghouse' under permitted development rights.
- Is not on Article 2(3) designated land*.

Limitations on the proposed development:
- Materials must be similar in appearance to the existing house.
- Volume of enlargement (including any previous enlargement) must not exceed the original roof space by more than:
  - 40 cubic metres for terraced houses; or
  - 50 cubic metres otherwise.
- Must not exceed the height of the existing roof.
- On the principal elevation of the house (where it fronts a highway), must not extend beyond the existing roof slope.
- Must not include:
  - verandas, balconies* or raised platforms; or
  - installation, alteration or replacement of any chimney, flue, or 'soil and vent pipe'.
- Side-facing windows must be obscure-glazed; and, if opening, to be 1.7 metres above the floor of the room in which they are installed.
- Construction must ensure that:
  - The eaves of the original roof are maintained (or reinstated)
  - Any enlargement is set back, so far as practicable, at least 20cm from the original eaves (see pages 35-36 of the online Permitted development rights for householders: technical guidance)
  - The roof enlargement does not overhang the outer face of the wall of the original house

With the exceptions that:
- Points 1 and 2 do not apply to the relevant parts of any hip-to-gable enlargement.
- None of these three points apply to the relevant parts of any enlargement that joins the original roof to the roof of a side or rear extension.

Definitions
Article 2(3) designated land
This is defined as land within:
- a conservation area; or
- an area of outstanding natural beauty; or

- an area specified by the Secretary of State for the purposes of enhancement and protection of the natural beauty and amenity of the countryside; or
- the Broads; or
- a National Park; or
- a World Heritage Site.

Balcony

The Government's technical guidance states that: "A balcony is understood to be a platform with a rail, balustrade or parapet projecting outside an upper storey of a building. A 'Juliet' balcony, where there is no platform and therefore no external access, would normally be permitted development."

Even if the loft conversion can be built under permitted development rights, it is recommended to get a Lawful Development Certificate which accredits that the proposed works are lawful. This is especially helpful if the property will be sold in the 10 years following the works. If the works are not seen to be lawful, planning permission will be required.

It is always recommended to seek advice and guidance from professionals if required.

A loft conversion must comply with the requirements of the building regulations. Building Control or an Approved Inspector must be consulted early in the process in order to ensure compliance and avoid costly changes later. You can find out more about the Building Regulation Approval and the process on the Planning Portal website (see resources).

Planning Portal Interactive Guide can be found at https://interactive.planningportal.co.uk/mini-guide/loft-conversion/0

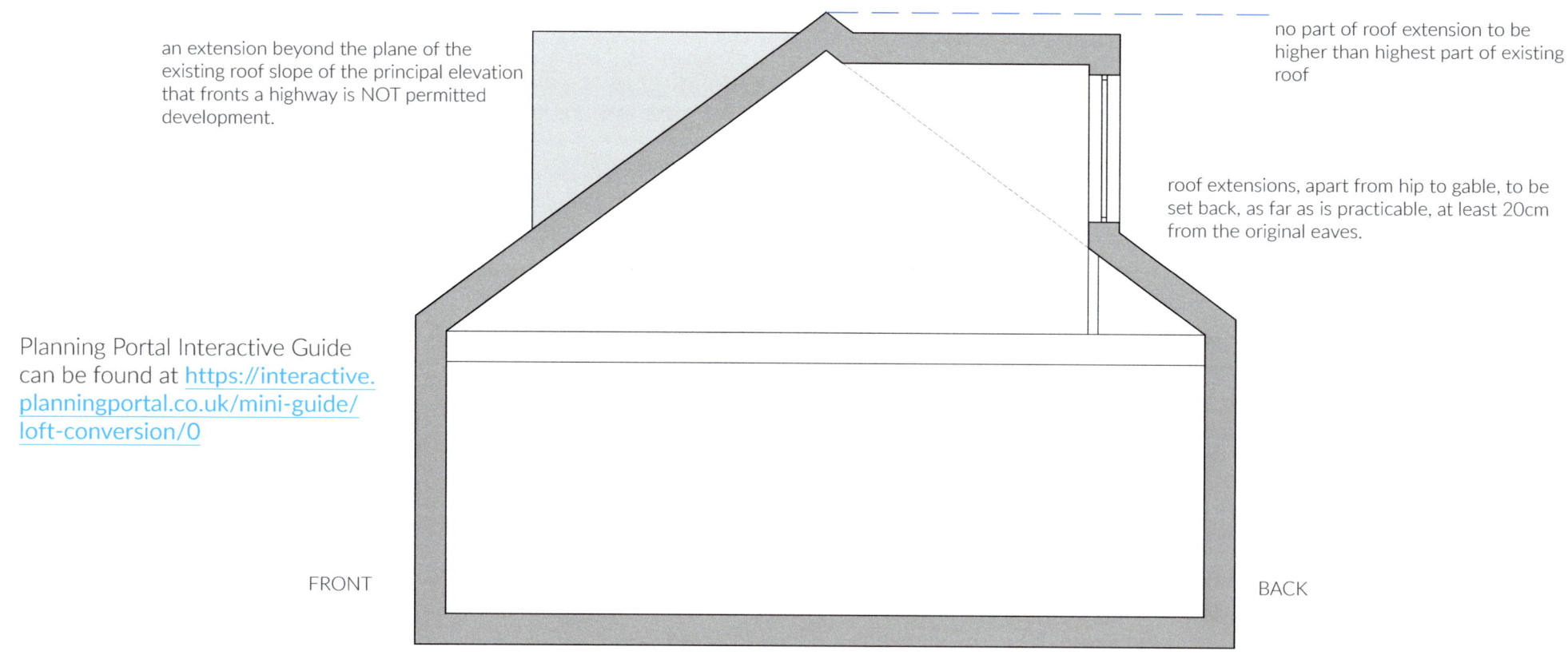

NEW STRUCTURE

Floors

The new floor structure will need to be able to support both the dead loads of the loft conversion - for example the new internal walls, new dormer windows etc. and also support the live loads - such as furniture and people in the loft space. Existing ceilings are rarely strong enough to fulfil this role, so a new floor or existing floor strengthening strategy is usually proposed by the structural engineer. In most cases, headroom is limited in a loft conversion, so the new floor will need to be as slim as possible to maximise the room height.

There are various ways a new floor can be installed; it is important to consult with a structural engineer to find the right solution for your specific project.

Options include placing the new floor joists alongside the existing ceiling joists, installing new structural steel beams to 'hang' the new joists on, or even completely rebuilding the floor structure and remove the existing ceiling.

Although it is possible to support the new floor structure on the existing external and internal walls, it is rarely feasible - a structural engineer will be able to confirm whether this is an option for your project.

In the first option, new joists are inserted adjacent to existing joists, sometimes bolted together, and hanging off new structural beams. This option is great for utilising the existing structure as bracing but may reduce the head height in the loft if floor beams are thicker than the existing are required.

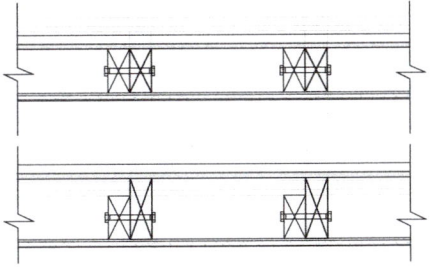

bolted to existing joists - matching joists

bolted to existing joists - larger joists

The second option sees new joists installed above the existing structure. These new joists then have the freedom to either run parallel to existing or perpendicular. This option reduces the internal loft space greatly but provides an independent ceiling and floor structure which is sometimes desired if creating separate apartments. It is also useful if pipework or large services are required to run perpendicular to the existing joists.

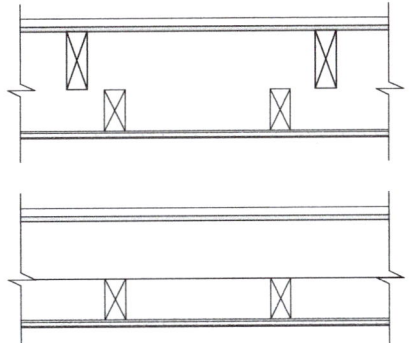

independent floor above existing joists hung off joist hangers at extremities - parallel to existing joists

independent floor above existing joists hung off joist hangers at extremities - perpendicular to existing joists

If there is insufficient headroom in the loft to install the new floor structure above the existing ceiling, and if there is adequate headroom in the bedrooms below - another option is to support the ceiling from the underside. New joists are installed with the top of timber flush with the existing. This will require new ceilings in the rooms below, existing lights will need to be moved and possible rewiring required. This can be an expensive option but sometimes the only option if the headroom in the loft is limited.

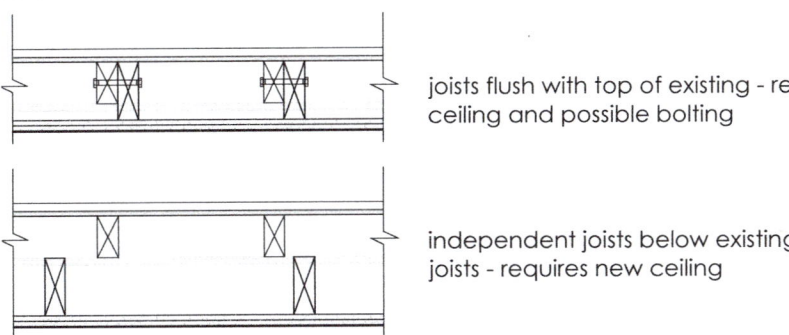

joists flush with top of existing - requires new ceiling and possible bolting

independent joists below existing ceiling joists - requires new ceiling

The design and layout will vary according to individual project requirements.

TRADA publish Span Tables which can be found www.trada.co.uk/ad-hoc/span-tables/ - a list of floor joists and the permissible clear spans which is a useful reference guide.

Roof Structure

A loft conversion will affect the existing roof structure, the walls and internal layout, in a number of ways depending on the type and scope of the conversion. It is advisable to engage a structural engineer to provide a structural assessment of the works along with calculations for new structural requirements. Your engineer will also determine the suitable lateral constraints for gable walls.
These calculations will be required by the building control officer or appointed approved inspector.

The preferred minimum ceiling height in a loft conversion is 2.3m, but this is not required throughout the usable space and lower ceiling heights are deemed acceptable.
Heights below 1.5m are not classed as habitable space as they are difficult to use. They are therefore usually transformed into fitted storage.

If the conversion is a relatively simple one, with the addition of some roof windows, but no dormers, the rafters can remain largely undisturbed. If a new dormer is specified, some significant alterations to the rafters will be necessary and possible steel or timber structural reinforcement.

Dormers and Roof Extensions

Dormers are a common design option for loft conversions. They create extra headroom, and allow for a light opening in the roof structure. A dormer has more structural requirements than a normal rooflight, due to the additional loading from the dormer. There are a couple of types of dormers which we will briefly explore here.

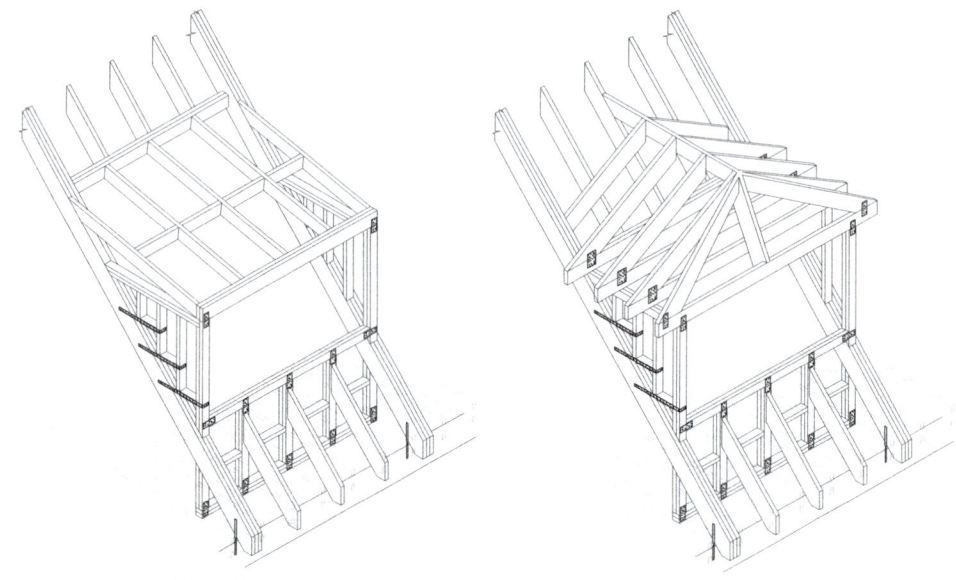

image credit: Dennis Buckell

Small dormer windows

A small dormer window usually has a pitched roof, and doesn't tend to exceed a width of 1.2m. This allows for the dormer to be created within trimmers, with only one or two rafters needing to be cut to create the opening. These are more common at the front of the property or to the rear, and are not usually covered by permitted development rights.

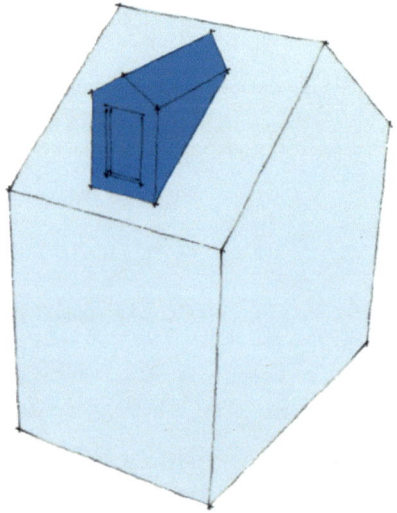

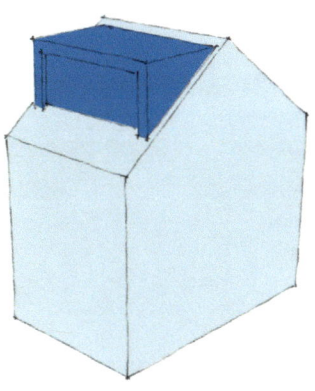

Large dormer windows

The larger dormer windows come in two sizes, offset dormers or full width dormers. Both types of dormer are generally constructed with a flat roof. The offset dormer will leave a small amount of sloping roof to either side of the dormer, the full width will completely replace the roof slope. They are usually set back from the existing rear wall, supported by steel work below or built off the existing purlins.

These are more common to the rear of the property but can sometimes be found to the side of end of terrace or semi detached properties.

Large box dormers

Similarly to the large dormer windows, there are two main types of box dormers. Ones which are built off the gable wall and the more common ones built offset and away from the gable wall. Both of these will usually be built off the existing rear wall usually in timber or masonry with steelwork where required.

The large box dormer will leave at least one rafter on each side that can be trimmed, but further reinforcement will be required in the form of a steel ridge beam at the apex of the loft which provides support to the new flat roof joists.

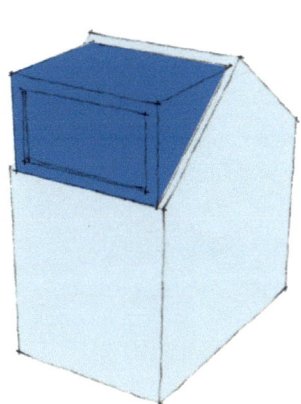

Full width dormers are more typical in Georgian terraced properties where a defined parapet and a party wall which extends beyond the roof can be easily extended to build the dormer off. Although the party walls can also extend beyond the roof in Victorian or Edwardian properties, it is a common planning requirements to have to offset the dormer from the gable walls.

L-shaped dormers

L-shaped dormers are only suitable for certain properties, mainly either Victorian or Edwardian houses where there is an existing addition at the rear, known as a two-storey outrigger. Usually one dormer will be built on the rear outrigger roof and the other on the main roof, constructed in a way that they join together. These extensions are great for increasing space. These properties tend to be on split levels; the main house on one level and the outrigger on an intermediate level, and a L shaped dormer can help in increasing the headroom of the staircase as well as creating extra space in the loft.

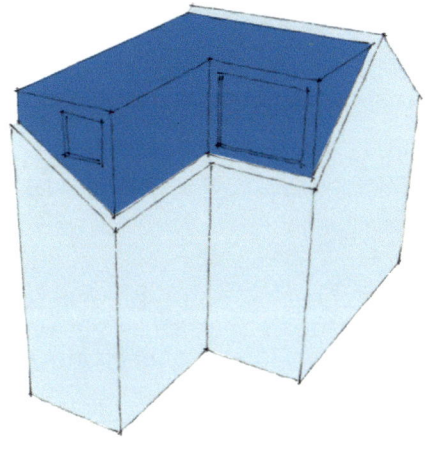

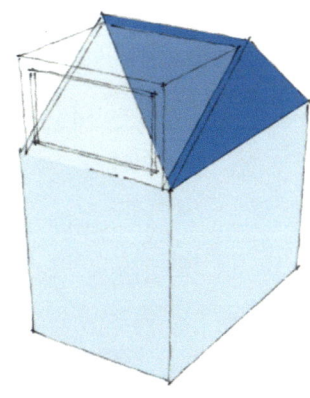

Hip to gable loft extensions

End-of-terrace or semi-detached post war properties tend to have a hipped roof which may not be suitable for a simple loft conversion as the proposed staircase would need to be located at the lowest point of the roof. However, as most of these properties are not within conservation areas and are not listed, it can be relatively simple to gain planning permission for a hip to gable wall loft extension. Additional box dormers to the rear and/or side can also greatly increasing the internal area of the loft.

Mansard loft extensions

Mansard loft extensions are less common in residential loft conversions and are more typically seen in mansion block roof conversions or larger properties. This conversion involves creating a new roof with two pitches, one shallower at the top and one almost vertical below. This increases the interior space greatly whilst maintaining the roof like volume compared to a simple dormer. The downside of this option is the need for a completely new roof structure and possible planning difficulties.

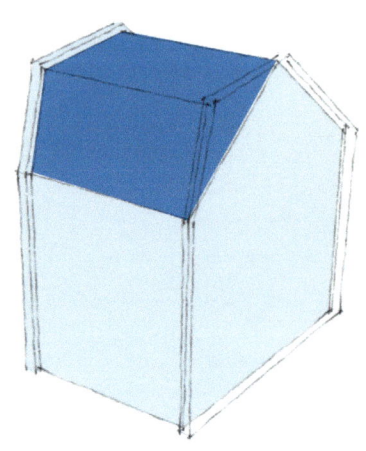

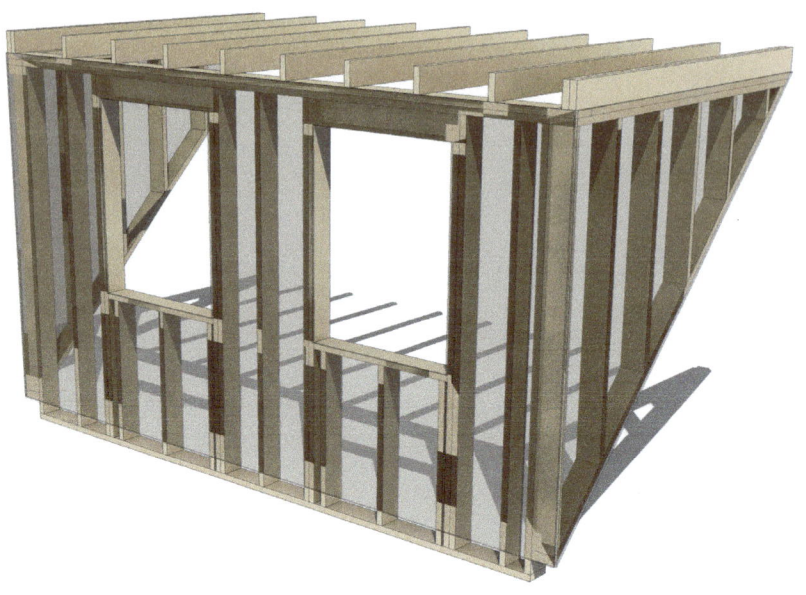

Large dormer structure - usually offset from party walls and built off the existing rear wall and roof structure

Butterfly roofs

The previous examples of roof extensions have shown possible solutions for gabled, hipped and L-shaped roofs. However, for butterfly roofs, a series of solutions are possible depending on the existing structure and layout. If the butterfly roof is stand-alone, infilling the existing roof may be the best option. However, due to planning restrictions, a mansard roof may be a more feasible option if there are larger brick party walls to either side. If the butterfly roof also has a lean-to roof over the extension, an L-shaped dormer may be the best option.

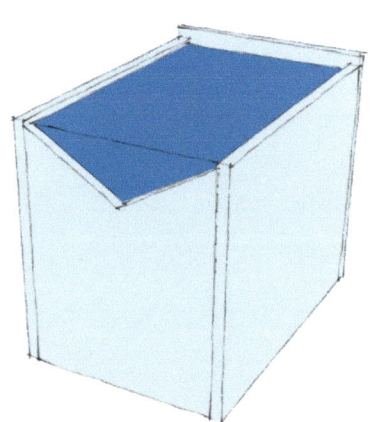
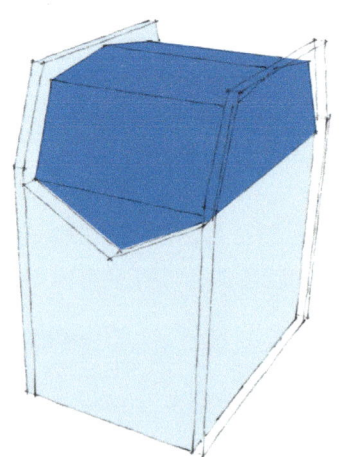

Small dormer window structure usually found at the front of properties

Thermal Performance

U-Values Explained

Insulating the new loft conversion serves a number of purposes including thermal performance and sound insulation. A U-value is used as a measure of the ability of a building element or component to conduct heat from a warmer environment to a cooler environment. The unit is W/m^2K. A higher U-value means more heat is conducted and therefore a worse insulater. A lower value means the element is less conductive and therefore a better insulater. Insulation companies will have online calculators to assist in the specification of construction build-ups. Other online calculators allow you to add the different elements and their conductivity to calculate the total U-value.

The Building Regulation document *Conservation of fuel and power: Approved Document L 2021 edition* has been recently updated and provides minimum U-value requirements for the different elements of a building.

Within the new document, the minimum U-value requirements have been updated to better reflect the growing need for homes which are more insulated and therefore require less heating and energy.

Be aware that these are the minimum requirements, and it is always advisable to aim for a better performance as insulating a building well is the easiest way to reduce energy usage throughout the building's life. Some local authorities may also request higher requirements. With increased insulation, ventilation must also be considered, Building Regulation document *Ventilation: Approved Document F* provides further information on this.

The table below summarises Approved Document L which makes three U-Value distinctions: Table 1.1 shows requirements for a new dwelling, Table 4.2 for new fabric elements in an existing dwelling and Table 4.3 threshold and required improved values to existing thermal elements in an existing dwelling. The differentiation of these are further explained on the following page.

Criteria	Approved Document Part L, Conservation of Fuel and Power, Volume 1: Dwellings, 2021 Edition - England			EnerPHit Requirement
	Table 1.1 - Summary of notional dwelling specification for new dwelling	Table 4.2 - Limiting U-values for new fabric elements in existing dwellings	Table 4.3 - Limiting U-values for existing elements in existing dwellings	
			Threshold/Improved	
Roof (Including flat roof)	0.11 W/m²K	0.15 W/m²K	0.35 W/m²K / 0.16 W/m²K	0.12 W/m²K
Wall (Including dormer cheeks)	0.18 W/m²K	0.18 W/m²K	-	-
Wall - cavity insulation	-	-	0.7 W/m²K / 0.55 W/m²K	0.15 W/m²K
Wall - internal or external insulation	-	-	0.7 W/m²K / 0.3 W/m²K	0.15 W/m²K
Party wall	0.0 W/m²K	-	-	-
Floor⁺	0.13 W/m²K	0.18 W/m²K	0.7 W/m²K / 0.25 W/m²K	0.15 W/m²K
Window	1.2 W/m²K	1.4 W/m²K *	-	≤0.85 W/m²K
Rooflight	1.2 - 1.7 W/m²K	2.2 W/m²K	-	-
Doors with >60% of internal face glazed	See window requirements	1.4 W/m²K **	-	-
Other doors	1.0 W/m²K	1.4 W/m²K *	-	-

* or Window Energy Ration Band B minimum

** or Window Energy Ration Band C minimum

⁺refers to floors adjacent to soil and unheated basements, not internal floors.

Part L Table 1.1 applies to new dwellings. A dwelling is defined as; a self-contained unit designed to accommodate a single household.
Part L Table 4.2 applies to new fabric elements in an existing dwelling such as:
a. Elements in extensions to existing dwellings.
b. New or replacement elements in existing dwellings. Such as works which are not covered by the definitions for Table 4.3 detailed below.

Part L Table 4.3 applies if you are renovating an existing thermal element. This means one of the following:
a. Providing a new layer through cladding or rendering the external surface of a thermal element.
b. Providing a new layer through dry-lining the internal surface of a thermal element.
c. Replacing an existing layer through stripping down the element to expose basic structural components (e.g. bricks, blocks, rafters, joists, frame) and then rebuilding.
d. Replacing the waterproof membrane on a flat roof.
e. Providing cavity wall insulation.

If a thermal element is renovated and one of the following applies, then the whole of the thermal element should be improved to achieve at least the improved U-value given in Table 4.3:
a. More than 50% of the surface of the individual thermal element is renovated.
b. The work constitutes a major renovation. A major renovation is when more than 25% of the surface area of the external building envelope is renovated.

The requirements for this category are less stringent than new fabric elements within an existing dwelling, however they tend to only apply when small changes are being made to an existing layer and not when a full renovation is being undertaken.

There are also a large number of exceptions, such as historic houses, and further detailed requirements. More about these can be found in Building Regulations Part L.
The last column shows EnerPHit requirements, which is the established standard for refurbishment of existing buildings using the Passivhaus basic principles and components.

Loft Insulation
Traditionally loft spaces were designed to be well ventilated, with any moisture occurring in the space able to easily evaporate away. This would help to keep the house cool in summer and warm in winter. The new loft space will now be insulated, which has the potential to create unwanted moisture build up. It is important to ensure a vapour control layer is fitted on the internal side of the insulation to prevent warm moist air passing through the assembly, and condensing within the structure. Roofs can also be ventilated to allow airflow, and thus drawing any moisture away. If the roof is not ventilated, all penetrations through the vapour control layer must be well sealed. Your insulation supplier should be able to advise on location and specification of vapour control layers.

Floor Insulation
New floors should be insulated for sound purposes. The use of sound insulation between joists is recommended to prevent airborne sound from passing between floors. It is also advised to use isolation strips on the top of floor joists, at the edge of floor finishes and base of stud walls to prevent impact sound from passing between floors and rooms.

Wall Insulation
External walls must be insulated to achieve minimum U-value requirements or better. If an existing masonry cavity gable wall is not sufficiently wide enough to achieve the minimum requirements it may be necessary to build a timber/steel frame wall on the inside face to provide suitable levels of insulation.

Roof insulation
Roof insulation can be applied in a number of ways to achieve the required standards. The most common option is for new insulation to be installed between and under the rafters. If completely re-roofing, the insulation can also be fitted over the rafters, or between and over the rafters. Thickness and arrangement will be according to required U-values and manufacturers specifications.

Stairs

The position and design of a new stair in a loft conversion is an important consideration. Fire regulations need to be considered, along with the best space saving opportunities.

Where possible, it is advisable to use the existing stairwell to create the new stair up to the next level, which saves space but also gives continuity. Of course, this is not always feasible, so each project needs to be assessed for its own design solutions.

The staircase also needs to be designed to create enough headroom at the top of the stair, therefore finishing at a point in the loft where the roof pitch is relatively high. The building regulations require at least a 2m headroom at the top of the stair. There is some flexibility, where a stair terminates at a sloping ceiling, the headroom must be a minimum 1.9m at the centre line of the stair.

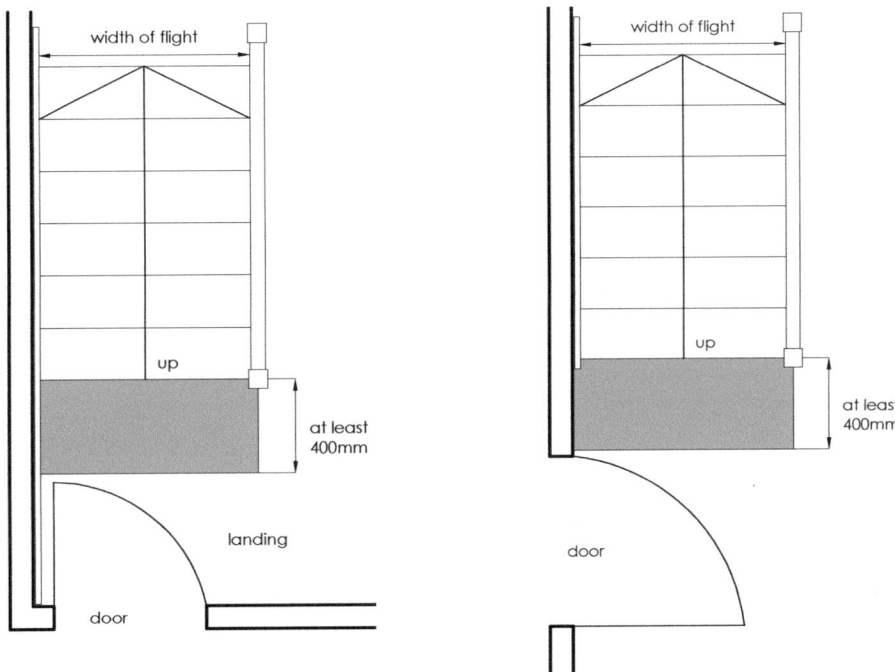

Although conventional stairs are the most common option for a loft conversion, it is possible to include other styles such as spiral staircases, or even alternating tread stairs.

Consider how often the loft room will be used, and how important easy access to the room/s will be.

The alternating tread stair is only permissible in stairs that lead to just one habitable room. If children or the elderly will be using the loft room, it is worth considering whether a safer conventional stair would be a better choice.

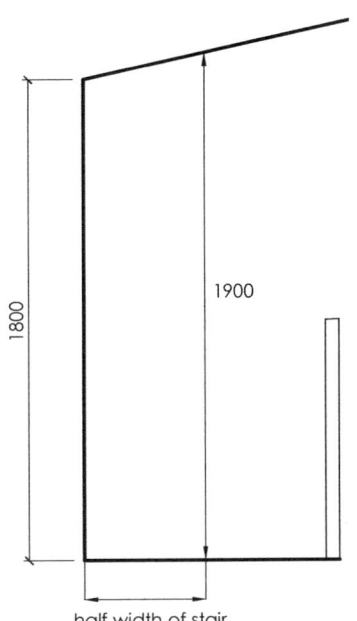

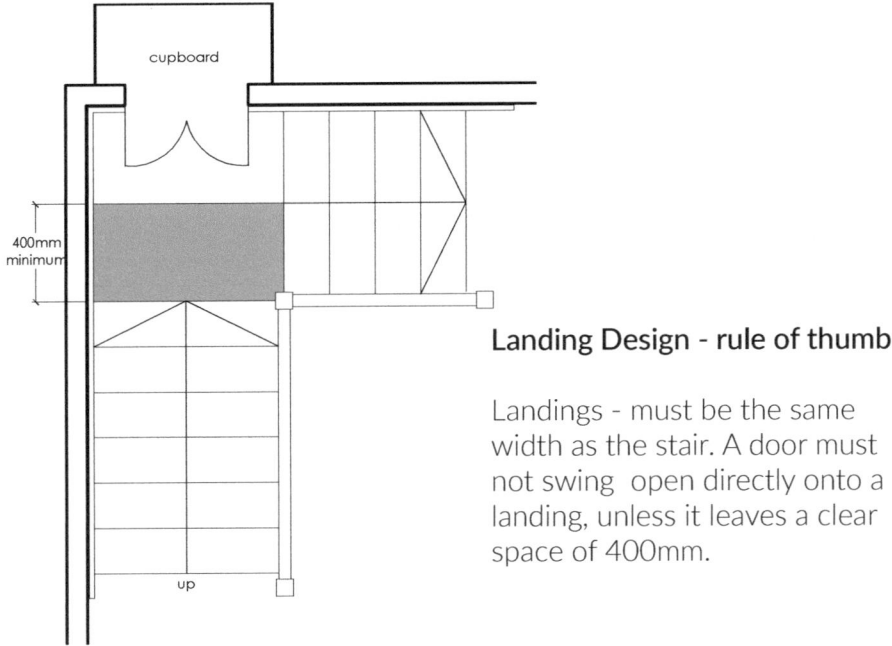

Landing Design - rule of thumb

Landings - must be the same width as the stair. A door must not swing open directly onto a landing, unless it leaves a clear space of 400mm.

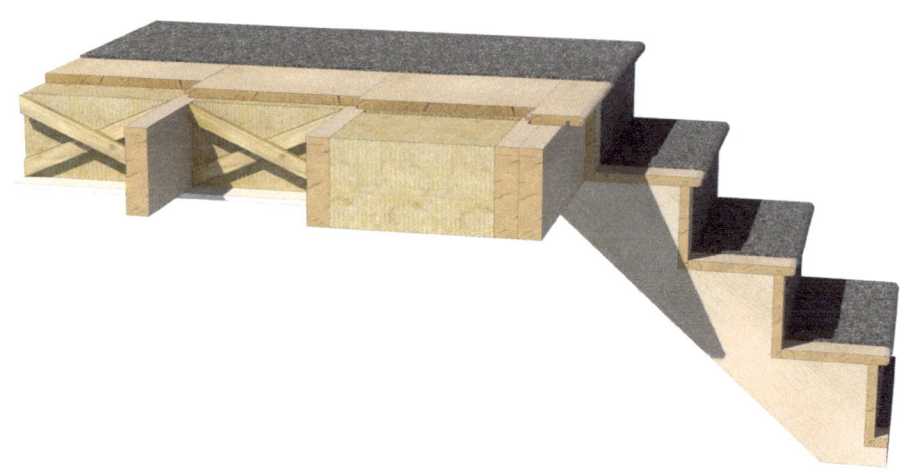

Windows and Doors

A loft conversion can include a few different window options:
- New windows to existing gable wall
- New dormer windows
- New roof windows

The building regulations provide a limit to the area of windows, roof windows and external doors in an extension to not more than 25% of the floor area of the extension. This restriction is in place to limit heat gains and losses as part of the Approved Document Part L. Approved Document Part O also requires reasonable provision must be made to limit unwanted solar gains in summer and provide an adequate means to remove heat from the indoor environment, usually through solar shading.

New windows should provide good thermal performance, with best practice U-values of less than 1.4 W/m²K for windows.

It is important to refer to the Building Regulations Approved Document K for glazing protection requirements for critical locations.

Guarding must be provided to windows and glazing with sills lower than 800mm. This can be in the form of fixed toughened safety glass or through guarding such as a Juliet balcony to the exterior.

There are a wide variety of roof windows available, with Velux being the best known manufacturer. There are a huge range of alternative products that offer a number of innovative designs. Centre pivots are the most popular choice of roof window, but can create an obstruction as the casement projects into the room.

An alternative to this is the top hung roof window, where the window opens outwards from the bottom. This gives a clear internal opening, and offers uninterrupted view to the outside. There are also roof balcony and roof terrace options where the opening is split to create an area to walk into. The upper window opens upwards, while the lower window can either remain fixed or can open outwards to walk through onto the terrace/ balcony area.

Stair Design - rules of thumb

- Headroom - minimum 2m metres, or 1.9m at the centre line with a pitched ceiling
- Pitch - no steeper than 42 degrees
- Goings - no smaller than 220mm deep
- Risers - no higher than 220mm
- Winders - must be a minimum 50mm at the narrowest point and no less than 220mm at the centre
- Handrails - must be on one side minimum, to a minimum height of 900mm. Any balusters must not have a gap that exceeds 90mm (or that a 100mm sphere cannot pass through any openings in the guarding.
- Landings - must be the same width as the stair. A door must not swing open directly onto a landing, unless it leaves a clear space of 400mm.

It is also necessary to consider how these windows will be cleaned in the future as accessing a sloped roof is not always safe or feasible. Many new windows offer fully reversible options so the outside pane of glass can be cleaned from the inside.

When roof windows are to be installed, trimming will be required to reinforce the existing rafters. In most cases a rafter will need to be cut to create the opening large enough for a window. Trimming is required to the top, bottom and sides of the opening. New rafters are fixed either side of the new opening, along with trimmers to the top and bottom, where the rafter has been cut. The ends of the rafters are butted to the trimmers.

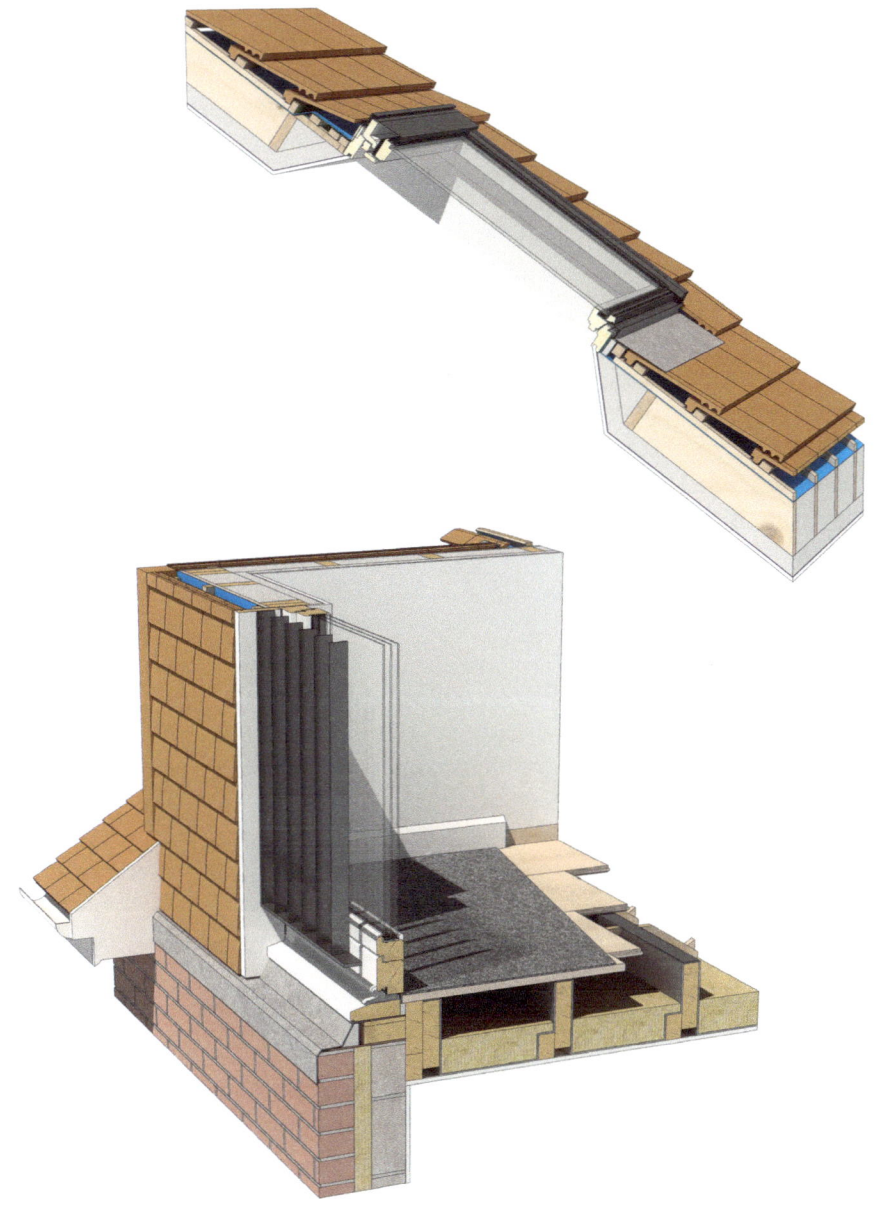

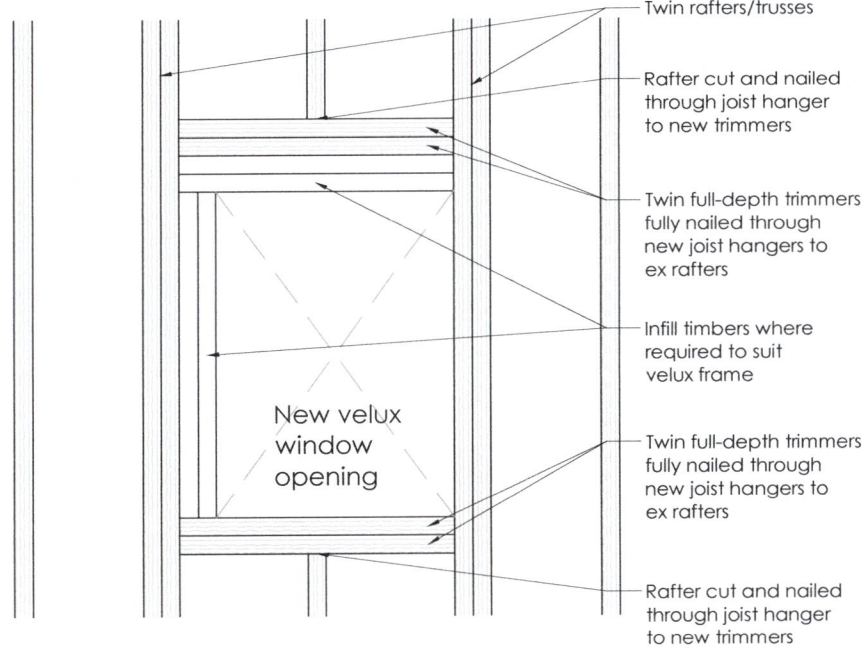

image credit: Dennis Buckell

Doors

External doors to loft conversions can be in the form of a Juliet balcony. The door is installed in the gable wall, with an inward opening swing and guarding to the exterior. The handrail must be at a minimum height of 1100mm.

Materials, choices and limitations

There are a huge range of material options which are suitable for loft conversions and extensions. Permitted development rights can sometimes limit materials to those found on the existing building, however, discussing options with the council can give you more flexibility. It is important to consider the location of the building when picking a roof or dormer material due to climate, extreme weather, local vernacular and knowledge. Some examples of common materials are listed below.

Clay Roof Tiles

Clay tiles are a common roofing material. The two main types of tiles are plain tiles and interlocking tiles, although within these two types there are a huge range of finishes, shapes and sub-types. Some plain tile options include handmade, hung, flat, pantile, Roman, panels and ornamental. Some interlocking tile options include hung, flat, rustic, angular, pantile and Roman.

The fixings of these tiles depend greatly on the type of tiles chosen but include nails, wooden pegs, hanging and nailing off timber battens, self-supporting, etc. Due to the variety, it is always recommended to contact the manufacture for specific installation requirements although most clay products can be installed around 25° to 90° (as a wall).

As clay is a natural material, different areas may have different clay colours and therefore different tile colours. Many modern clay tiles are also finished to a huge variety of colours and roughness' as well as glazing options for bright colours.

Clay tiles can be quite an expensive up front cost and are quite heavy. They do however last for many years and are very resistant to weather and temperature.

Slate roof tiles

Slate is another fairly common roofing material. It can be used both on pitched roofs and dormer walls. However, it is not usually suitable for pitches below 25°. Slate is a natural material and is very resistant, although the quality also depends on where the slate is sourced from.

The most common way of installing slate is with clout nails through preformed holes onto timber battens however some steeper roofs or walls use stainless steel slate hooks as an alternative fixing.

Zinc & other sheet metal roofs

Zinc is a fairly common roofing material, and is especially good when doing transitions between roofs and walls. This is why they are such a common material in Paris's mansard roofs. Zinc also works at nearly all angles and is therefore great for creating sculptural elements to buildings.

Zinc comes in sheet form and can be installed in lots of different forms including standing seam vertical and horizontal, flat lock panels, interlocking panels, overlapping panels and tiles.

There are a large range of finishes including those that imitate other metals such as copper, although the standard pre-weathered or raw zinc are the most common. Zinc roofs can however have a relatively expensive upfront cost as the installation must be completed by an approved installer.

Timber

Timber cladding is a less common loft conversion material although modern techniques and finishes can help extend the life span of timber. Sustainably sourced timber can be great for reducing the carbon footprint of a building and can be quite simple to install.

Timber cladding types include, but are not limited to shiplap, tongue and groove, open board and shingles. These types come in a variety of timbers, shapes and sizes and can be installed in different ways such as horizontally or vertically to create a huge variety of aesthetics.

Timber cladding is more common as just that, a cladding material, but it can also be used on pitched roofs when detailed correctly.

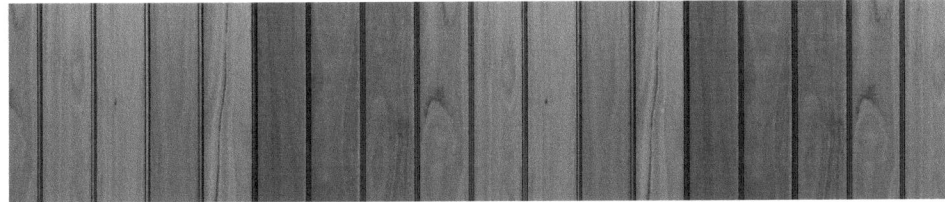

Flat roofing materials

There are a huge range of flat roofing materials and brands to choose from. Below is a short summary of some of the most popular.

Single ply (mainly EDPM and Thermoplastic Polyolefin)

Development of rubbers and plastics has allowed materials to be produced that accommodate differential movement without disrupting the integrity of the membrane. The membrane is applied to the deck by adhesion, mechanical fixing or loose laying. These polymer-based membranes, known as single ply membranes are durable and reliable. They also provide a near seamless coating and are a cost effective solution for new flat roofs.

GRP Roofing (Glass Reinforced Plastic or fibreglass)

GRP roofs consists of glass fibres which are layered or laid as sheets on external grade chipboard or plywood and typically bonded with a polyester resin. GRP is typically used in boat hull manufacturing as is therefore lightweight and resistant to water. It also provides a seamless finish with many standard pre-fabricated edge options possible. It can be relatively easy to install and some high volume house builders even create pre-fabricated GRP dormers.

Built up felt roofing

Built up felt roofing uses a series of sections overlapped to form a continuous coating. The sections are partially bonded to the deck to allow for movement between the deck and the covering. The next layers will be fully bonded using bitumen to provide a two or three layer system. The older pour and roll method of installation is commonly seen in extensions that have unfortunately failed and have now therefore been superseded by torch-on felt which is melt welded onto a flat roof. This can sometimes be dangerous to install and coordinate on site due to the flame. Overall, this is a type of roofing which is used less and less as it tends not to be as durable as single ply membranes and GRP roofs.

Other liquid systems

For larger areas of flat roof or those with more foot traffic such as roof terrace, asphalt or bitumen roofing can be used. The material is applied in liquid form to create a continuous impervious membrane to the roof. A separating layer is positioned between the roof deck and the asphalt to allow for differential movement. The liquid system tends to soften in direct sunlight and heat, so can often be covered in stone chippings to protect it and keep the material cool. Stone chippings are not the only option, and often paving slabs can be positioned over the waterproofing layer using spacers that lift and level the slabs. This system often incorporates an insulation layer between the bitumen and the covering. These concealed membrane roofs can be termed 'inverted', where the insulation is above the waterproof covering. This form of materials may necessitate torch-on systems which require a highly skilled installer, they can also be toxic to handle if not installed but trained professionals. This and their durability is one of the reasons why they tend to be seen on larger flat roofs rather than a small domestic dwelling.

Asphalt and bitumen, along with other polymer based cold liquid applied membranes, which do not require a separation layer, are popular roof options for fixing existing flat roofs which have failed and let water in.

Other materials

Further to the materials mentioned above, there are a large range of other materials and man-made variations such as cement tiles.

BUILDING REGULATIONS
Fire Safety

There are a number of important considerations with regard to fire safety when carrying out a loft conversion. We will briefly look at some of those factors here. All loft conversion projects must be designed in accordance with the relevant Building Regulations and checked with their Building Control Advisor.

Protection of life in the event of fire is extremely important, the requirements for fire safety must be studied and applied diligently.

Fire Safety: Approved Document B; Volume 1: Dwellings, 2019 edition incorporating 2020 amendments - for use in England

Fire Detection
When a new habitable room is installed into a building above ground level, a new fire detection and fire alarm system must be installed.

Smoke alarms should usually be situated in the circulation spaces between sleeping areas (i.e. bedrooms) and places where fires are most likely to start. There should be at least one smoke alarm on each storey of the building.

Smoke and heat alarms must be mains operated, and where there is more than one alarm they should be linked. Refer to the Building Regulations for detailed information on fire detection and alarm requirements.

Means of Escape
Building Regulations Approved Document Part B provides guidance on means of escape.

A safe means of escape must be provided from any converted loft space. In most cases a protected stairway is a preferable option. The protected stair leads from the new loft room to the 'final exit' (external door), providing a protected enclosure that will give 30 minutes fire resistance. Fire resistance is provided by adequate fire rated doors to any rooms that lead off the protected stairway, fire resisting walls/ceilings and floors that provide protection for 30 minutes.
Other options include a partially protected escape combined with a sprinkler system; or the provision of an alternative escape such as an external stair.

Building Fabric - passive fire prevention
Fire resisting internal partitions must achieve 30 minutes fire resistance.

Fire resisting ceilings must provide 30 minutes fire protection.

External walls must achieve a fire rating of 30 minutes minimum. Refer to the Building Regulations with regard to boundaries and protected vs. unprotected areas.

A separating or party wall must be constructed as a compartment wall, and achieve a fire rating of 60 minutes.

Fire Doors
All doors leading onto a protected area (including cupboard doors) must be fire doors that achieve a minimum 20 minutes fire resistance although many come in 30 minutes +. Fire doors and surrounds can be purchased as door sets and are labelled with identification markers to certify their rating.

Automatic Fire Suppression System (Sprinkler Systems) - active fire suppression
Sprinklers and water spray mist systems are becoming a very popular option for many home owners and are a requirement in all new homes in Wales. A sprinkler system provides active fire suppression when smoke and heat in a room reach a certain level, activating the water system.

These are a great solution to allow a completely open floor plan onto a staircase of escape route, or if walls or doors are not fire rated such as certain metal framed glazing systems. Systems such as these may require water storage tanks and expert knowledge to specify and install.

Building Regulations Notes

There are many aspects of the Building Regulations that need to be considered when designing a loft conversion. Below are some of the areas to check compliance - this list is not exhaustive and can be updated at any time. If expanded upon, it can be submitted to the building control officer to show how the chosen design solution complies with current building regulation.

Structure: Approved Document A, 2004 edition incorporating 2004, 2010 and 2013 amendments
A structural engineer may be required to comply with building regulations.

Fire Safety: Approved Document B; Volume 1: Dwellings, 2019 edition incorporating 2020 amendments - for use in England and June 2022 amendments
There must be early warning fire detection and alarm system.
There must be suitable means of escape, and escape routes in the event of a fire.
Any safe routes must be protected from effects of fire.
In the event of a fire, occupants must be able to safely escape from the building without external assistance. (B1)

Resistance to the passage of sound: Approved Document E, 2003 edition incorporating 2004, 2010, 2013 and 2015 amendments.
New internal walls must be designed to provide reasonable resistance to the passage of sound.

Ventilation: Approved Document F, 2021
There must be adequate means of ventilation provided for people in the building.

Overheating: Approved Document O: 2022 edition - for use in England
There must be adequate means to limit unwanted solar gains in summer and provide an adequate means to remove heat from the indoor environment.

Sanitation, hot water safety and water efficiency: Approved Document G, 2015 edition with 2016 amendments.
Drainage and waste disposal: Approved Document H, 2015 edition.
Adequate sanitation and drainage must be provided if increasing roof area or adding a bathroom to a loft.

Combustion appliances and fuel storage systems: Approved Document J, 2010 edition incorporating 2010 and 2013 amendments.
If a combustion appliances is included, such as a boiler, working or gas fireplace, its installation, flue positioning and warning systems of carbon monoxide should be in accordance with the regs Part J.

Protection from falling, collision and impact: Approved Document K, 2013 edition - for use in England.
Stairs shall be designed, constructed and installed to be safe for people moving between different levels of the building. (Part K1)
Stairs shall be provided with barriers where necessary to protect people in or about the building from falling. (Part K2)
Guarding must be provided where necessary to any balcony, roof or opening.
Ensure that glazing, if breaks, will break safely, or is robust, or can be permanently protected. (Part K4)

Conservation of Fuel and Power: Approved Document L Dwellings 2021 Edition
Suitable U-values must be achieved for the building fabric.

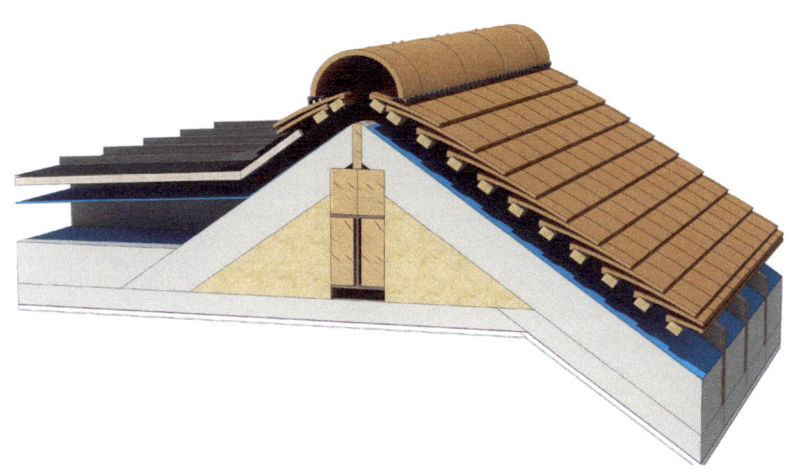

CONSTRUCTION DETAILS

The following pages include a number of construction details relating to loft conversions. First you will see a selection of standard build-ups that have been used throughout the book. These provide a quick glance view to the different types of construction with detailed information of the assemblies.

The details have been broken down into segments for easy navigation. The segments include:
General Loft Details
Front Dormer Window Details
Rear Dormer Extension Details
Zinc Standing Seam Details
Faceted Zinc Dormer Details
Velux Details

At the beginning of each segment there is a section diagram to show where the details are taken, along with a contact sheet of all details in that section. You can click on any of these images to jump directly to the detail.

The details are best viewed in two page format so that you can see the 2D detail alongside the 3D detail. Depending on your PDF viewer, you can usually adjust your settings in the View menu.

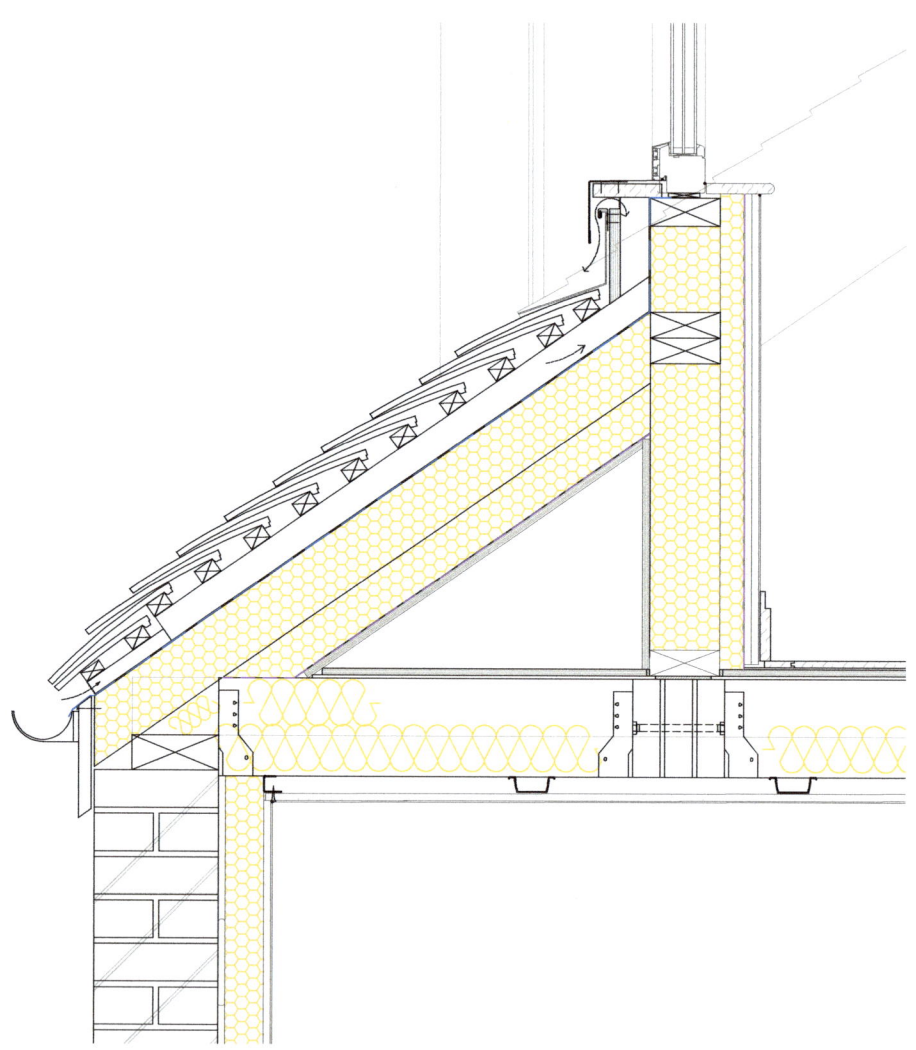

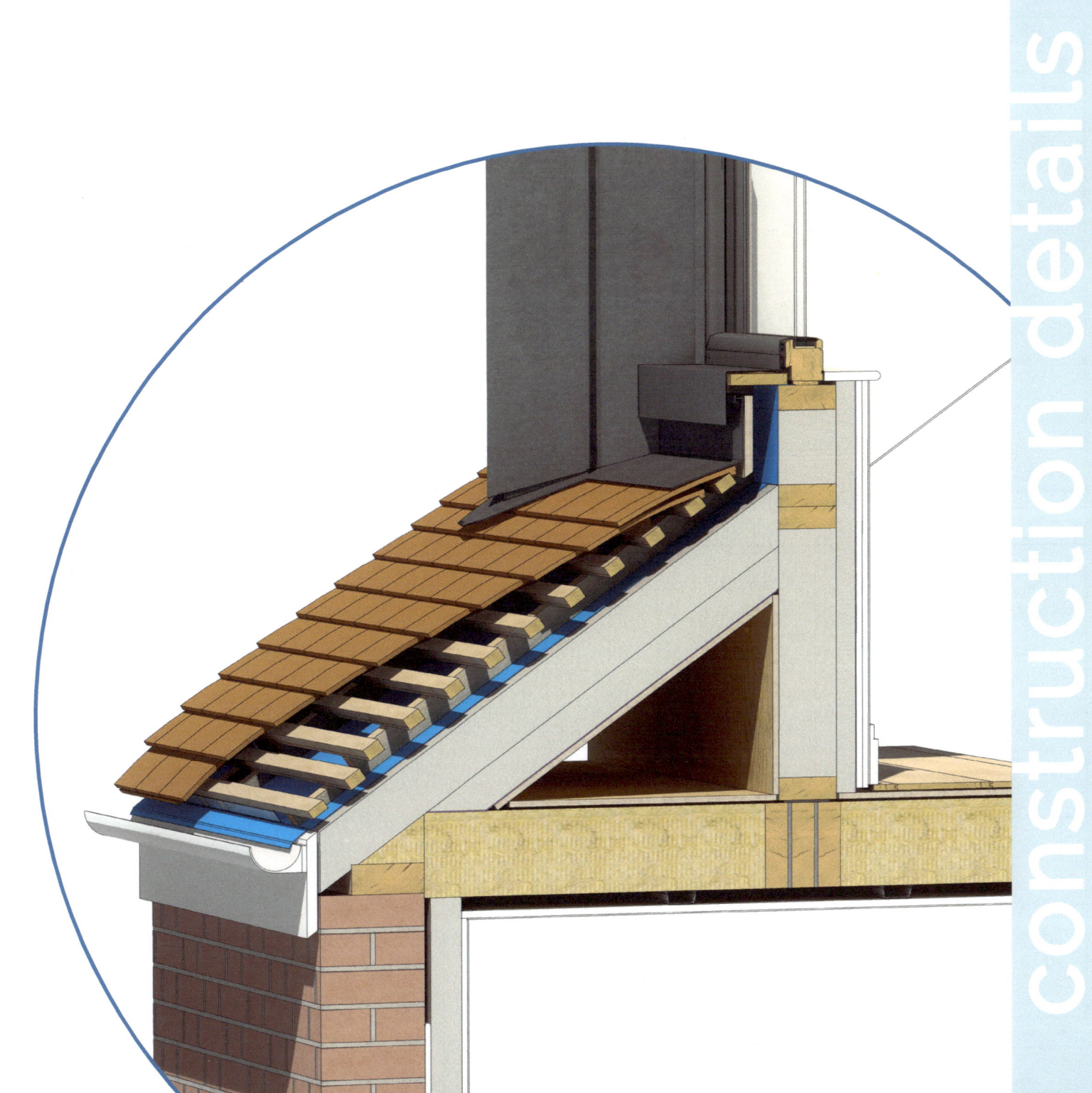

construction details

External Wall Types

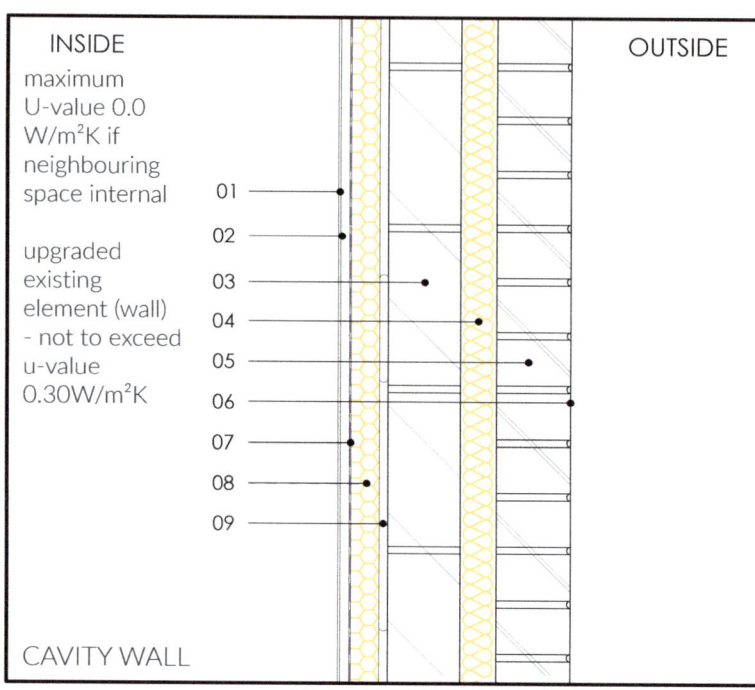

CAVITY WALL

INSIDE — maximum U-value 0.0 W/m²K if neighbouring space internal

upgraded existing element (wall) - not to exceed u-value 0.30W/m²K

OUTSIDE

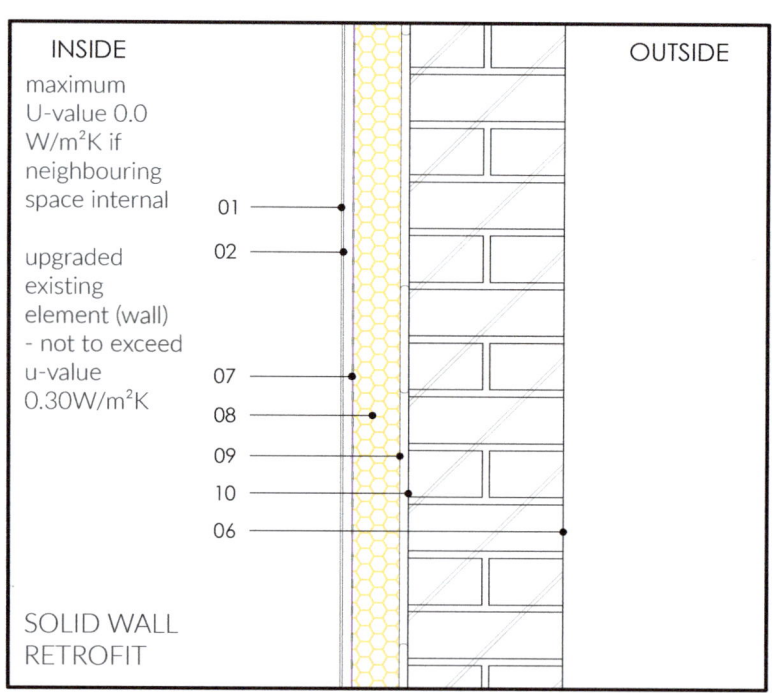

SOLID WALL RETROFIT

INSIDE — maximum U-value 0.0 W/m²K if neighbouring space internal

upgraded existing element (wall) - not to exceed u-value 0.30W/m²K

OUTSIDE

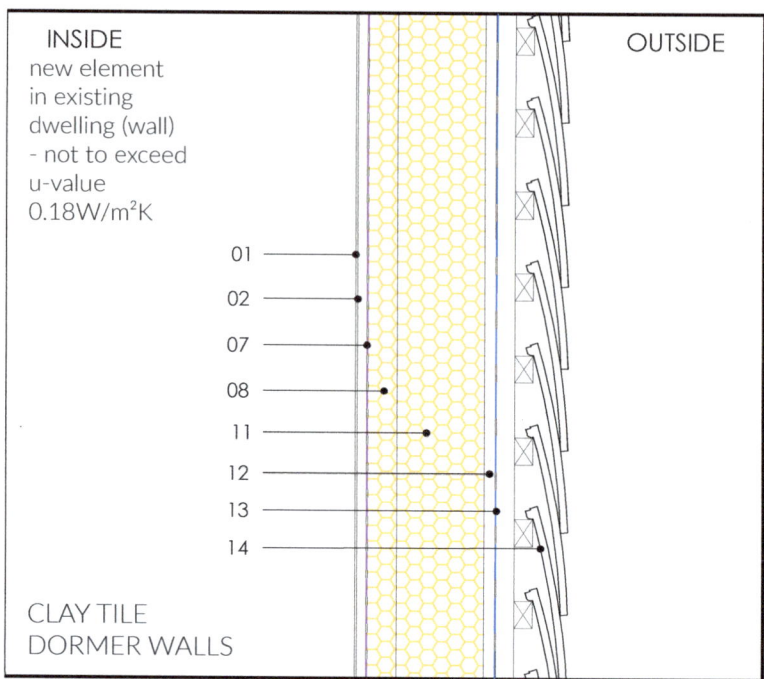

CLAY TILE DORMER WALLS

INSIDE — new element in existing dwelling (wall) - not to exceed u-value 0.18W/m²K

OUTSIDE

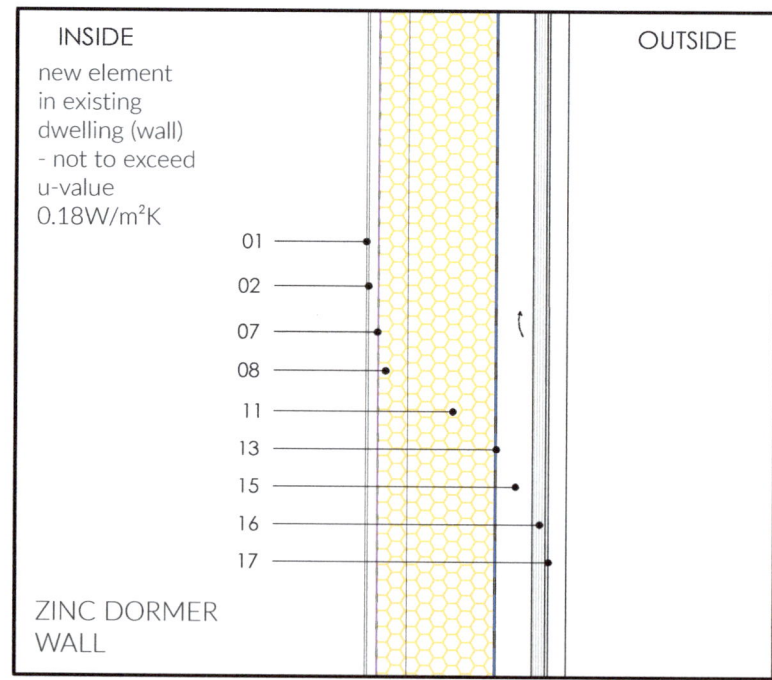

ZINC DORMER WALL

INSIDE — new element in existing dwelling (wall) - not to exceed u-value 0.18W/m²K

OUTSIDE

1. 3mm plaster skim and paint finish
2. 12.5mm single coat plaster
3. 100mm blockwork to SE specification
4. 50mm full-fill mineral wool insulation
5. 102.5mm single leaf brickwork
6. external finishes or neighbouring property finishes
7. VCL or tape and jointed insulation if VCL inbuilt into insulation
8. 40-100mm rigid insulation, thickness to suite U-Value requirement
9. dot and dabs, attaching insulation to wall and creating small service cavity
10. existing party wall construction - typically 215mm solid brickwork
11. 120mm high performance rigid insulation or thickness to suite U-Value requirement
12. 15mm fibre cement board, alternative or omission to SE specification
13. breather membrane to BS 5250: 2011
14. clay hung tiles on 25 x 38mm battens and counter battens to BS 5534: 2014
15. 50mm unobstructed ventilated cavity to be created with external grade timber, cavity reduction or increase dependant on zinc manufacturer's recommendations
16. 18mm marine grade or external grade plywood
17. zinc - vertical standing seam shown, finish to desired specification

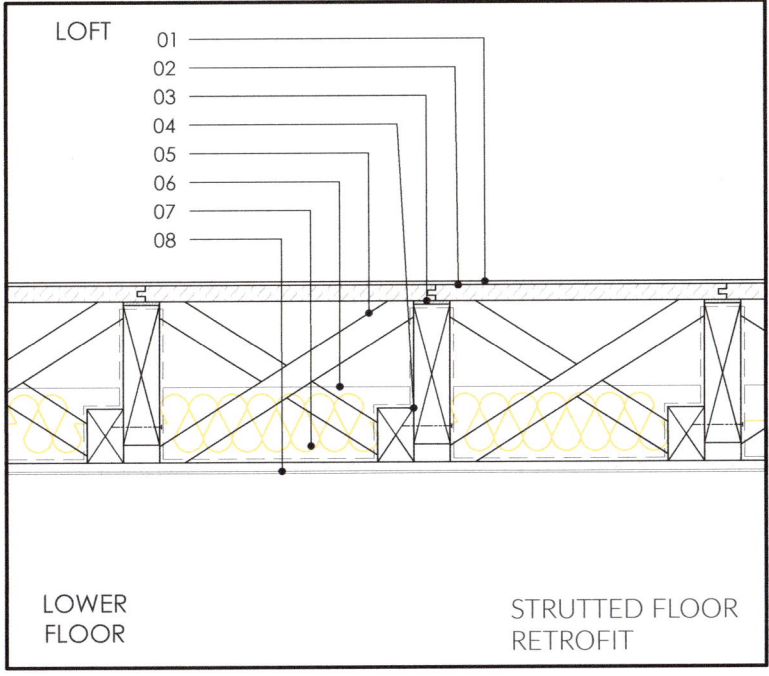

STRUTTED FLOOR RETROFIT

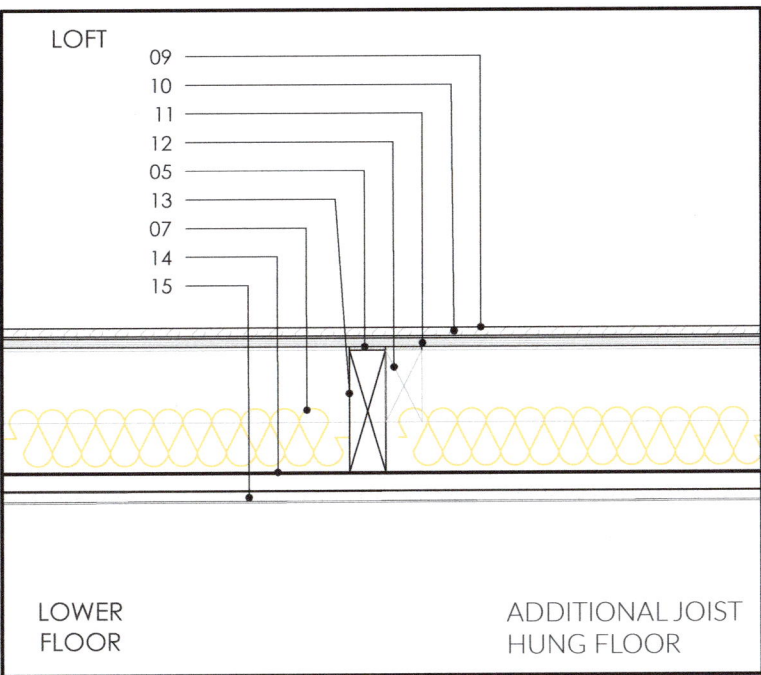

ADDITIONAL JOIST HUNG FLOOR

Floor Types

01. floor finish
02. 18-22mm thick flooring grade tongue & grooved floor boarding screwed & glued together & screwed down to new floor joists
03. 5mm thick acoustic isolation strip screwed or glued to top of floor joist, base of stud wall & edge of floor finish/soleplate junction for sound deadening purposes
04. doubled-up floor joists with noggins under all new non-loadbearing timber stud partitions, bottom of new floor joists set with a 25mm deflection gap to bottom of existing ceiling joists
05. provide strutting by herringbone, solid or pre-galvanised mild steel - 1 row at middle of floor span between 2.5-4.5m, with 2 rows equally spaced above a 4.5m span
06. fixed galvanised chicken wire mesh for fire & sound insulation purposes - alternatively use a high quality PIR insulation board cut to fit tightly between the floor joists and higher grade plasterboard below
07. 100mm fire proof insulation
08. existing plasterboard & skim or lath & plaster ceiling
09. 12mm engineered timber floor boards
10. 3mm adhesive
11. 12mm tongue and groove plywood or chipboard
12. existing ceiling joists
13. 170 x 50mm new ceiling & floor joists, sizing, connection and spacing to SE specification
14. 26mm standard suspended ceiling section
15. 12.5mm plasterboard with 3mm plaster skim & paint finish

Sloped Roof Types

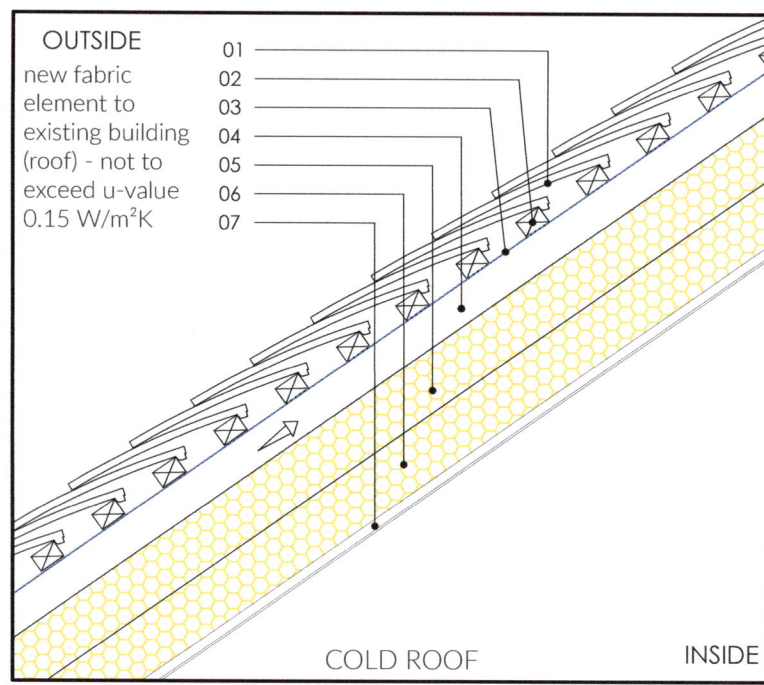

COLD ROOF

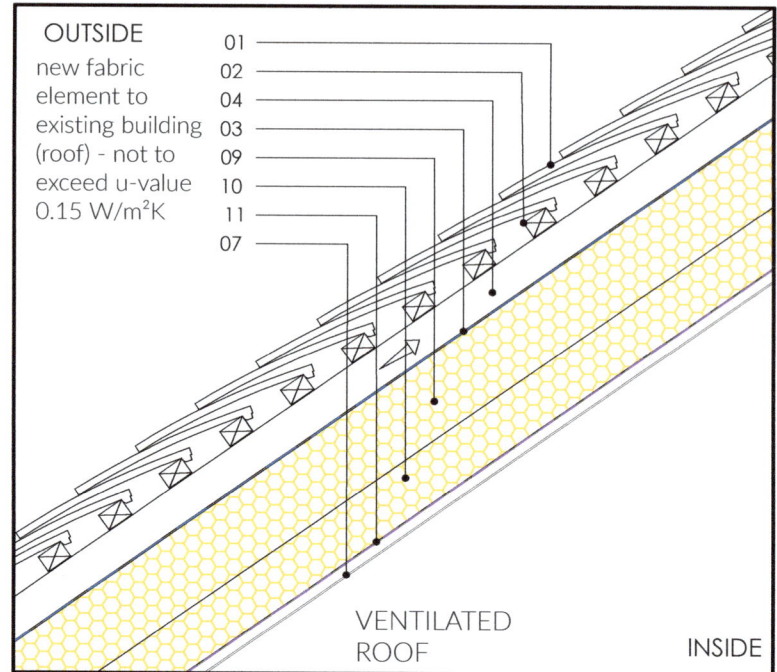

VENTILATED ROOF

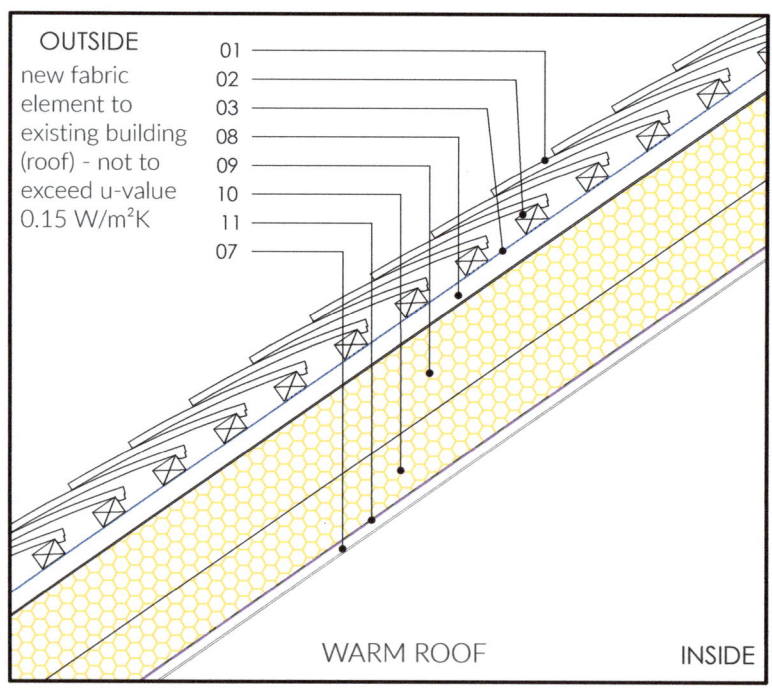

WARM ROOF

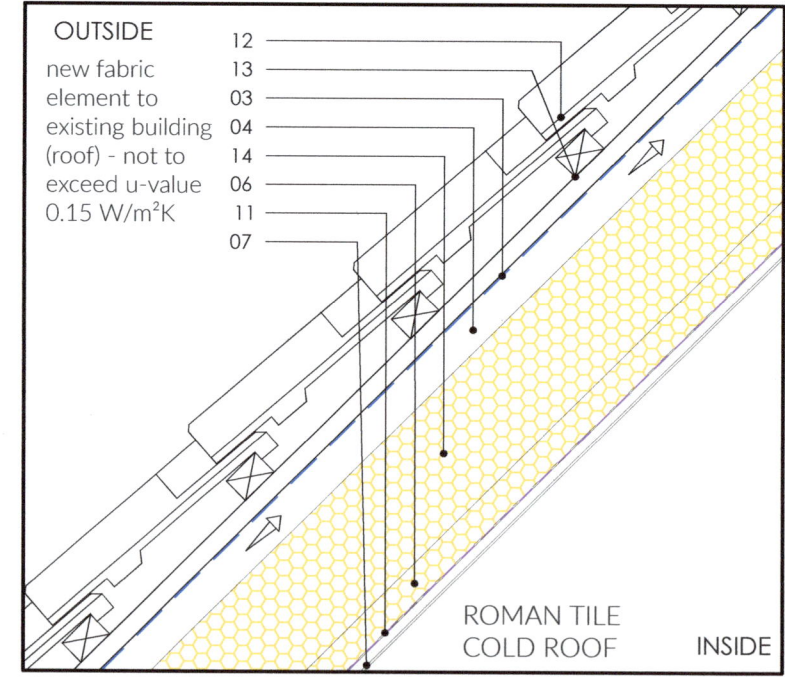

ROMAN TILE COLD ROOF

01. clay tiles
02. 25 x 38mm timber battens to BS 5534: 2014
03. breather membrane to BS 5250: 2011
04. 50mm min. unobstructed airgap over rafter insulation or created with external grade timber battens on existing rafters
05. 50-200mm high performance rigid insulation dependant on rafter width, fitted between rafters
06. 40-120mm high performance rigid insulation fitted under rafters with taped joints to provide a vapour control layer & air leakage barrier
07. 12.5mm plasterboard with 3mm plaster skim coat & paint finish
08. 10-25mm unobstructed airgap to insulation manufacturer's recommendations
09. 100-150mm high performance rigid insulation dependant on rafter width, fitted between rafters
10. 40-120mm high performance rigid insulation fitted under rafters
11. VCL or tape & jointed insulation if VCL inbuilt into insulation
12. interconnecting clay pantiles or roman tiles
13. 38x50mm battens on 25x38mm counter battens
14. 150mm high performance rigid insulating fitted between rafters

Flat Roof Types

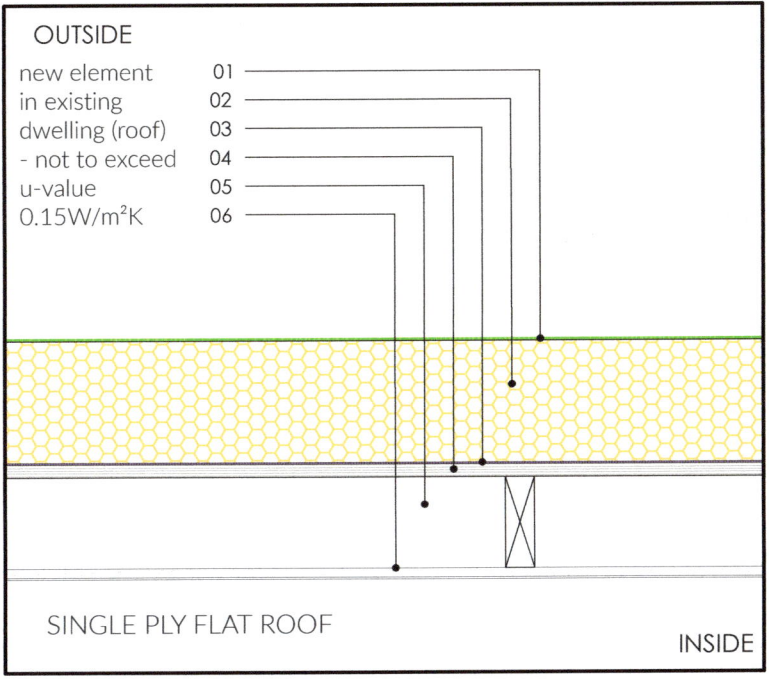

SINGLE PLY FLAT ROOF

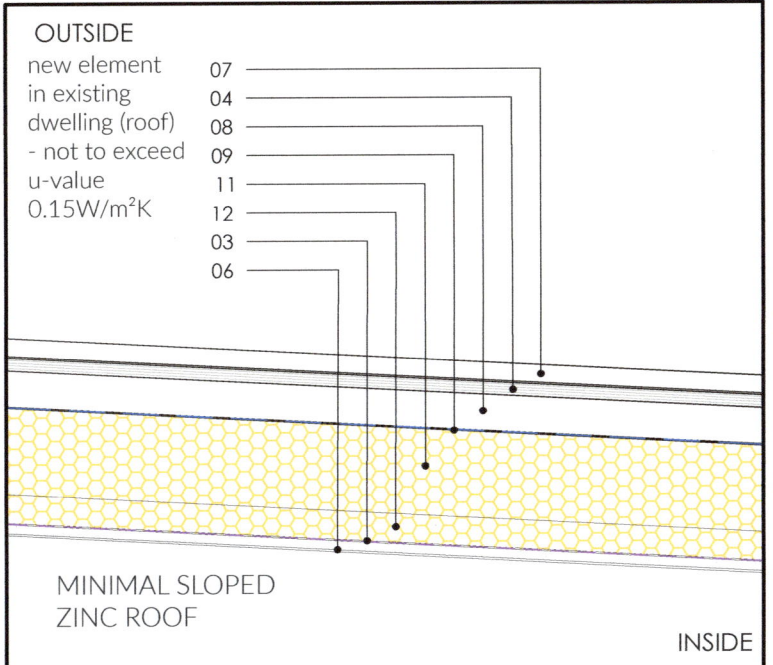

MINIMAL SLOPED ZINC ROOF

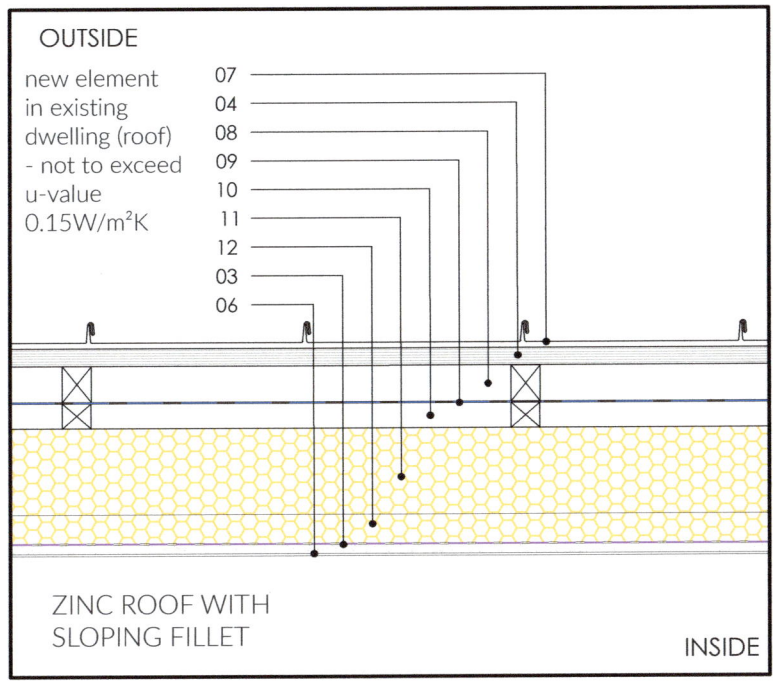

ZINC ROOF WITH SLOPING FILLET

01. high performance single ply roofing membrane / finish shown fully adhered to top of insulation with hot air welds - this can also be mechanically fixed & the detail will vary between manufacturers, typically with 100-150mm laps
02. 170mm high performance rigid insulation or thickness to suite U-Value requirement
03. vapour control layer
04. 18mm marine grade plywood
05. 100-250mm timber structured roof, void created for lighting, services and to create a flush ceiling with structure, depth dependant on SE calculations
06. 12.5mm plasterboard with 3mm plaster skim coat & paint finish, an extra layer of plasterboard or higher grade plasterboard may be chosen for a better finish or fire requirements
07. zinc - vertical standing seam shown, finish to desired specification
08. 50mm unobstructed ventilated cavity to be created with external grade timber, cavity reduction or increase dependant on zinc manufacturer's recommendations
09. breather membrane to BS 5250: 2011
10. timber tilting fillet, slope according to zinc manufacturers recommendations
11. 120mm high performance rigid insulation between studs or thickness to suite U-Value
12. 40mm high performance rigid insulation inside studs or thickness to suite U-Value

General Loft Details

This first set of details includes the most standard junctions that are encountered in a loft conversion. This set includes stair and floor details, various eaves arrangements and wall upgrade details.

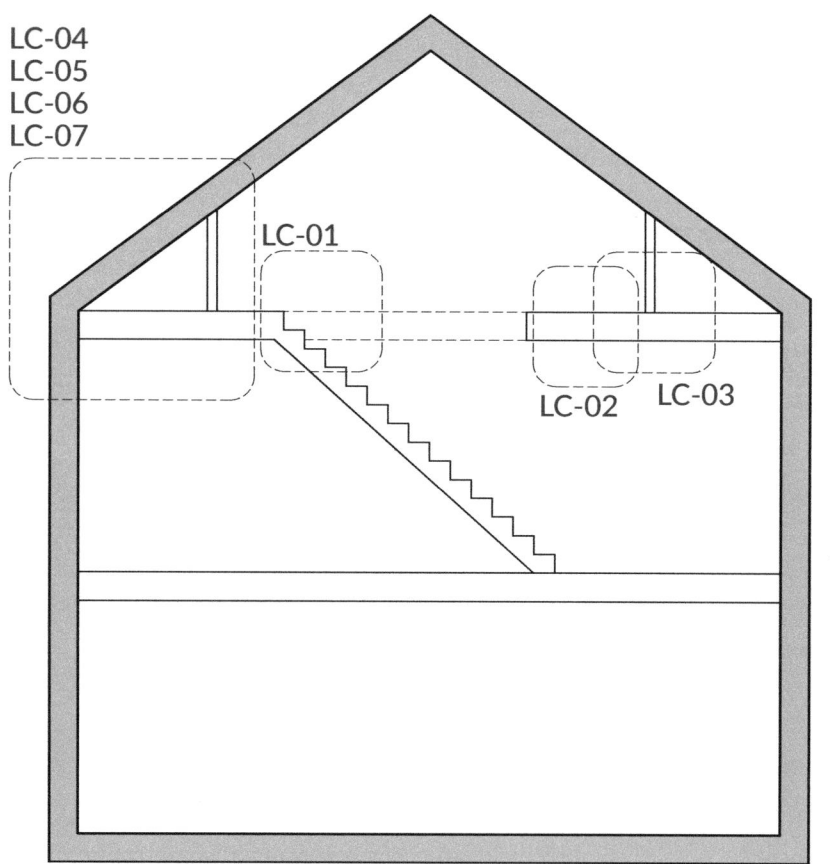
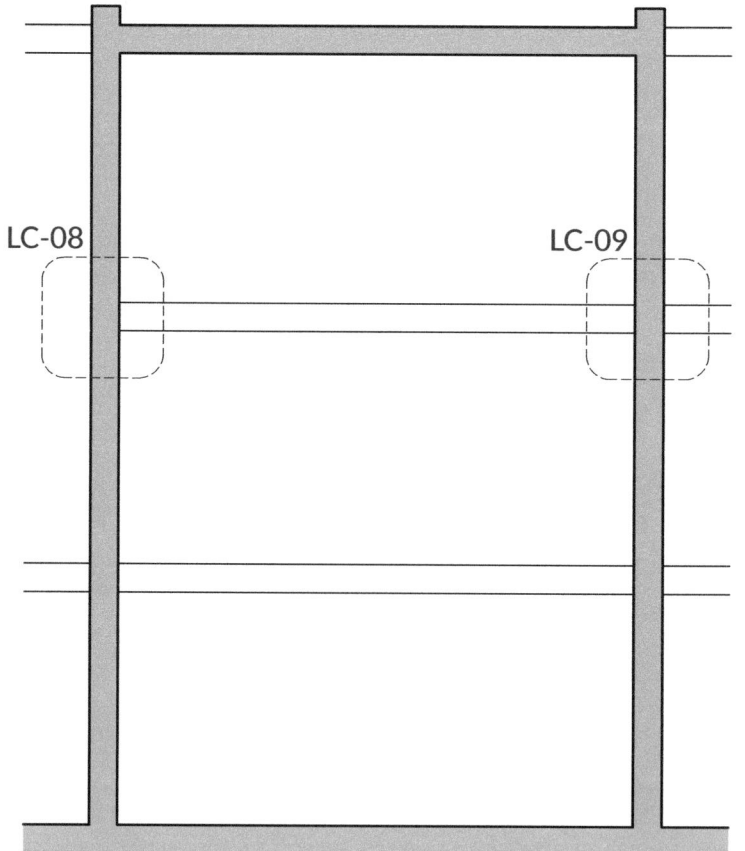

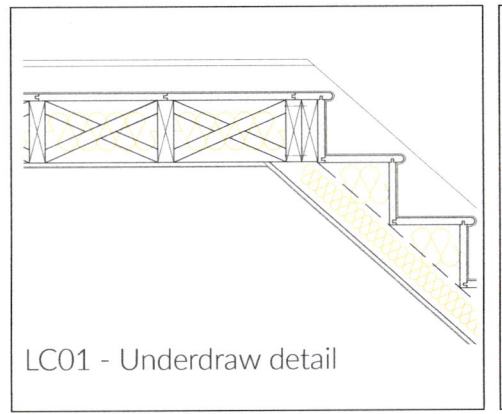
LC01 - Underdraw detail

LC02 - New floor detail

LC03 - Support under stud walls

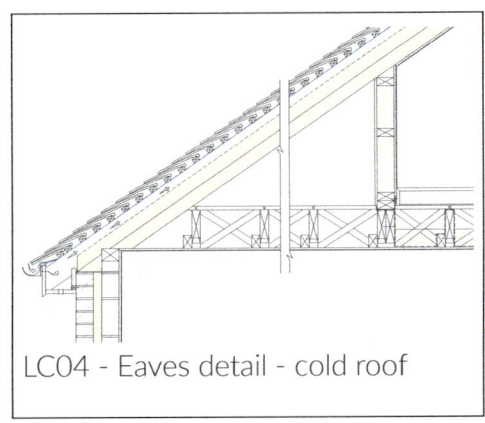
LC04 - Eaves detail - cold roof

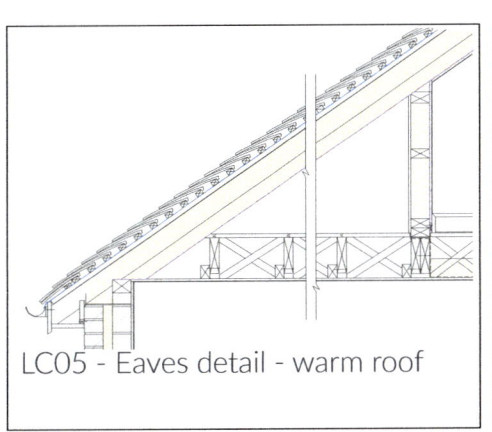
LC05 - Eaves detail - warm roof

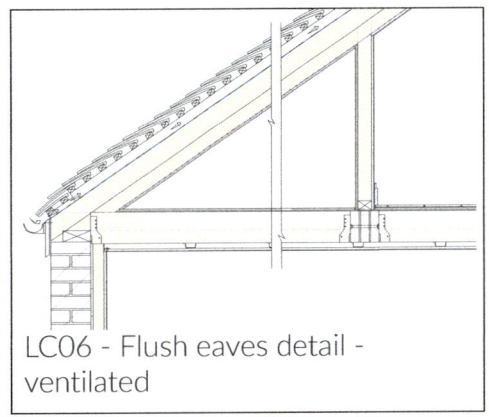
LC06 - Flush eaves detail - ventilated

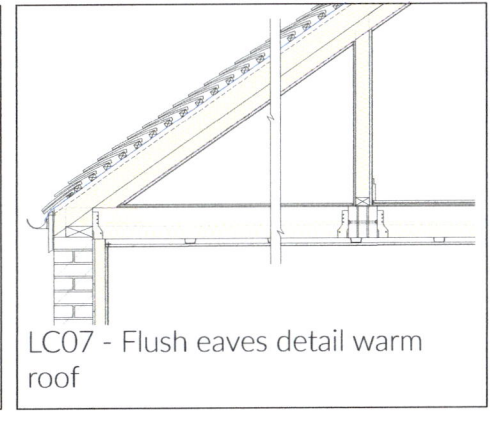
LC07 - Flush eaves detail warm roof

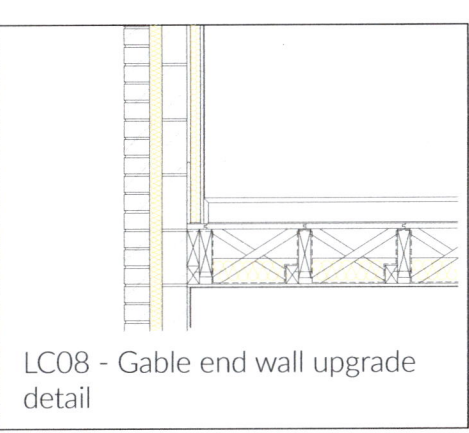
LC08 - Gable end wall upgrade detail

LC09 - Party wall upgrade detail

LC-01
UNDERDRAW DETAIL / LANDING TRIMMER

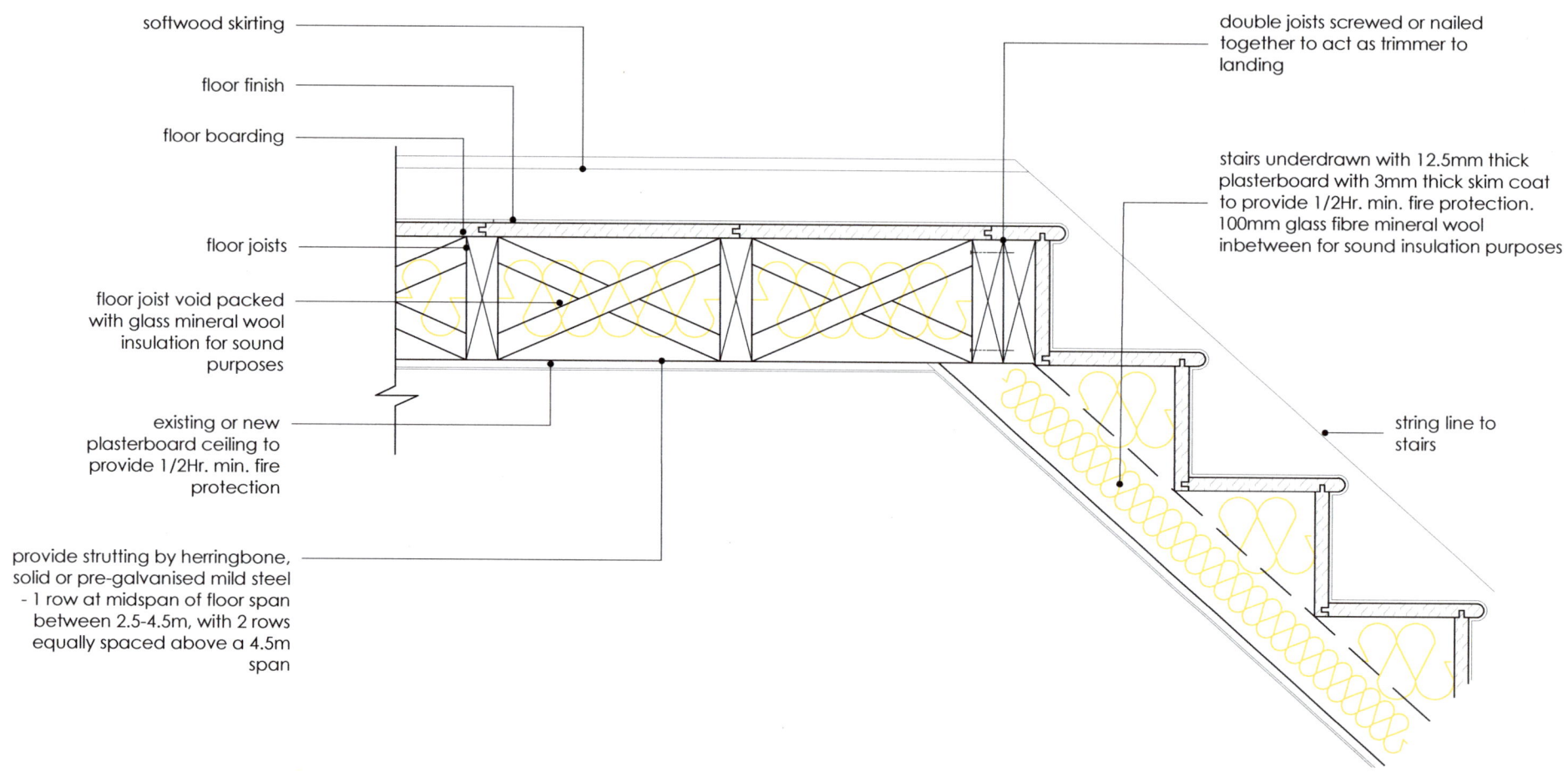

2D Detail LC-01 - Underdraw detail / landing trimmer

Drawing note:
this is a typical detail of a new staircase up to the loft conversion which shows that the stairs & floor when moving into a 3rd storey of a dwelling require 1/2Hr. min. fire protection - usually achieved by using a mineral wool insulation to provide both fire & sound protection alongside the existing plasterboard ceiling / new plasterboard to ensure an adequate amount of fire protection.
note the double joist trimmer at the top of the stairs; sometimes this will need to be calculated by structural engineer dependant on the span of the trimmer & if any additional loads are to be transferred on to them

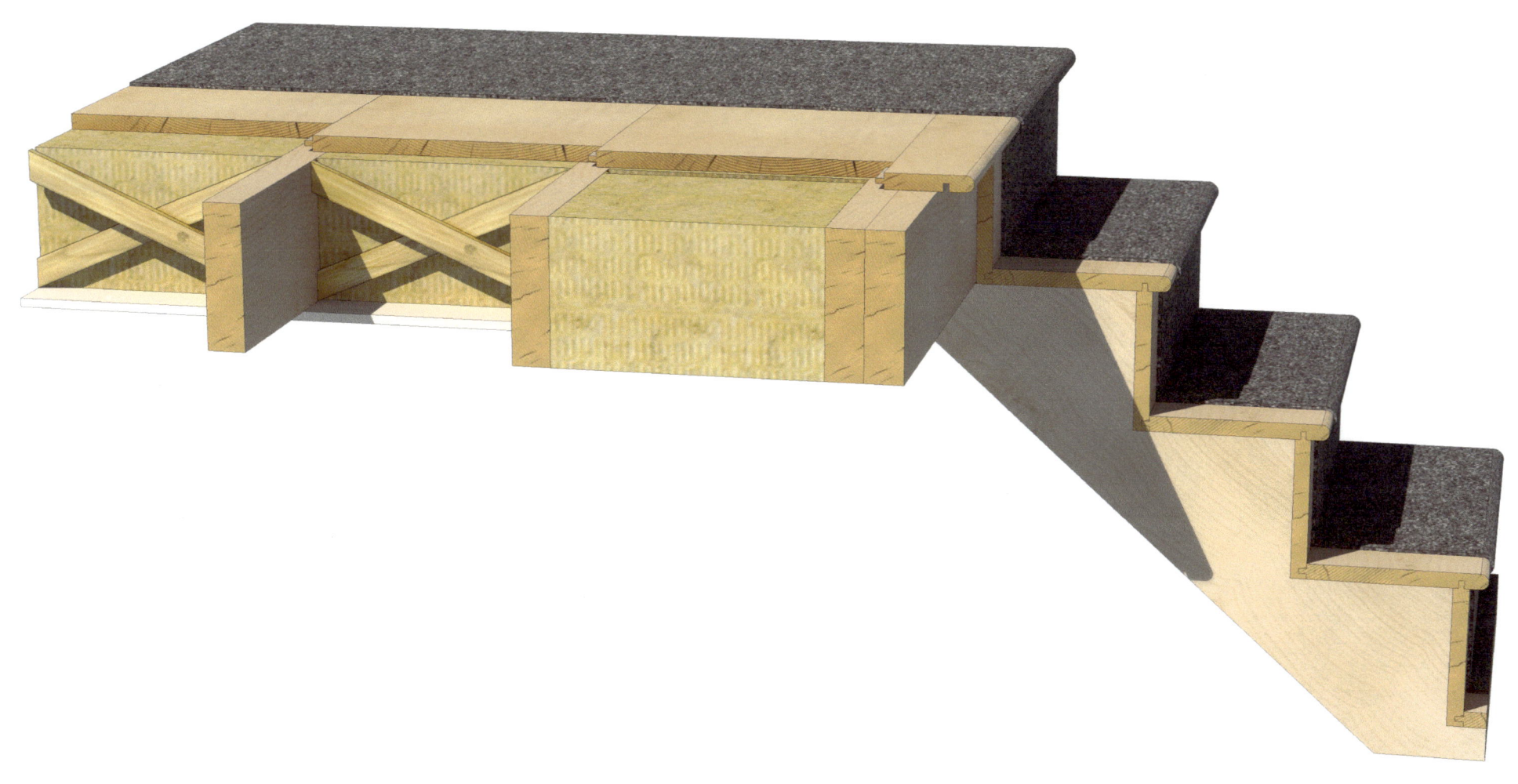

3D Detail LC-01 - Underdraw detail / landing trimmer

LC-02

FIRE AND SOUND PROOFING SHOWING NEW JOISTS ALONGSIDE EXISTING

- softwood skirting
- floor finish
- 18-22mm thick flooring grade tongue & grooved floor boarding screwed & glued together & screwed down to new floor joists
- 5mm thick acoustic isolation strip screwed or glued to top of floor joists for sound deadening purposes
- new floor joists (typically 195-250mm long) screwed, nailed or strapped alongside the existing ceiling joists
- provide lateral support with mild steel straps at 2.0m max. c/c's taken across at least 3No. joists all to Part "A" of the current Building Regulations.
- void between floor joists filled with 100mm fire proof insulation (such as Rockwool Flexi) on fixed galvanised chicken wire mesh for fire & sound insulation purposes
- provide strutting by herringbone, solid or pre-galvanised mild steel - 1 row at midspan of floor span between 2.5-4.5m, with 2 rows equally spaced above a 4.5m span
- bottom of new floor joists set with a 25mm deflection gap to bottom of existing ceiling joists
- existing plasterboard & skim or lath & plaster ceiling

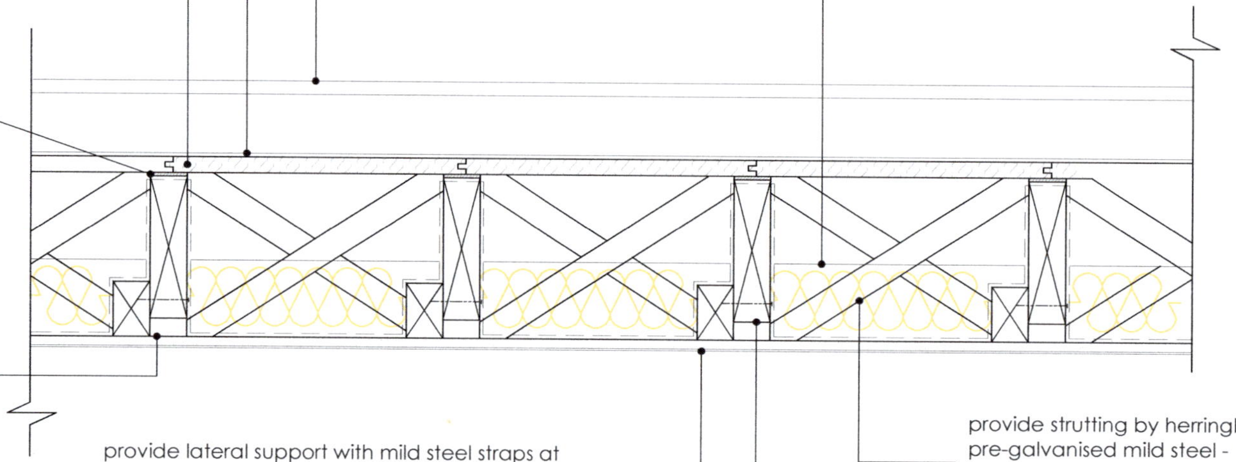

2D Detail LC-02 - Floor detail showing new joists alongside existing

Drawing note:
this is a typical detail of the new 2nd floor / existing 1st floor ceiling of to provide 1/2Hr. min. fire protection - usually achieved by using a mineral wool insulation to provide both fire & sound protection alongside the existing plasterboard ceiling.
note that floor joist spans above 2.5m will require strutting to brace the floor joists & help prevent twisting.

3D Detail LC-02 - Floor detail showing new joists alongside existing

LC-03
FLOOR DETAIL SHOWING SUPPORT UNDER STUD WALLS

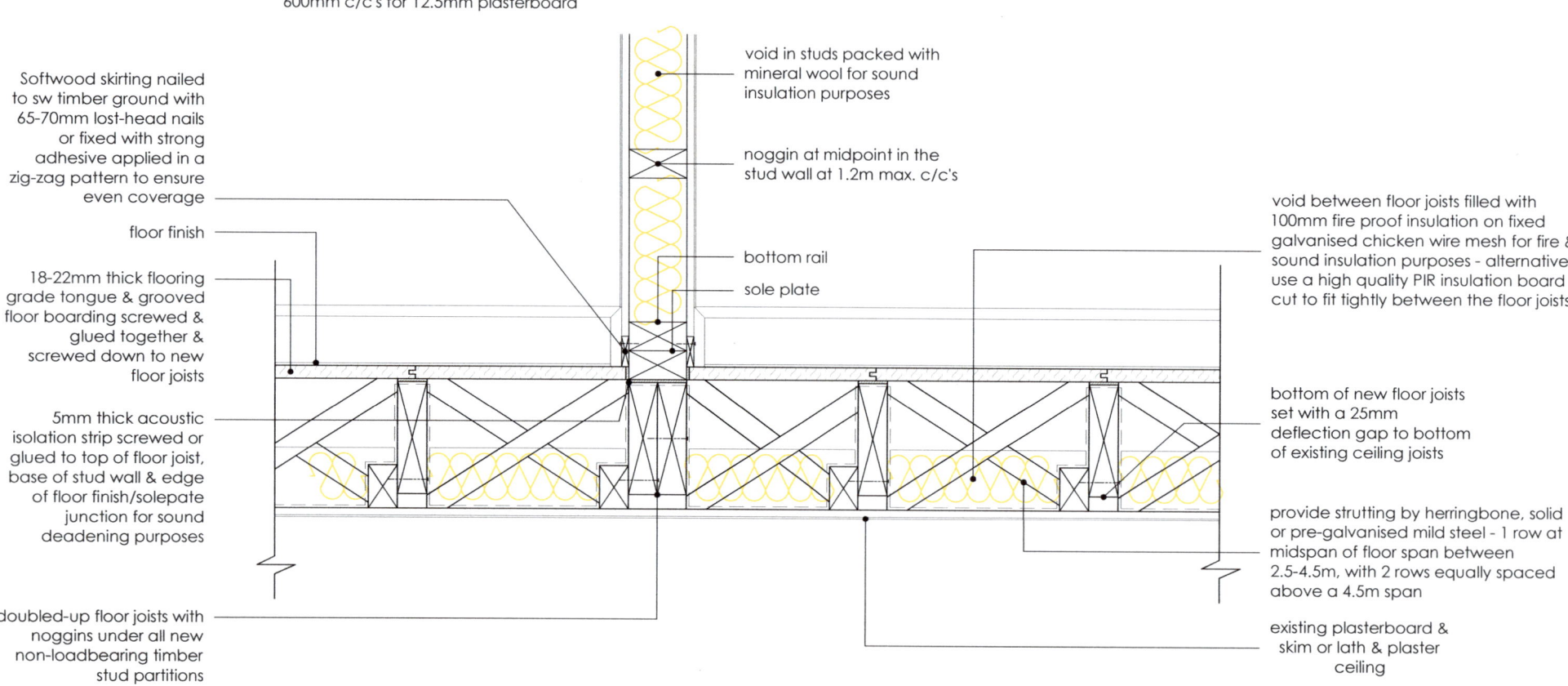

2D Detail LC-03 - Floor detail showing support under stud walls

Drawing note:
this is a typical detail showing a new non-loadbearing stud wall in the loft conversion with doubled-up floor joists below it as support & a base / sole plate.
sometimes a stud wall can also be loadbearing to help support the existing roof structure which will need to be designed & detailed by a structural engineer.

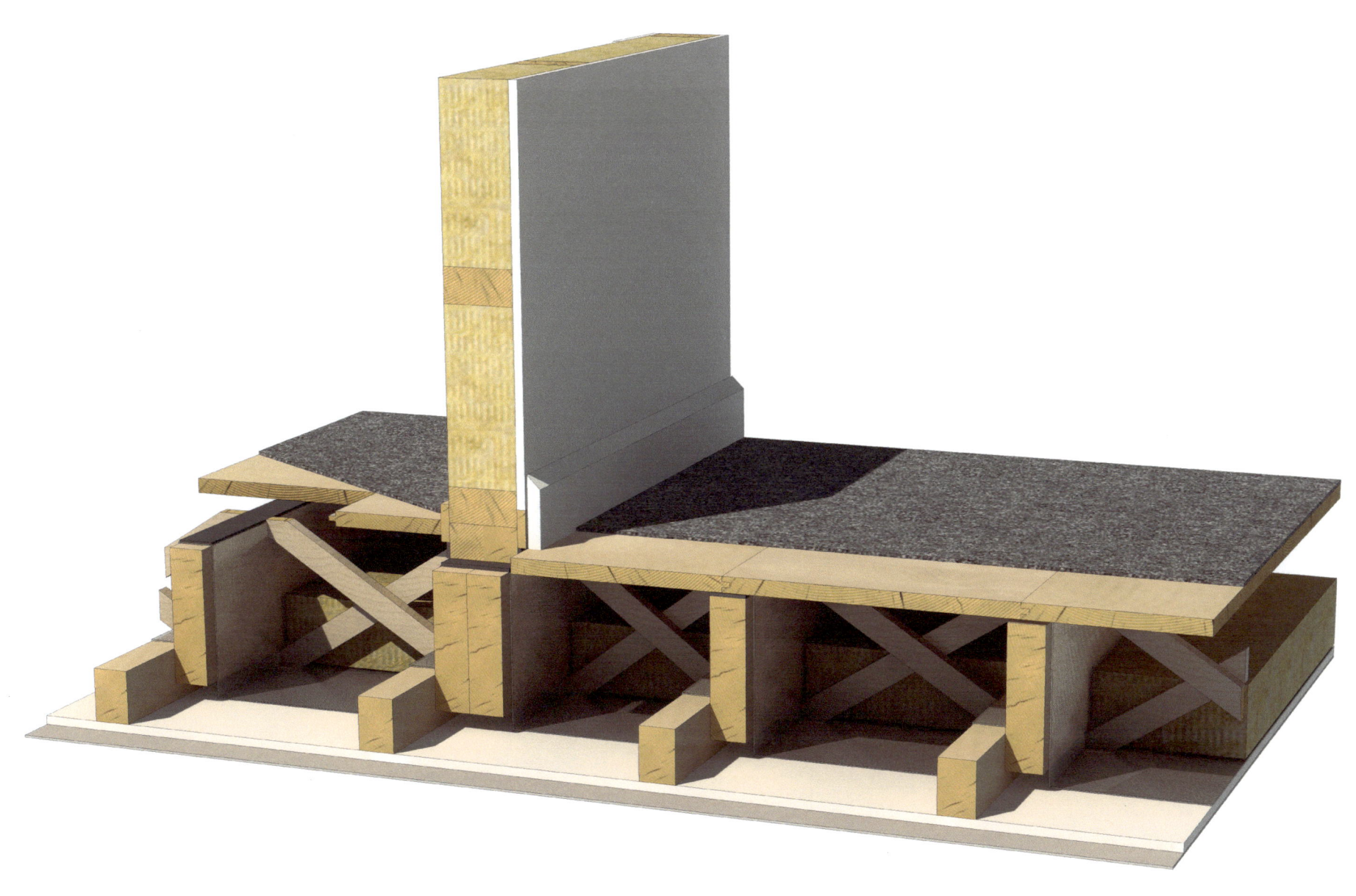

3D Detail LC-03 - Floor detail showing support under stud walls

LC-04

EAVES DETAIL - COLD ROOF

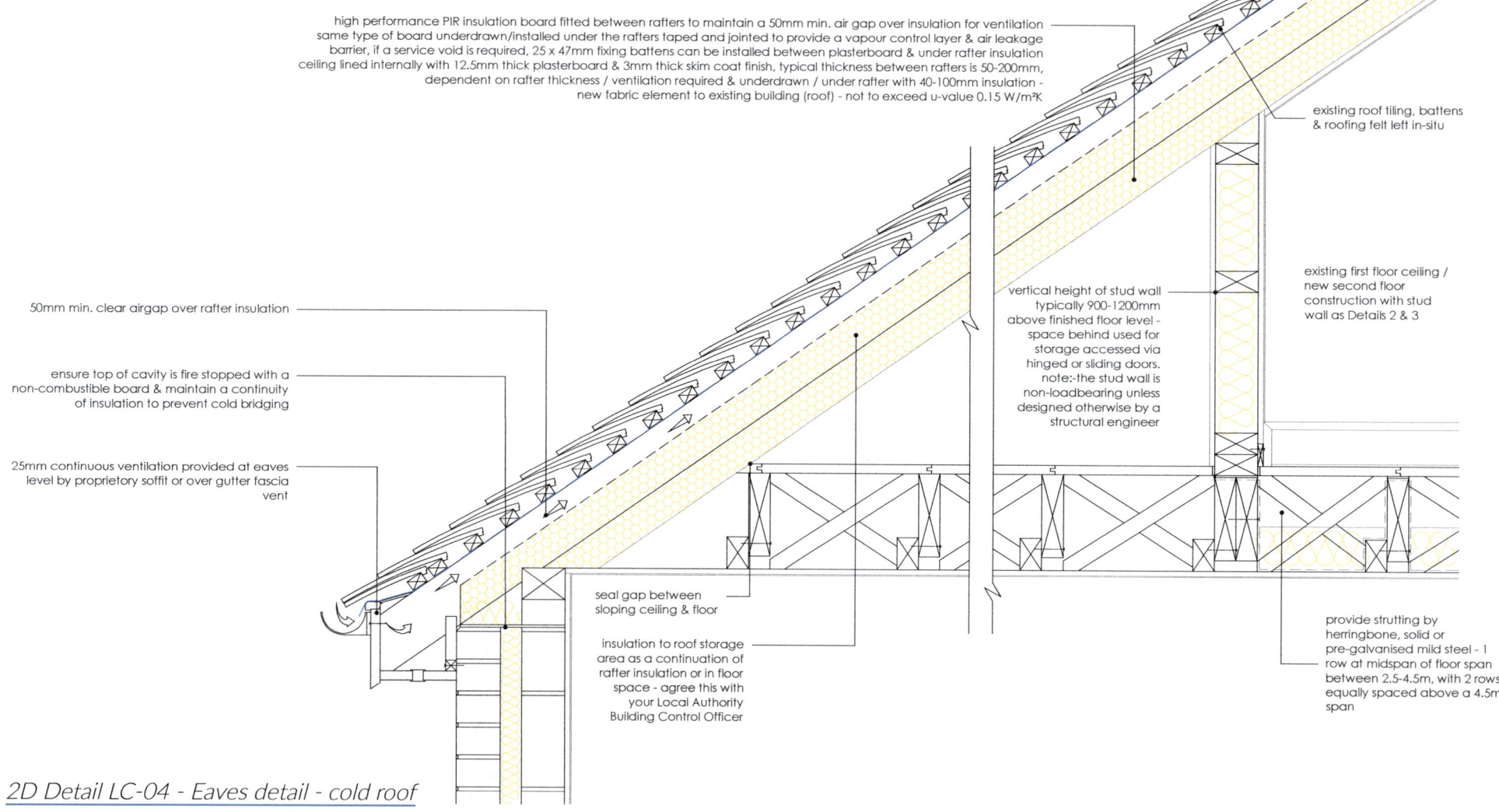

2D Detail LC-04 - Eaves detail - cold roof

Drawing note:
this is a "cold" roof situation that is typically used in a loft conversion when the roof tiles are being left in-situ. See Detail LC05 for "warm" roof detail that can be used when the roof tiles & roofing felt are being replaced.
ensure 50mm continuous ventilation is provided at ridge / high level by proprietary ridge vent or tile vents - this maintains cross ventilation throughout the roof space.

3D Detail LC-04 - Eaves detail - cold roof

LC-05
EAVES DETAIL - WARM ROOF

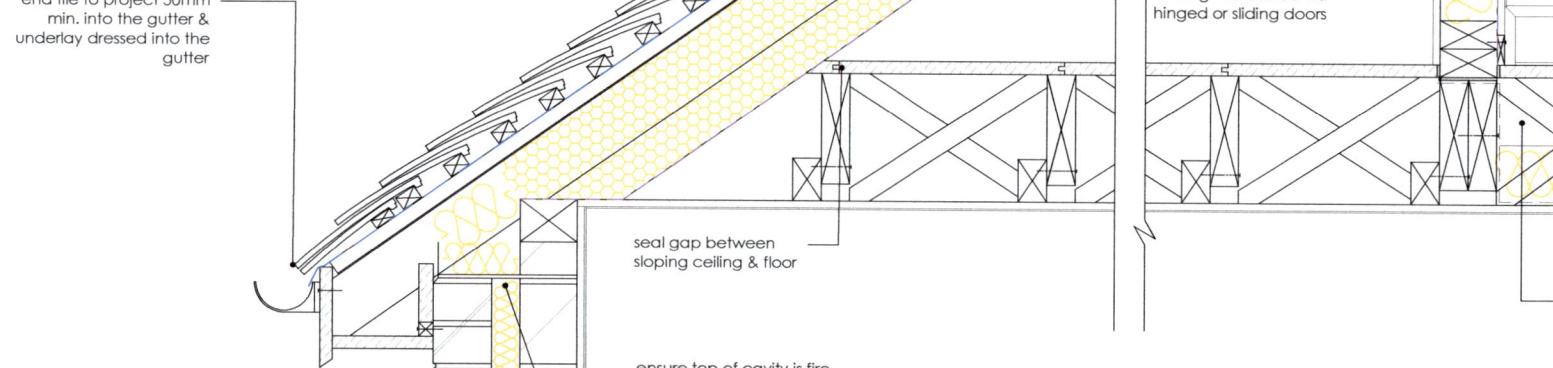

2D Detail LC-05 - Eaves detail - warm roof

Drawing note:
this is a "warm" roof situation that is typically used when the roof tiles & roofing felt are being replaced. See Detail LC04 for "cold" roof detail that can be used when the existing roof tiles are remaining in-situ. If re-roofing, the insulation can be fitted in a variety of ways - over the rafters, between & over the rafters, between the rafters, or as shown between & under the rafters - see your chosen insulation manufacturers installation guidelines for full details.

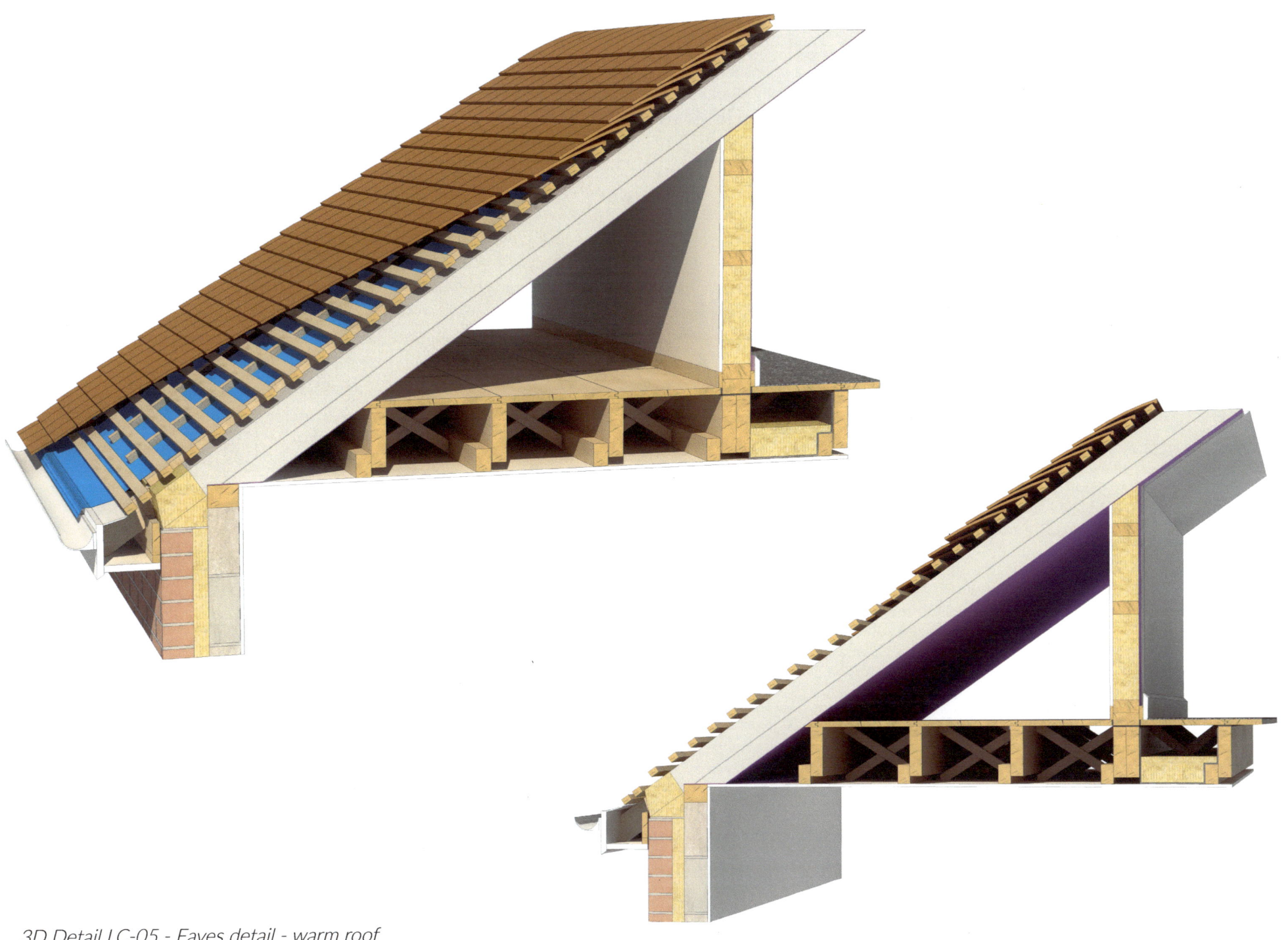

3D Detail LC-05 - Eaves detail - warm roof

LC-06

ALTERNATIVE FLUSH EAVES DETAIL - VENTILATED

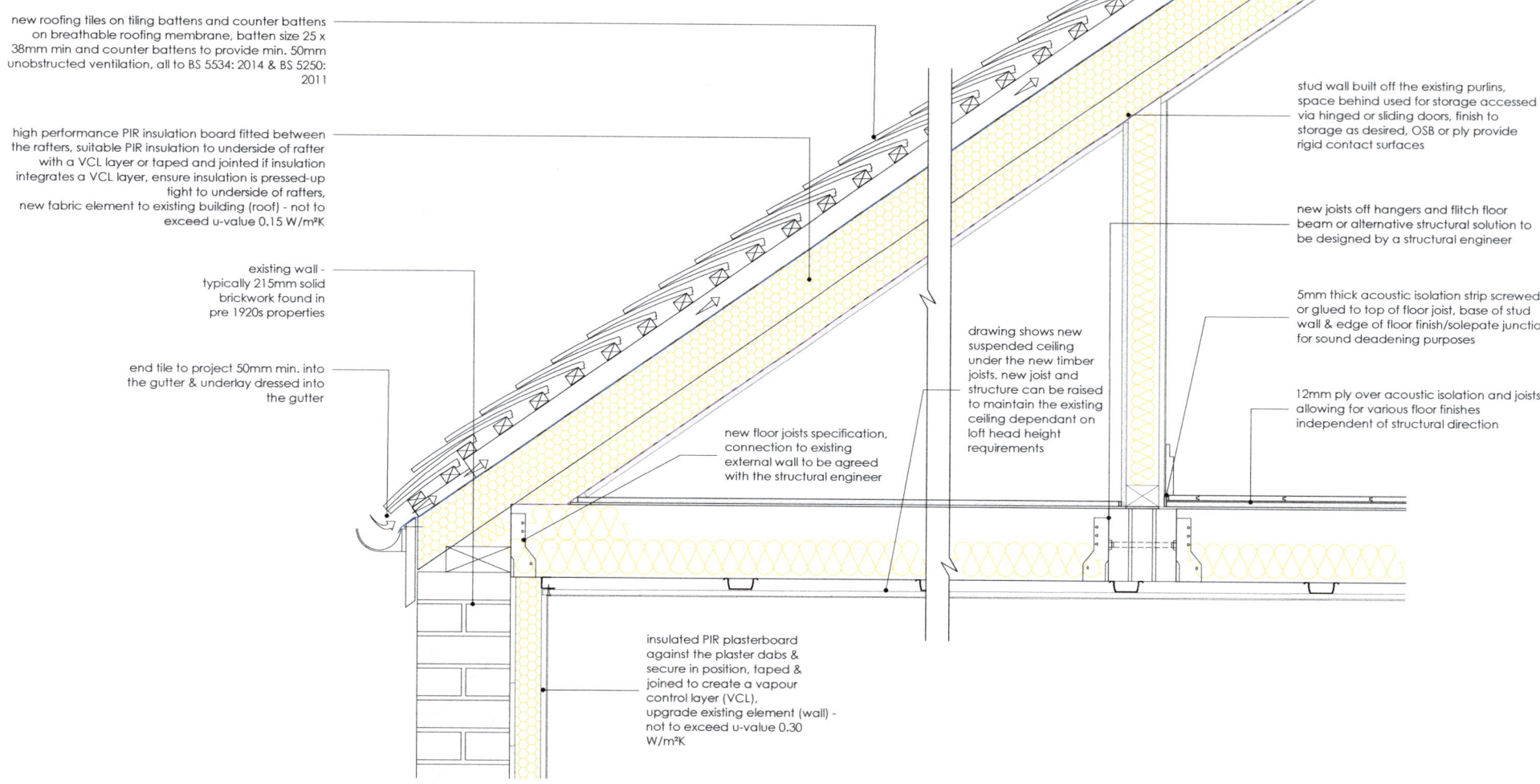

2D Detail LC-06 - Alternative flush eaves detail - ventilated

Drawing note:
this is a "cold" roof situation that is typically used if the existing rafters are small and a large ventilation area needs to be maintained. See Detail LC07 for "warm" roof detail that can be used when the existing rafters are larger and allow for small ventilation area between rafters if re-roofing, the insulation can be fitted in a variety of ways - over the rafters, between & over the rafters, between the rafters, or as shown between & under the rafters - see your chosen insulation manufacturers installation guidelines for full details.

3D Detail LC-06 - Alternative flush eaves detail - ventilated

LC-07

ALTERNATIVE FLUSH EAVES DETAIL - WARM ROOF

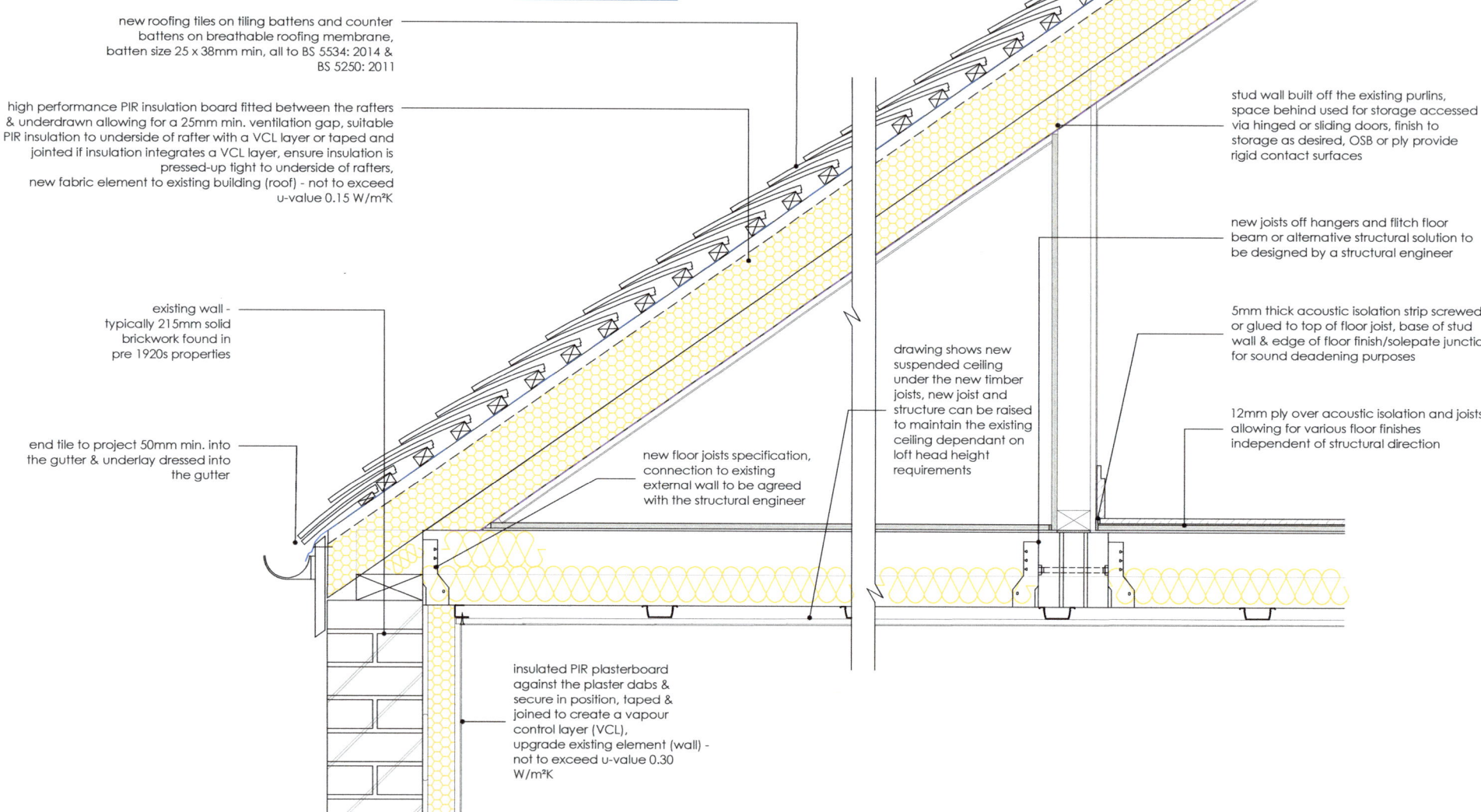

2D Detail LC-07 - Alternative flush eaves detail - warm roof

Drawing note: this is a "warm" roof situation that is typically used when the roof tiles & roofing felt are being replaced. See Detail LC06 for "cold" roof detail that can be used when the existing rafters are larger and allow for small ventilation area between rafters.
if re-roofing, the insulation can be fitted in a variety of ways - over the rafters, between & over the rafters, between the rafters, or as shown between & under the rafters - see your chosen insulation manufacturers installation guidelines for full details.

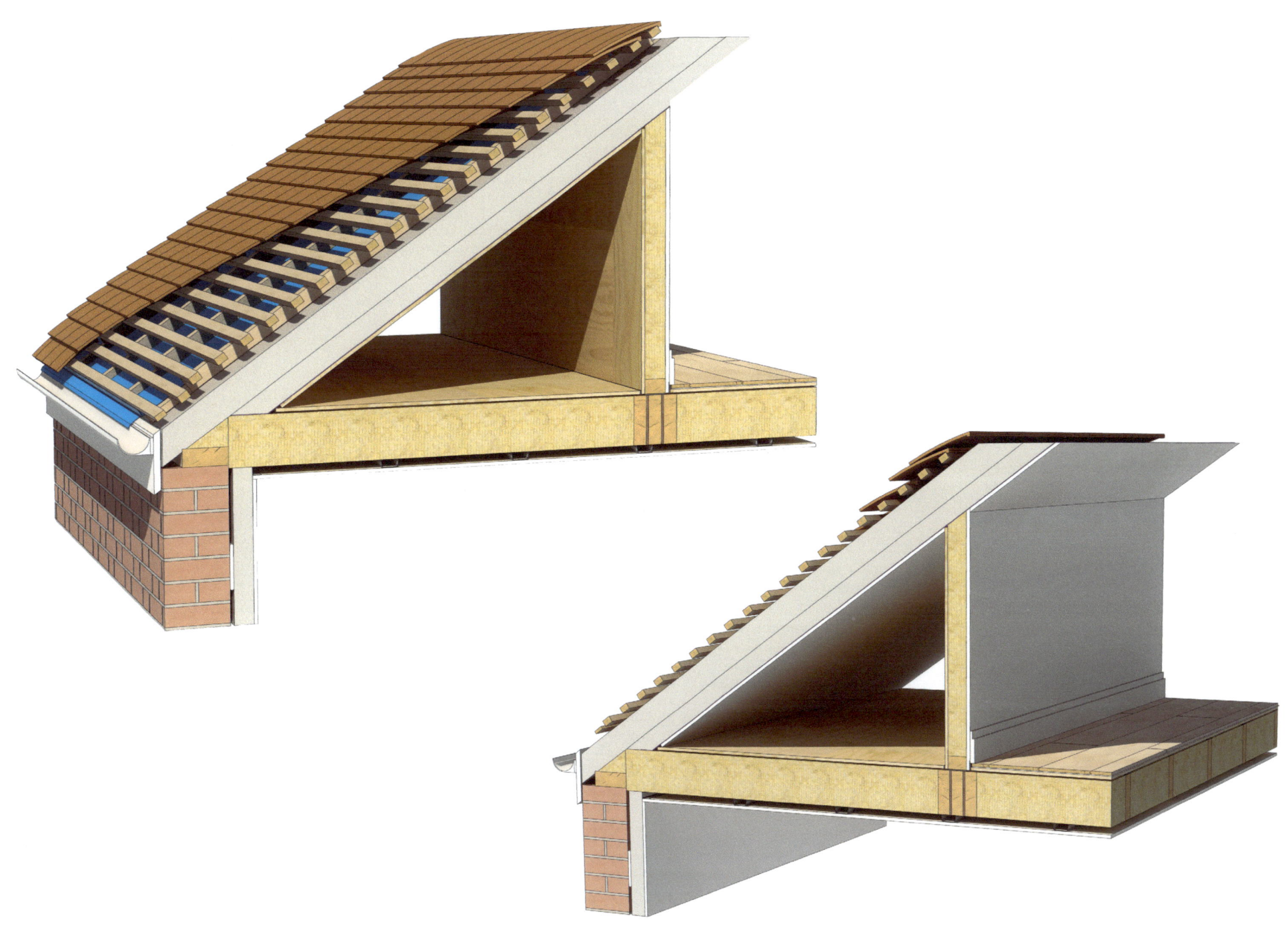

3D Detail LC-07 - Alternative flush eaves detail - warm roof

LC-08
GABLE END WALL UPGRADE DETAIL

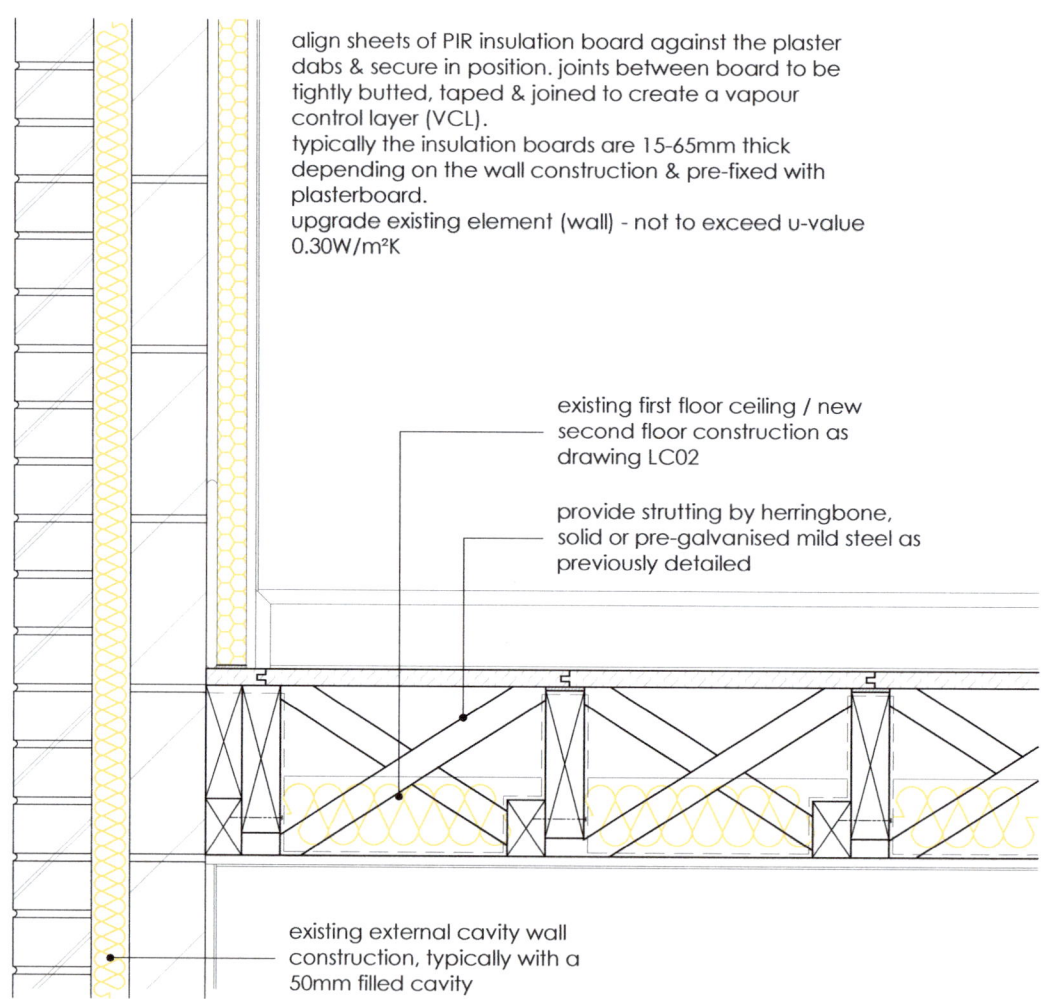

internal face of external wall in the roofspace to be converted - treat this wall with a soap based chemical treatment to leave the surface clean & free of dirt & dust.
apply a continuous seal of plasterboard adhesive (plaster dab) at skirting level 10-15mm thick, 50-75mm wide & approx. 250mm long in 3 vertical rows per board. alternativey use 25 x 50mm min. treated sw timber battens mechically fixed at 600mm max. c/c's. allow for additional secondary fixings if specified by your chosen insulation manufacturer

align sheets of PIR insulation board against the plaster dabs & secure in position. joints between board to be tightly butted, taped & joined to create a vapour control layer (VCL).
typically the insulation boards are 15-65mm thick depending on the wall construction & pre-fixed with plasterboard.
upgrade existing element (wall) - not to exceed u-value $0.30 W/m^2K$

existing first floor ceiling / new second floor construction as drawing LC02

provide strutting by herringbone, solid or pre-galvanised mild steel as previously detailed

existing external cavity wall construction, typically with a 50mm filled cavity

2D Detail LC-08 - Gable end wall upgrade detail

Drawing note: this is a typical existing gable wall upgrade detail showing a high quality PIR insulation board to maximise the usable floor area in the loft conversion - another option is to stud-out the wall internally & fill the void with glass-fibre insulation but this option will take-up more of the floor area as it needs a thicker amount of insulation to achieve the required U-value

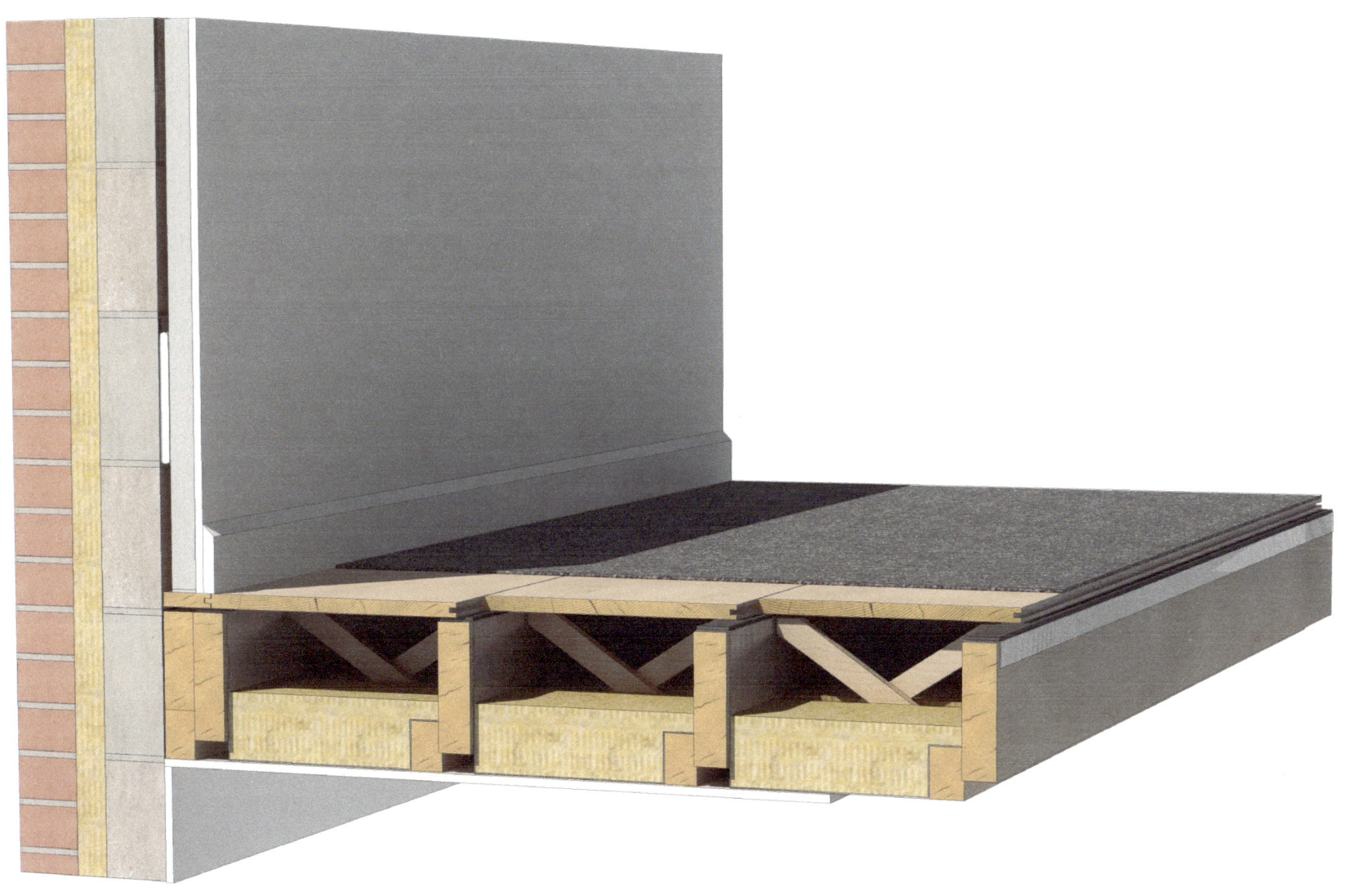

3D Detail LC-08 - Gable end wall upgrade detail

LC-09
PARTY WALL UPGRADE DETAIL

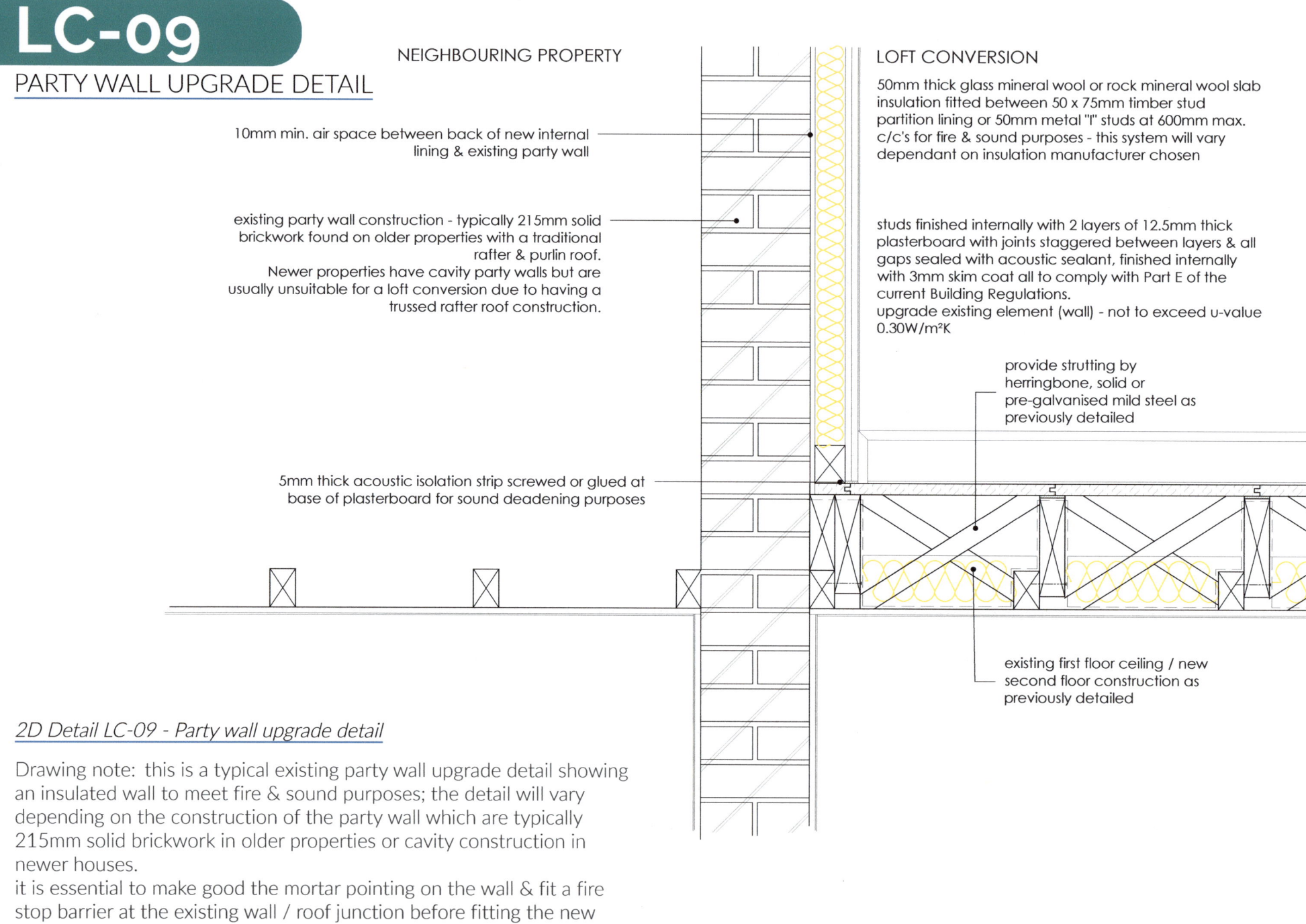

NEIGHBOURING PROPERTY

10mm min. air space between back of new internal lining & existing party wall

existing party wall construction - typically 215mm solid brickwork found on older properties with a traditional rafter & purlin roof. Newer properties have cavity party walls but are usually unsuitable for a loft conversion due to having a trussed rafter roof construction.

5mm thick acoustic isolation strip screwed or glued at base of plasterboard for sound deadening purposes

LOFT CONVERSION

50mm thick glass mineral wool or rock mineral wool slab insulation fitted between 50 x 75mm timber stud partition lining or 50mm metal "I" studs at 600mm max. c/c's for fire & sound purposes - this system will vary dependant on insulation manufacturer chosen

studs finished internally with 2 layers of 12.5mm thick plasterboard with joints staggered between layers & all gaps sealed with acoustic sealant, finished internally with 3mm skim coat all to comply with Part E of the current Building Regulations.
upgrade existing element (wall) - not to exceed u-value 0.30W/m²K

provide strutting by herringbone, solid or pre-galvanised mild steel as previously detailed

existing first floor ceiling / new second floor construction as previously detailed

2D Detail LC-09 - Party wall upgrade detail

Drawing note: this is a typical existing party wall upgrade detail showing an insulated wall to meet fire & sound purposes; the detail will vary depending on the construction of the party wall which are typically 215mm solid brickwork in older properties or cavity construction in newer houses.
it is essential to make good the mortar pointing on the wall & fit a fire stop barrier at the existing wall / roof junction before fitting the new insulation & plasterboard.

3D Detail LC-09 - Party wall upgrade detail

Front Dormer Window Details

This set of details explores the different arrangements and junctions associated with from dormer windows. These dormer details all feature a pitched roof.

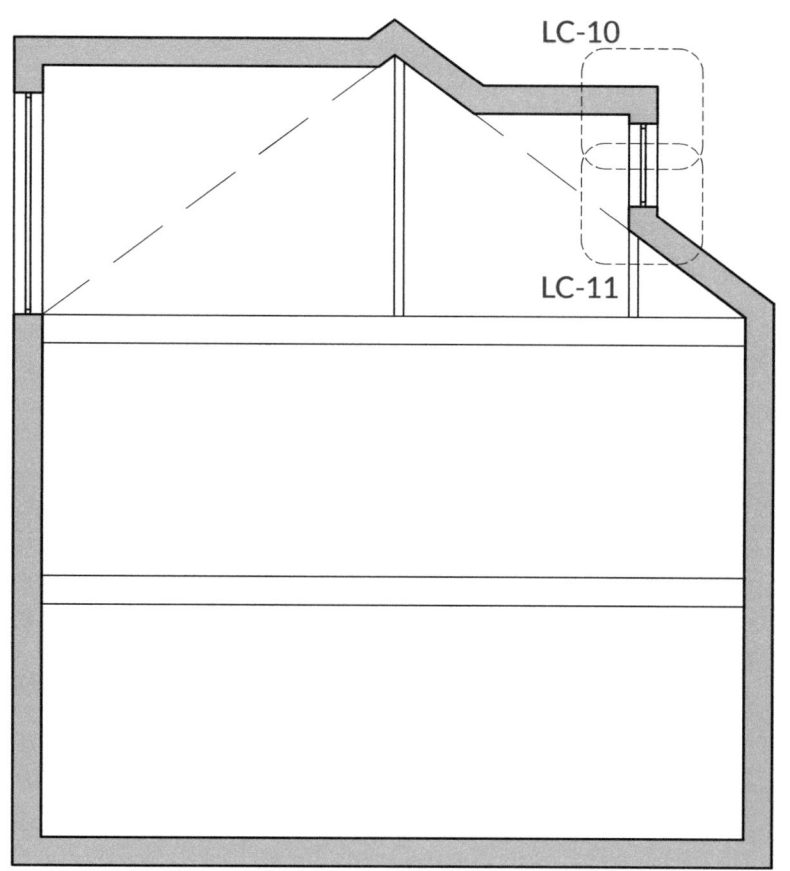
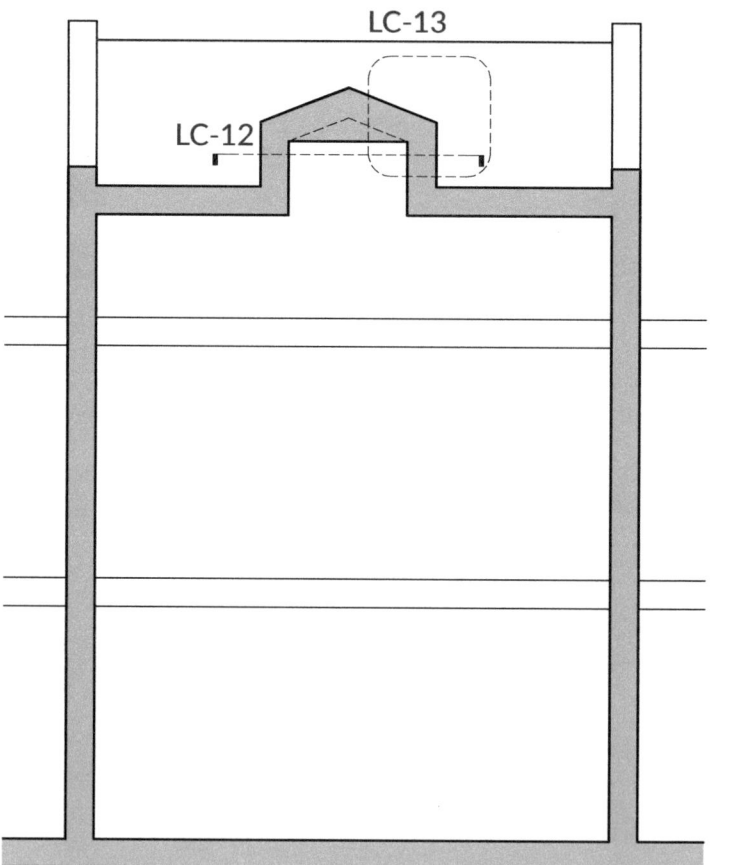

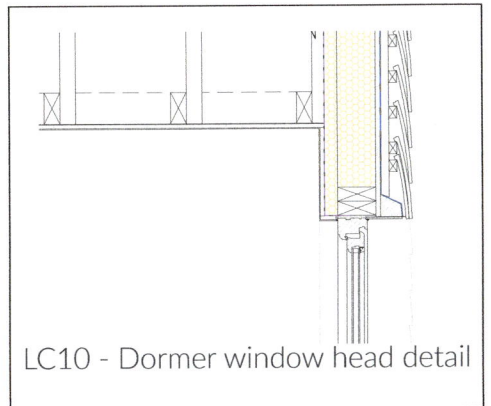

LC10 - Dormer window head detail

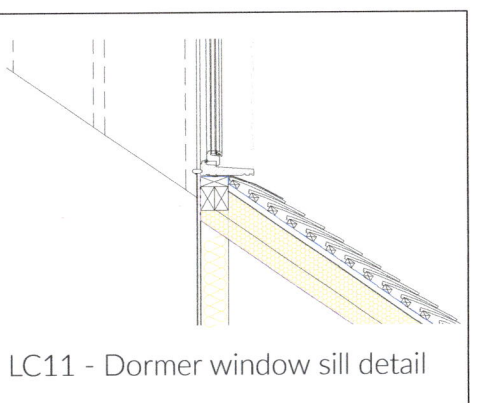

LC11 - Dormer window sill detail

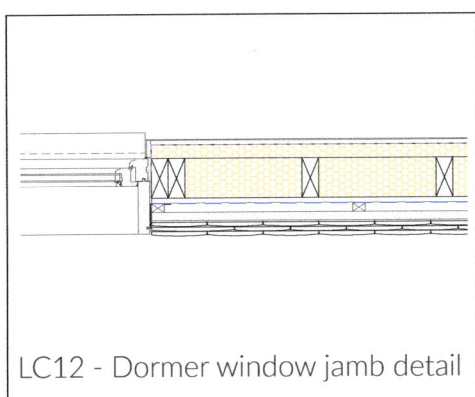

LC12 - Dormer window jamb detail

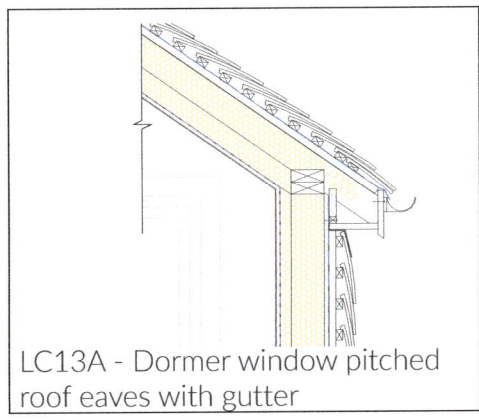

LC13A - Dormer window pitched roof eaves with gutter

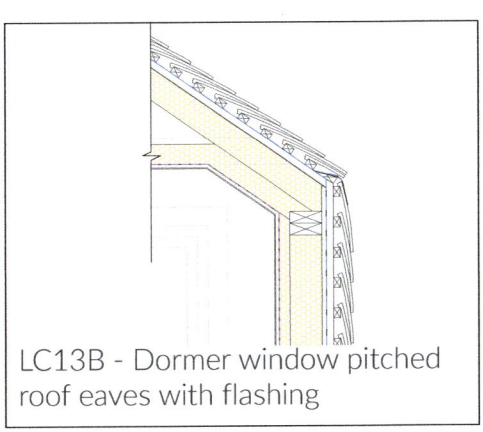

LC13B - Dormer window pitched roof eaves with flashing

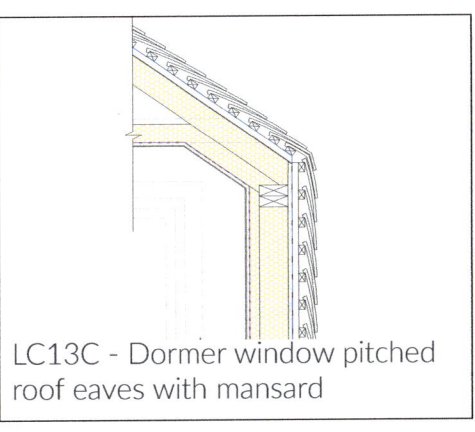

LC13C - Dormer window pitched roof eaves with mansard

LC-10
DORMER WINDOW HEAD DETAIL

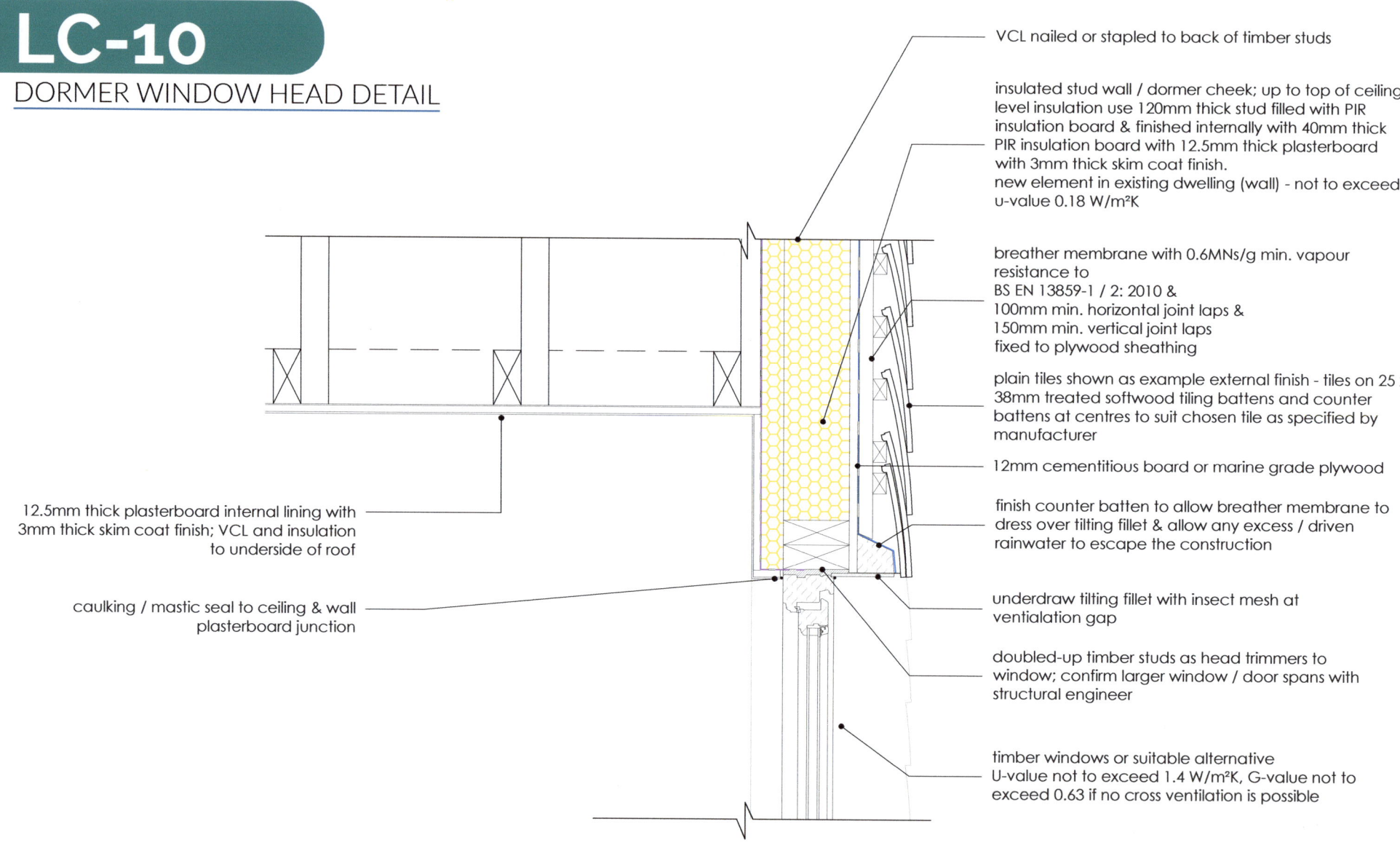

2D Detail LC-10 - Dormer window head detail

Drawing note:
this is a typical dormer window head detail with a sloped ceiling to allow for the greatest floor to ceiling height, comfortable finished floor to ceiling height around 2.3m, see detail LC13A for section running through the dormer cheeks.
one important part of the detail is the tilting fillet at the head - ensure there is enough angle & gap to allow any excess driven rainwater to escape the construction otherwise this will lead to premature rotting of the structure.

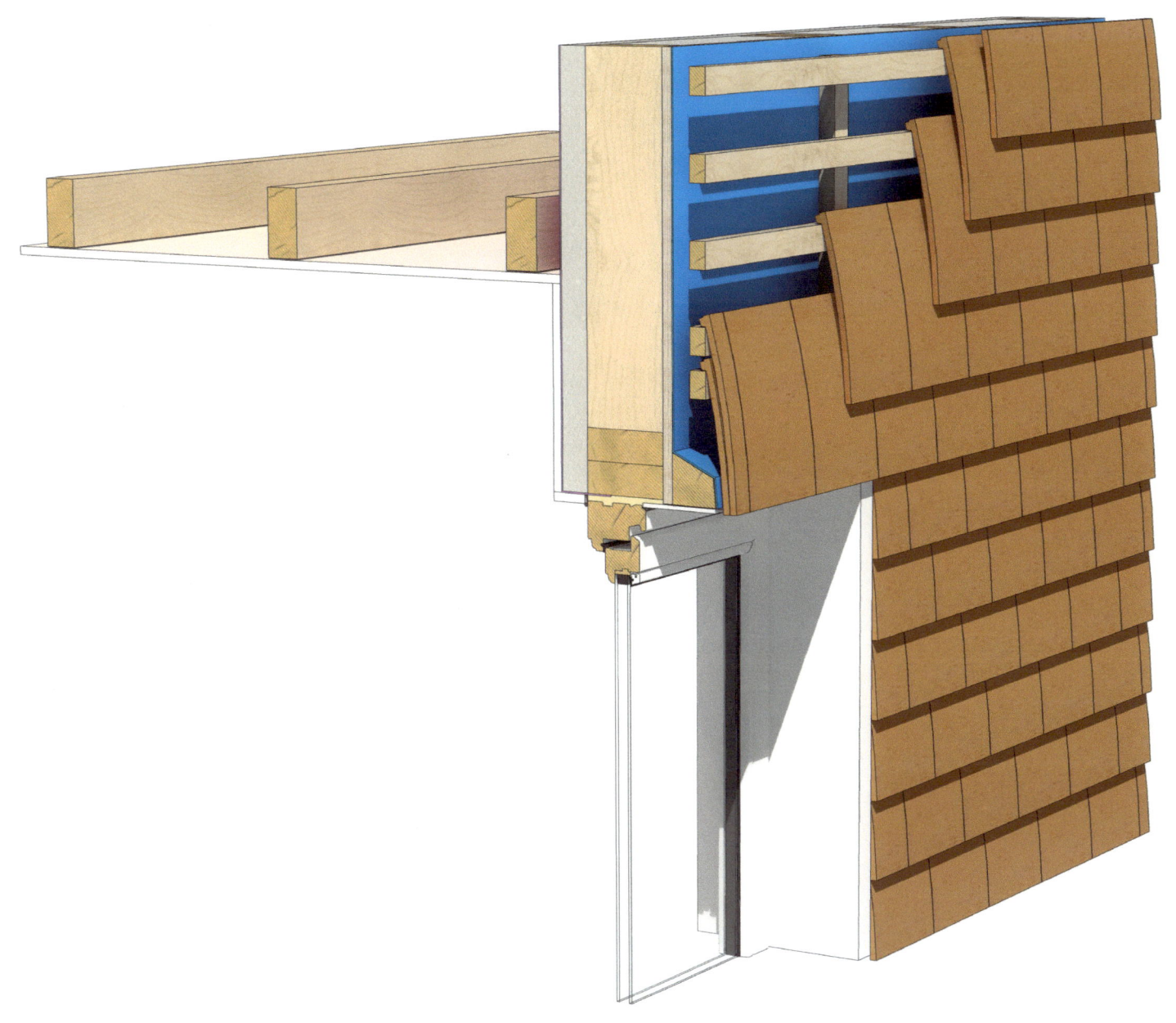

3D Detail LC-10 - Dormer window head detail

LC-11
DORMER WINDOW CILL DETAIL

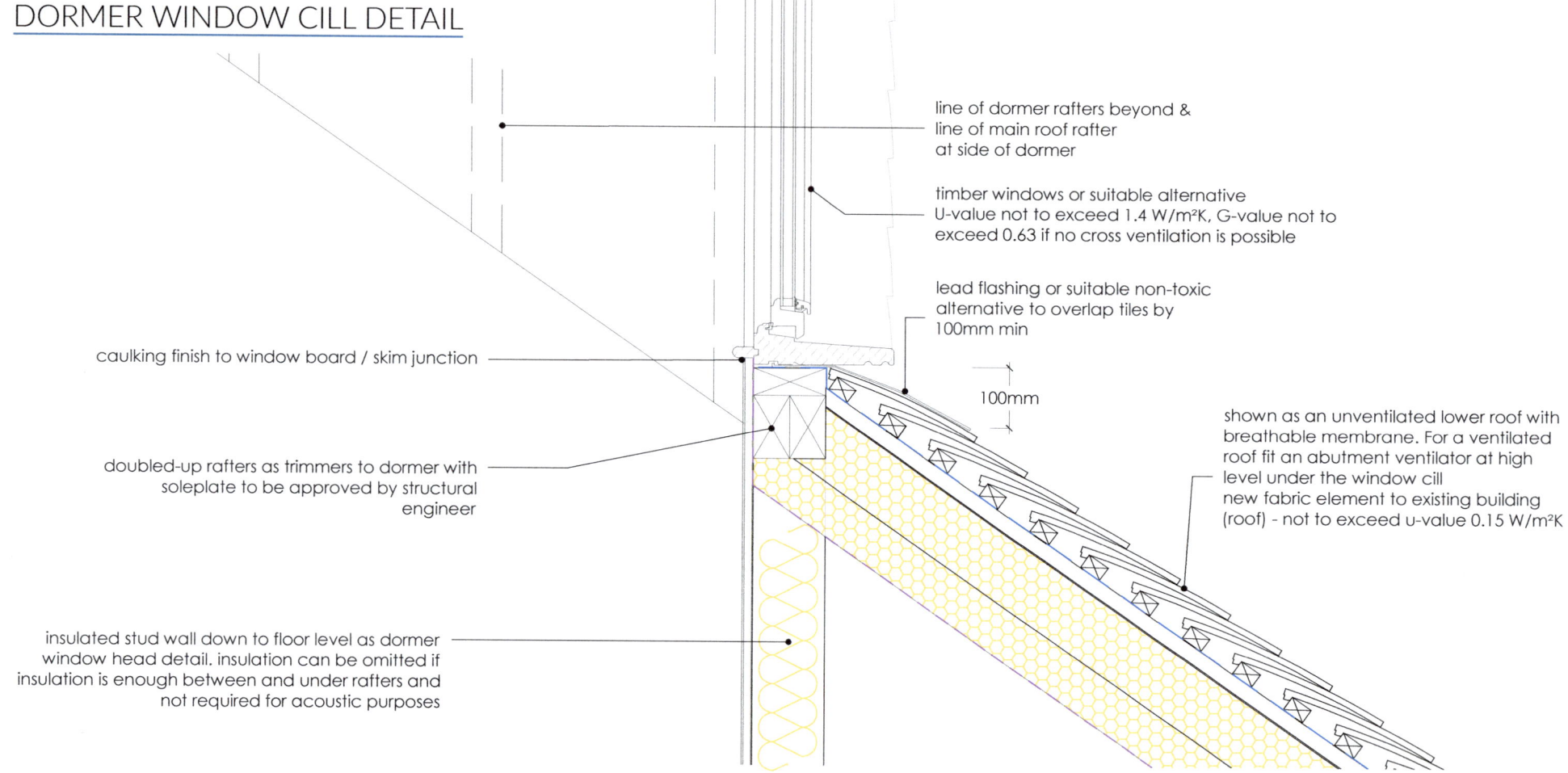

2D Detail LC-11 - Dormer window cill detail

Drawing note: this is a typical dormer window cill detail were the cill is at the junction with the main house pitched roof - this detail will also often have a small section of wall from the junction of the pitched roof up to the cill level due to the existing roof timber structure. the flashing detail & construction are very important to maintain a watertight finish, this is particularly important in highly exposed areas that are subject to a lot of wind-driven rain. a loft conversion that provides one storey more than 4.5m above ground level (typically a 3rd storey in a traditional dwelling) must provide means of escape in the event of a fire by a protected stairway as shown in Section 2 of Approved Document B volume 1 of current Building Regulations. a loft conversion that provides one storey 4.5m max. above ground level (typically a 2nd storey in a traditional bungalow) can provide means of escape in the event of a fire by stairs & an emergency escape window or external door, or direct access to a protected stairs as shown in Section 2 of Approved Document B volume 1 of current Building Regulations.

3D Detail LC-11 - Dormer window cill detail

LC-12
DORMER WINDOW JAMB DETAIL

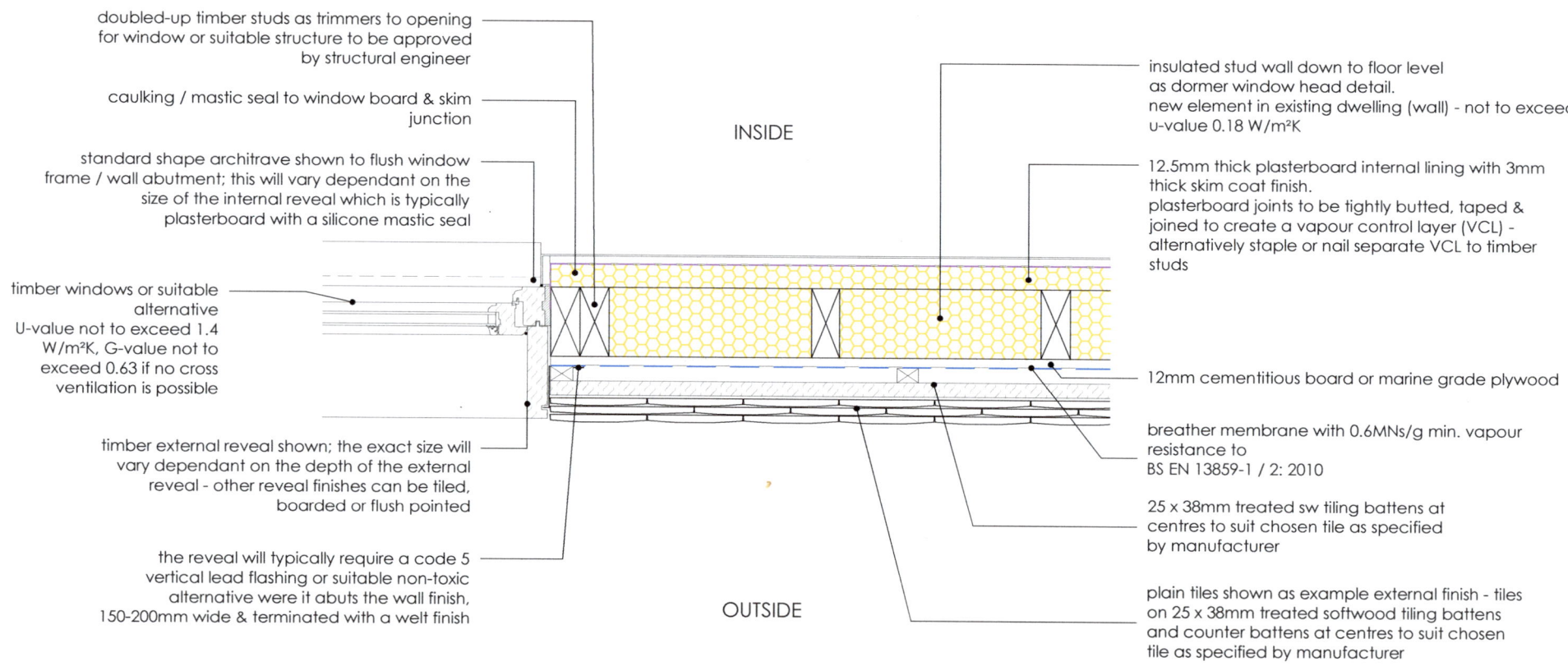

2D Detail LC-12 - Dormer window jamb detail

Drawing note: this is a typical dormer window jamb detail with the external wall finish shown as plain horizontal tiles; other common dormer wall finishes are uPvc or timber horizontal or vertical cladding, traditional slate, lead flashing & glazed - more modern methods are pre-formed GRP & standing seam zinc

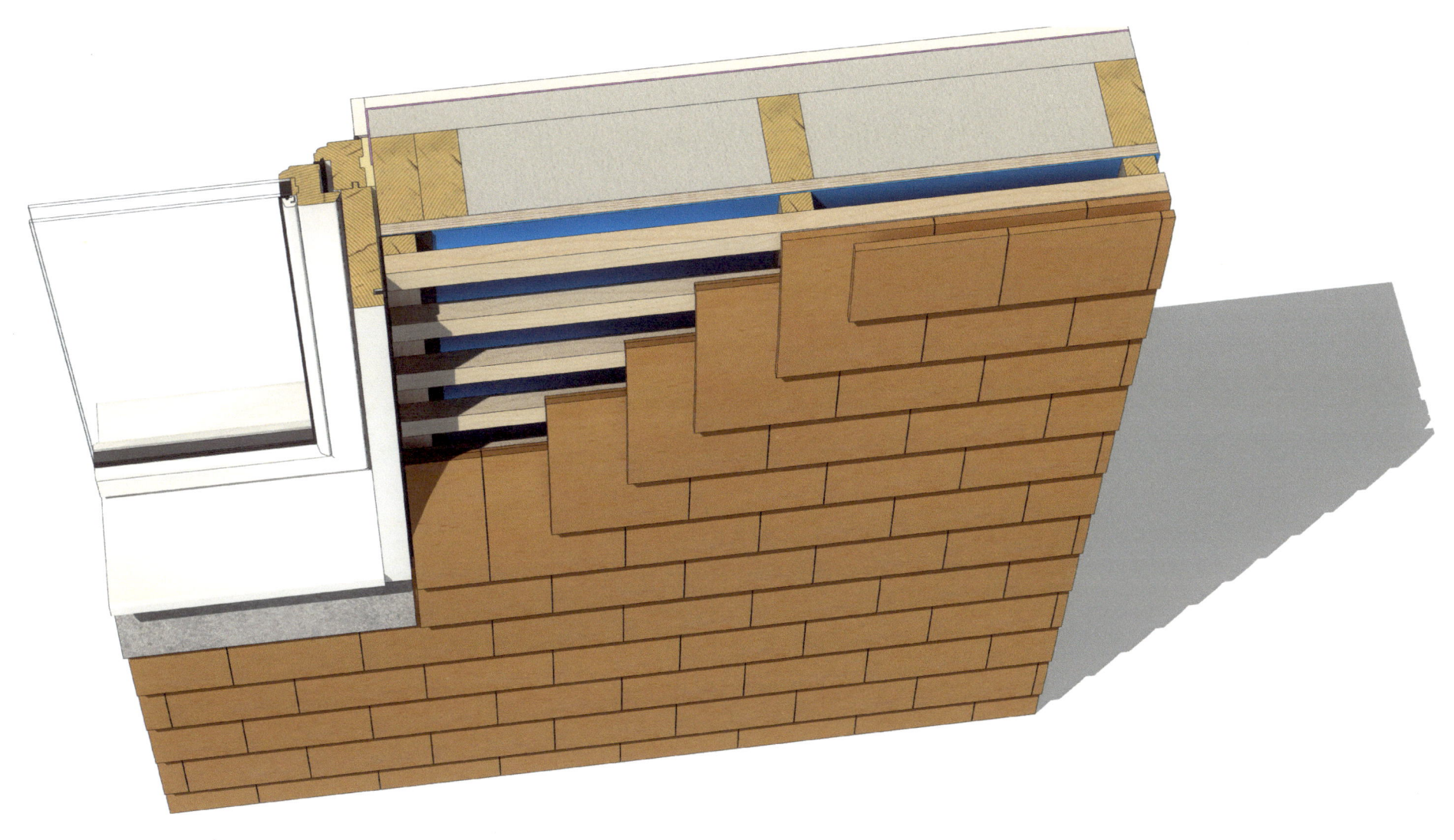

3D Detail LC-12 - Dormer window jamb detail

LC-13A

DORMER WINDOW PITCHED ROOF EAVES DETAIL WITH GUTTER

roof tiles & eaves as detail number LC04/5 - these will vary project to project depending on if it is a new build or extension / conversion scheme
new fabric element to existing building (roof) - not to exceed u-value 0.15 W/m²K

plain roof tiles shown as example external finish, other options suitable - tiles on 25 x 38mm treated sw tiling battens at centres to suit chosen tile as specified by manufacturer

insulation shown between & under the rafters to form a "warm" roof as detail number LC05 - for a new build, this can be formed as a warm or cold roof, & with rafter or ceiling level insulation to form a flat or sloping ceiling

rafters birdsmouthed over head plate / top plate timbers that are sized as the dormer cheek to be approved by structural engineer

100mm

finish under roof eaves with a continuous course of tops tiles with code 5 lead flashing or suitable non-toxic alternative fixed to face of tiling batten dressed 100mm min. over top course tile

insulated stud wall down to floor level as dormer window head detail.
new element in existing dwelling (wall) - not to exceed u-value 0.18W/m²K

plain tiles shown as example external finish, other options suitable - tiles on 25 x 38mm treated softwood tiling battens and counter battens at centres to suit chosen tile as specified by manufacturer

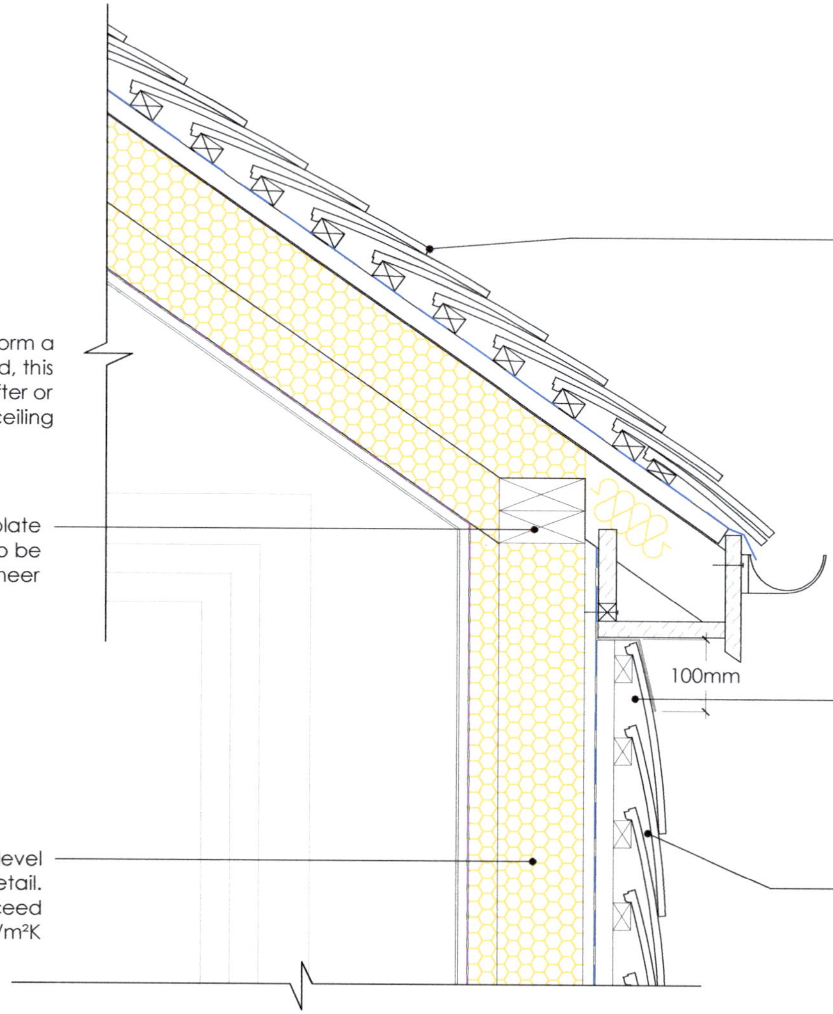

2D Detail LC-13A - Dormer window pitched roof eaves detail with gutter

Drawing note:
this is a typical dormer head / eaves detail; note that the counter batten should be tightly fixed up to the underside of the insulation as an active barrier against vermin & that the insulation in the roof should partially overlap the insulation in the wall construction to ensure no cold bridging occurs.

3D Detail LC-13A - Dormer window pitched roof eaves detail with gutter

LC-13B

DORMER WINDOW PITCHED ROOF EAVES DETAIL WITH FLASHING

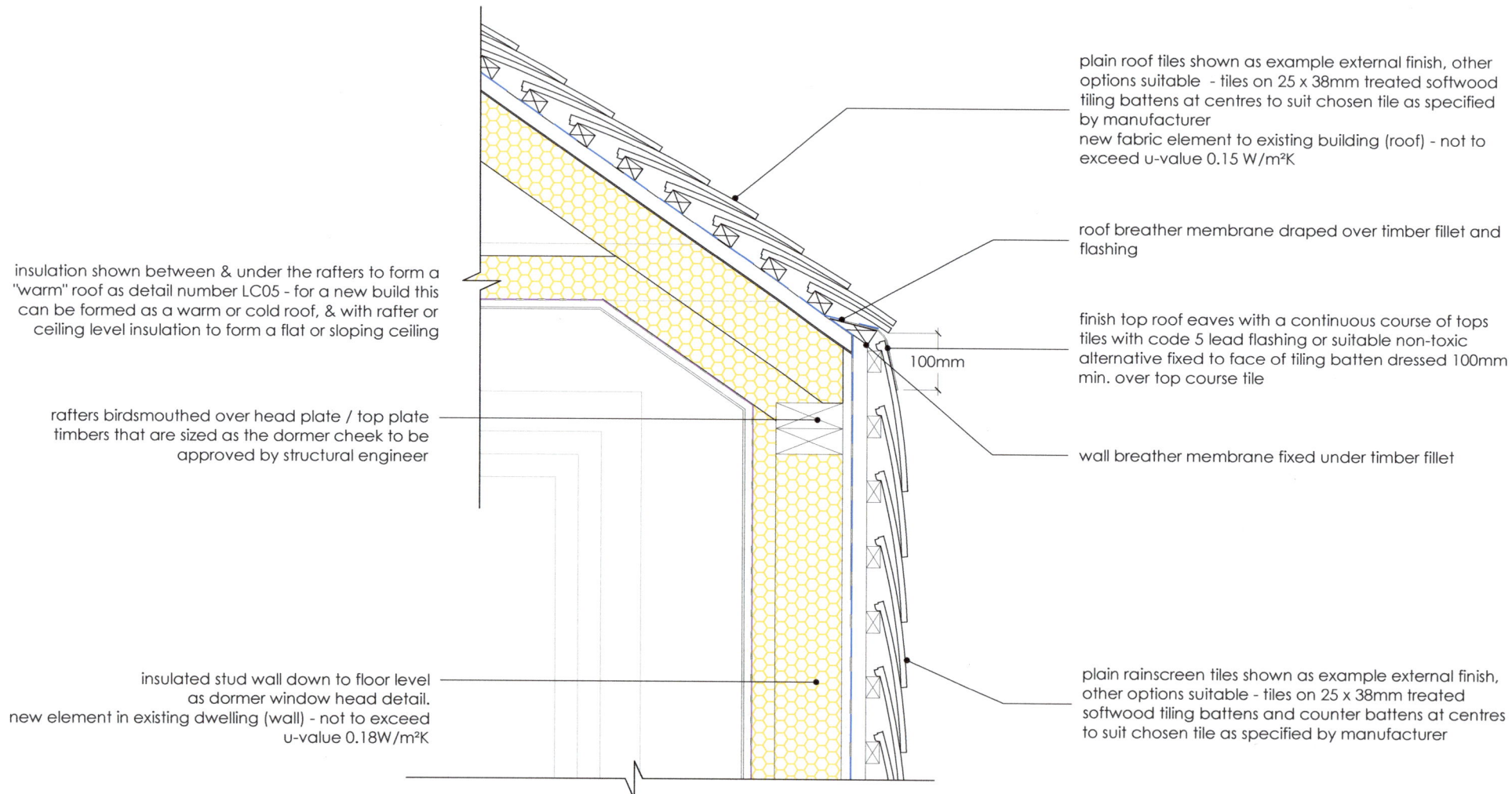

plain roof tiles shown as example external finish, other options suitable - tiles on 25 x 38mm treated softwood tiling battens at centres to suit chosen tile as specified by manufacturer
new fabric element to existing building (roof) - not to exceed u-value 0.15 W/m²K

roof breather membrane draped over timber fillet and flashing

finish top roof eaves with a continuous course of tops tiles with code 5 lead flashing or suitable non-toxic alternative fixed to face of tiling batten dressed 100mm min. over top course tile

wall breather membrane fixed under timber fillet

plain rainscreen tiles shown as example external finish, other options suitable - tiles on 25 x 38mm treated softwood tiling battens and counter battens at centres to suit chosen tile as specified by manufacturer

insulation shown between & under the rafters to form a "warm" roof as detail number LC05 - for a new build this can be formed as a warm or cold roof, & with rafter or ceiling level insulation to form a flat or sloping ceiling

rafters birdsmouthed over head plate / top plate timbers that are sized as the dormer cheek to be approved by structural engineer

insulated stud wall down to floor level as dormer window head detail.
new element in existing dwelling (wall) - not to exceed u-value 0.18W/m²K

2D Detail LC-13B - Dormer window pitched roof eaves detail with flashing

Drawing note:
this is a typical dormer head / eaves detail for roofs under 6sqm which do not require a rain water pipe; note that the counter batten should be tightly fixed up to the underside of the insulation as an active barrier against vermin & that the insulation in the roof should partially overlap the insulation in the wall construction to ensure no cold bridging occurs.

3D Detail LC-13B - Dormer window pitched roof eaves detail with flashing

LC-13C

DORMER WINDOW PITCHED ROOF EAVES DETAIL WITH MANSARD

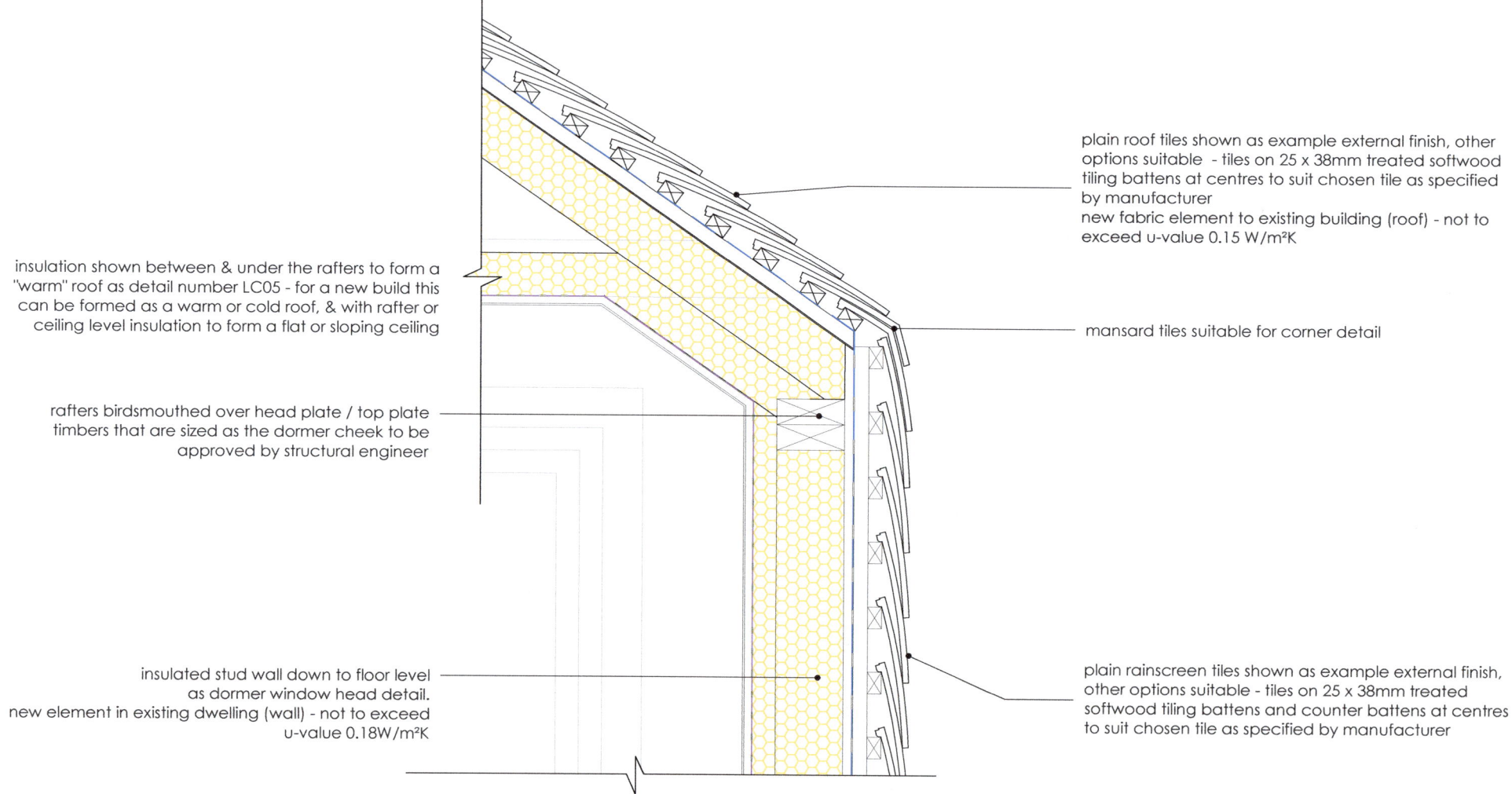

plain roof tiles shown as example external finish, other options suitable - tiles on 25 x 38mm treated softwood tiling battens at centres to suit chosen tile as specified by manufacturer
new fabric element to existing building (roof) - not to exceed u-value 0.15 W/m²K

insulation shown between & under the rafters to form a "warm" roof as detail number LC05 - for a new build this can be formed as a warm or cold roof, & with rafter or ceiling level insulation to form a flat or sloping ceiling

mansard tiles suitable for corner detail

rafters birdsmouthed over head plate / top plate timbers that are sized as the dormer cheek to be approved by structural engineer

insulated stud wall down to floor level as dormer window head detail.
new element in existing dwelling (wall) - not to exceed u-value 0.18W/m²K

plain rainscreen tiles shown as example external finish, other options suitable - tiles on 25 x 38mm treated softwood tiling battens and counter battens at centres to suit chosen tile as specified by manufacturer

2D Detail LC-13C - Dormer window pitched roof eaves detail with mansard

Drawing note:
this is a typical dormer head / eaves detail for roofs under 6sqm which do not require a rain water pipe; note that the counter batten should be tightly fixed up to the underside of the insulation as an active barrier against vermin & that the insulation in the roof should partially overlap the insulation in the wall construction to ensure no cold bridging occurs.

3D Detail LC-13C - Dormer window pitched roof eaves detail with mansard

Rear Dormer Extension Details

The rear dormer extension details demonstrate the various junctions of a flat roof rear dormer. This ranges from the dormer sole plate, junction with existing roof, through to junction with roof ridge and more.

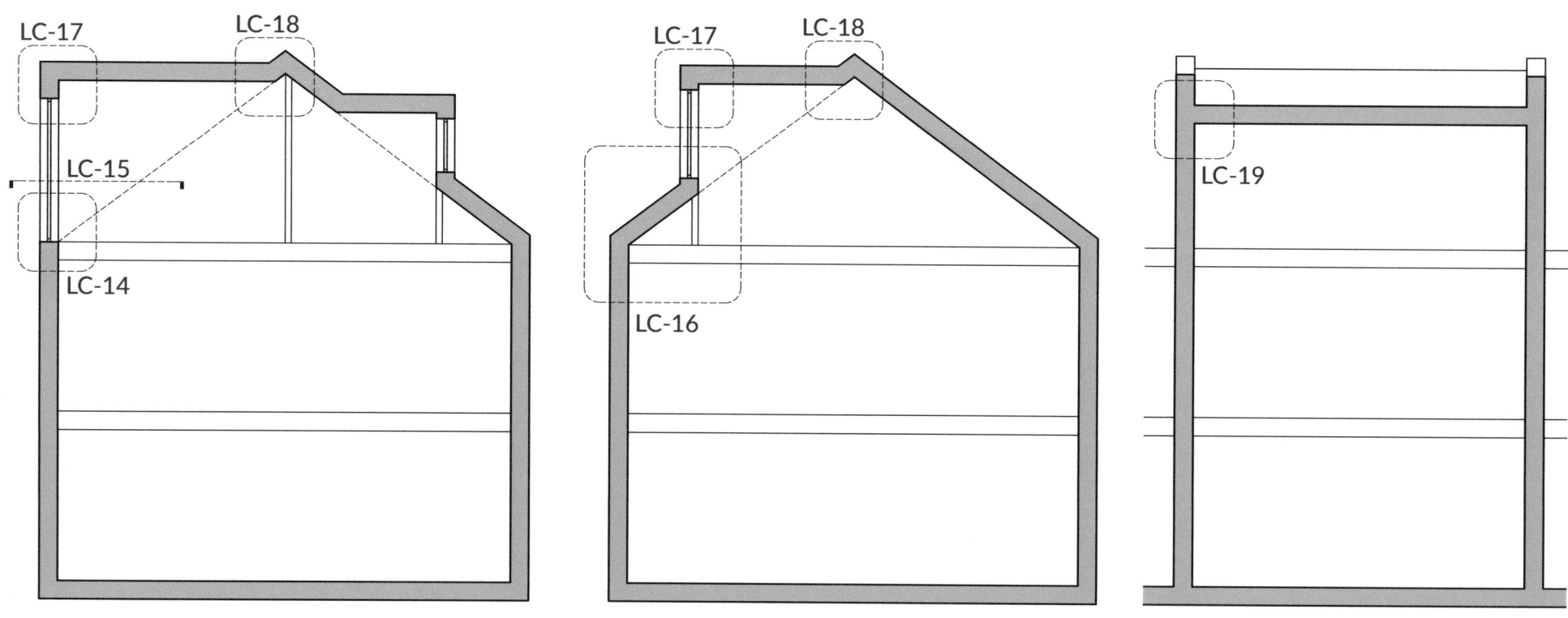

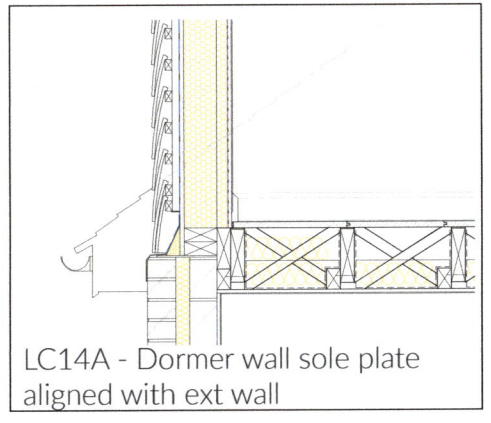
LC14A - Dormer wall sole plate aligned with ext wall

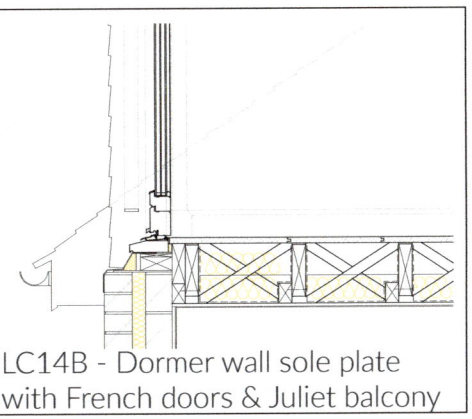
LC14B - Dormer wall sole plate with French doors & Juliet balcony

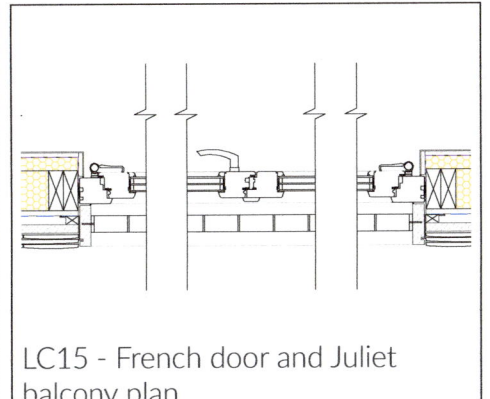
LC15 - French door and Juliet balcony plan

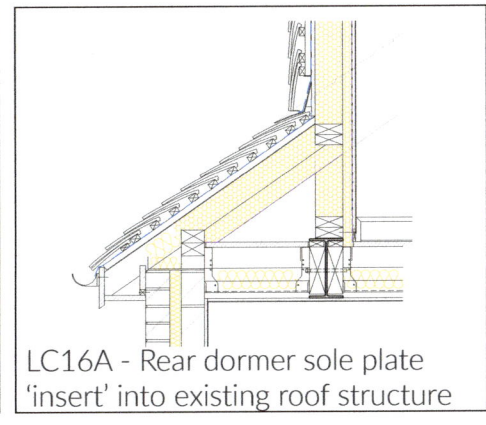
LC16A - Rear dormer sole plate 'insert' into existing roof structure

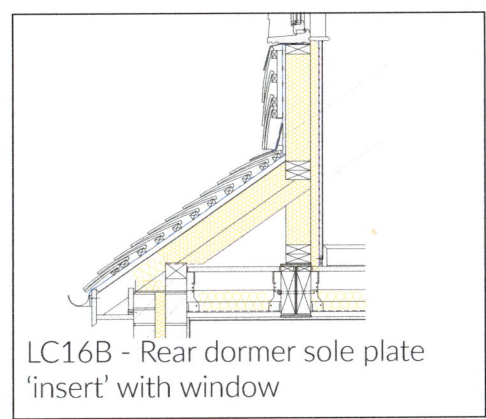
LC16B - Rear dormer sole plate 'insert' with window

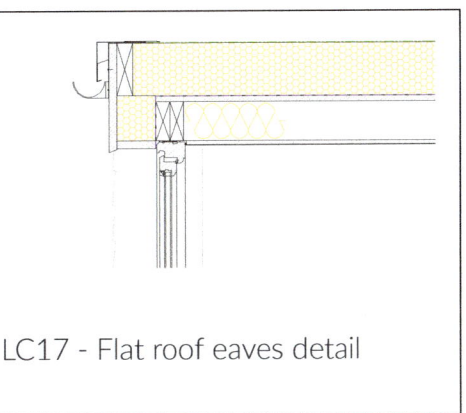
LC17 - Flat roof eaves detail

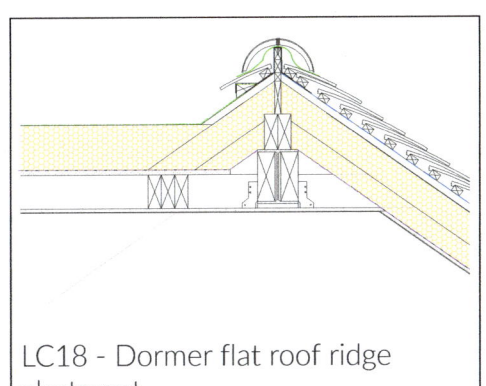
LC18 - Dormer flat roof ridge abutment

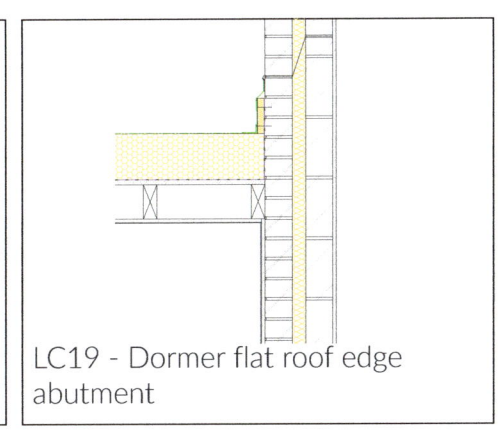
LC19 - Dormer flat roof edge abutment

LC-14A
DORMER WALL SOLE PLATE ALIGNED WITH INSIDE FACE OF EXT WALL

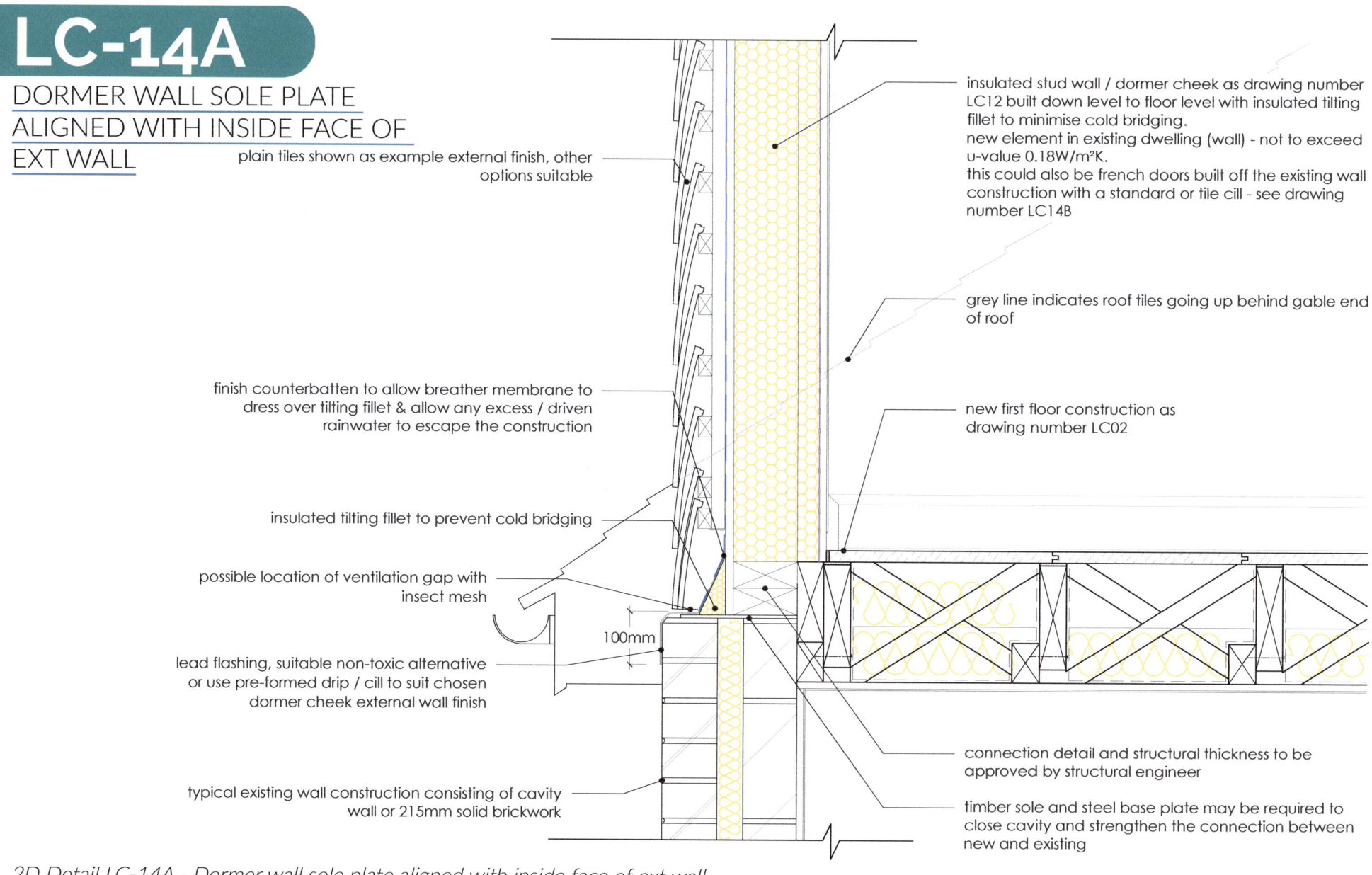

2D Detail LC-14A - Dormer wall sole plate aligned with inside face of ext wall

Drawing note: this is a typical dormer window sole plate detail that is aligned with the inside face of the existing external wall (note that planning restrictions in your local area may require the dormer to be positioned further up a roof slope rather than off the existing external wall to appear more like an "insert" in the roof structure rather than an "extension" to it - see also drawing number LC16A/16B for details). to totally eliminate the possibility of cold bridging at the wall junctions, a tilting fillet of insulation can be fitted at the structural level.

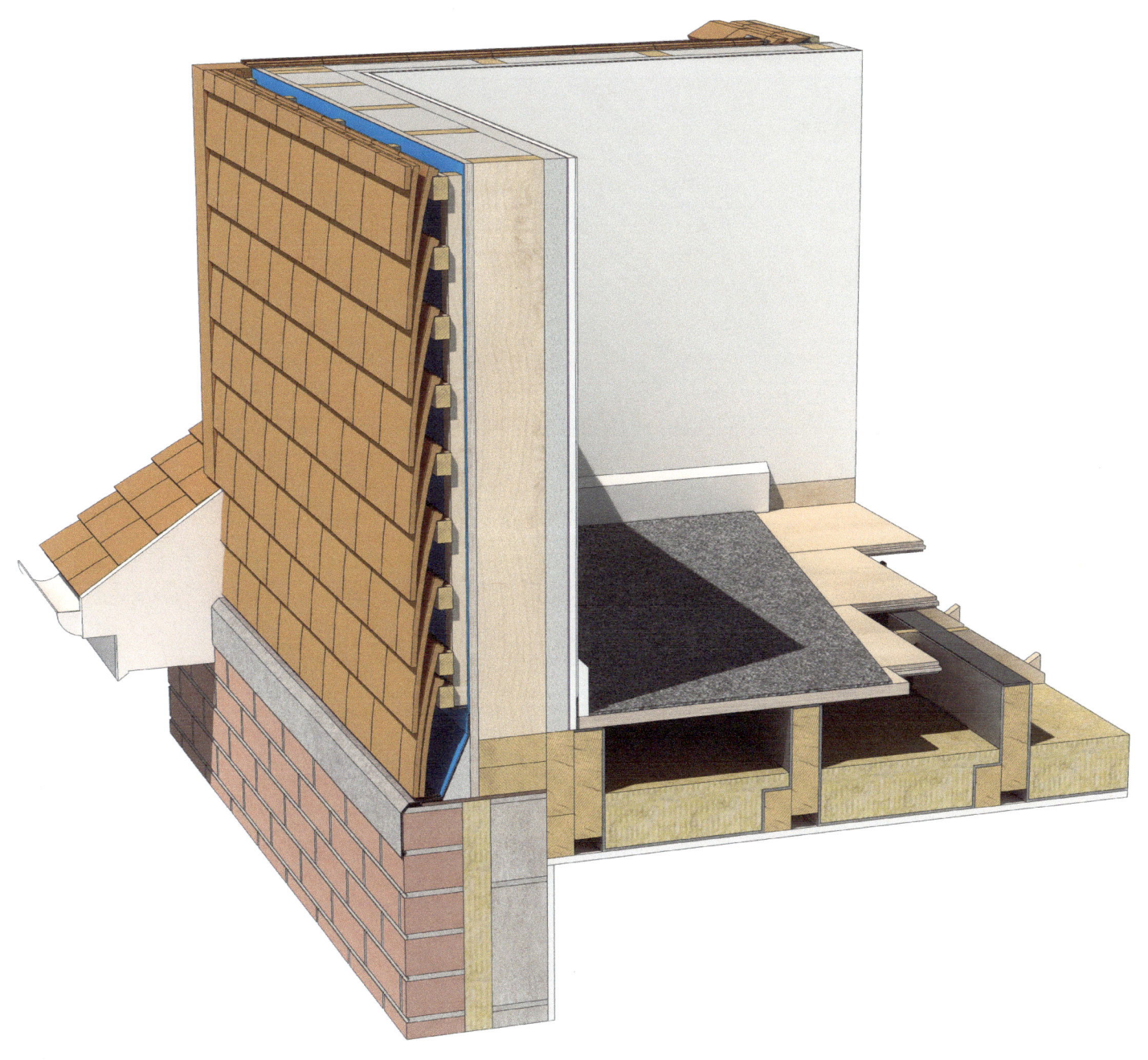

3D Detail LC-14A - Dormer wall sole plate aligned with inside face of ext wall

LC-14B

DORMER WINDOW SOLE PLATE WITH FRENCH DOORS AND JULIET BALCONY

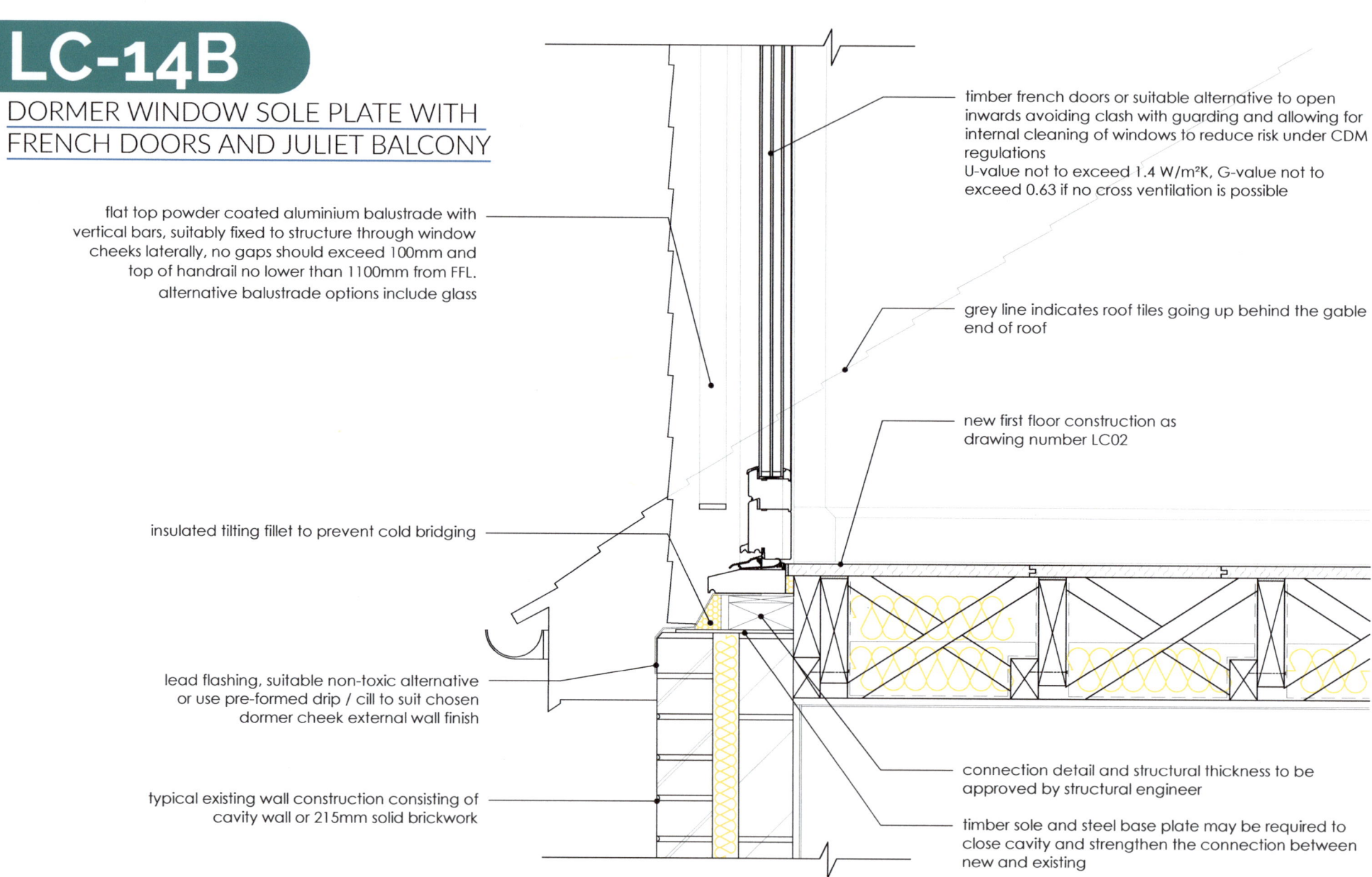

timber french doors or suitable alternative to open inwards avoiding clash with guarding and allowing for internal cleaning of windows to reduce risk under CDM regulations
U-value not to exceed 1.4 W/m²K, G-value not to exceed 0.63 if no cross ventilation is possible

grey line indicates roof tiles going up behind the gable end of roof

new first floor construction as drawing number LC02

flat top powder coated aluminium balustrade with vertical bars, suitably fixed to structure through window cheeks laterally, no gaps should exceed 100mm and top of handrail no lower than 1100mm from FFL. alternative balustrade options include glass

insulated tilting fillet to prevent cold bridging

lead flashing, suitable non-toxic alternative or use pre-formed drip / cill to suit chosen dormer cheek external wall finish

connection detail and structural thickness to be approved by structural engineer

typical existing wall construction consisting of cavity wall or 215mm solid brickwork

timber sole and steel base plate may be required to close cavity and strengthen the connection between new and existing

2D Detail LC-14B - Dormer window sole plate with French doors and Juliet balcony

Drawing note: this is a typical dormer window sole plate detail that is aligned with the inside face of the existing external wall (note that Planning restrictions in your local area may require the dormer to be positioned further up a roof slope rather than off the existing external wall to appear more like an "insert" in the roof structure rather than an "extension" to it - see also drawing number LC16A/16B for details). to totally eliminate the possibility of cold bridging at the wall junctions, a thin tilting fillet of insulation can be fitted at the cill level.

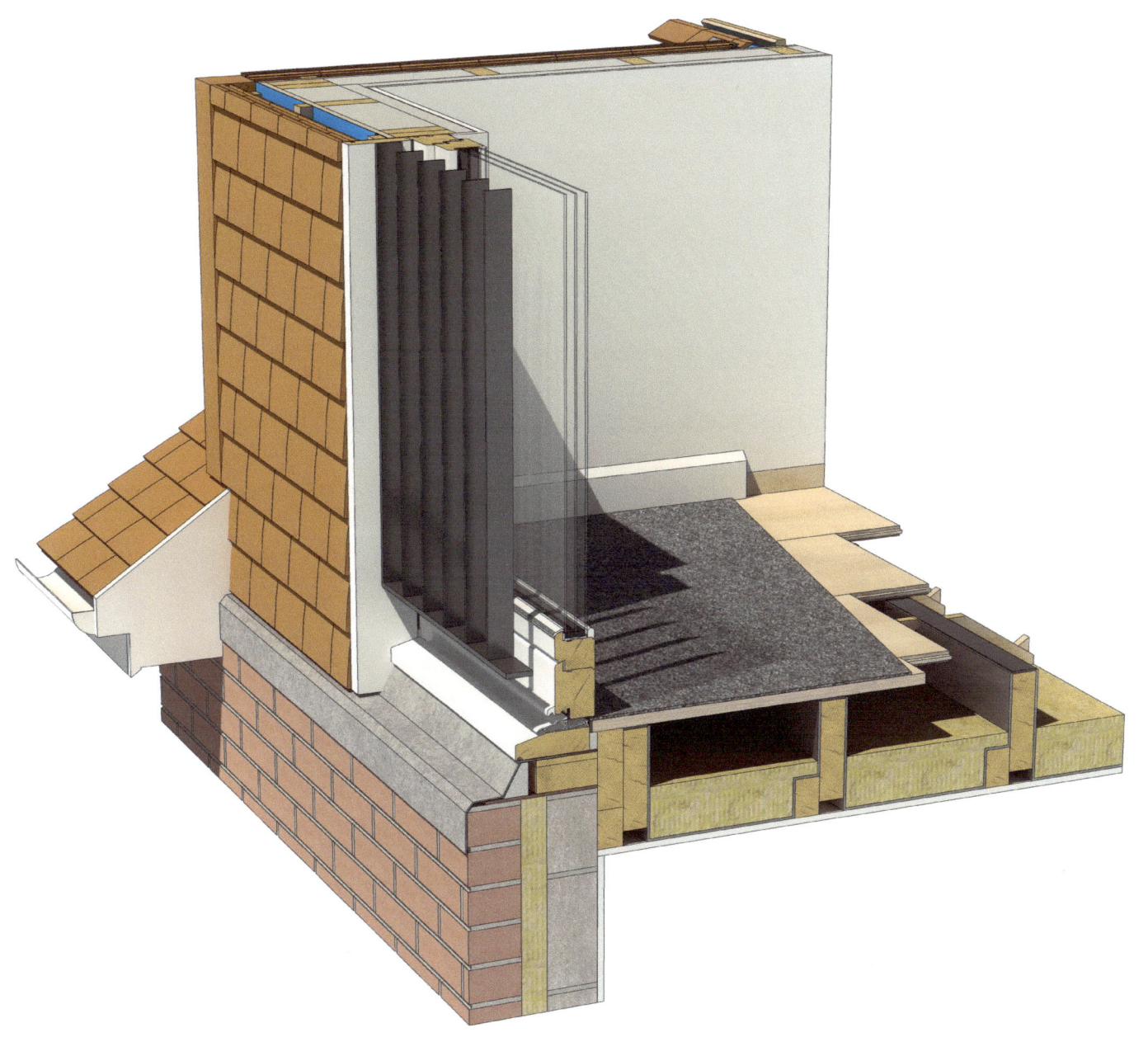

3D Detail LC-14B - Dormer window sole plate with French doors and Juliet balcony

LC-15

FRENCH DOOR AND JULIET BALCONY PLAN DETAIL

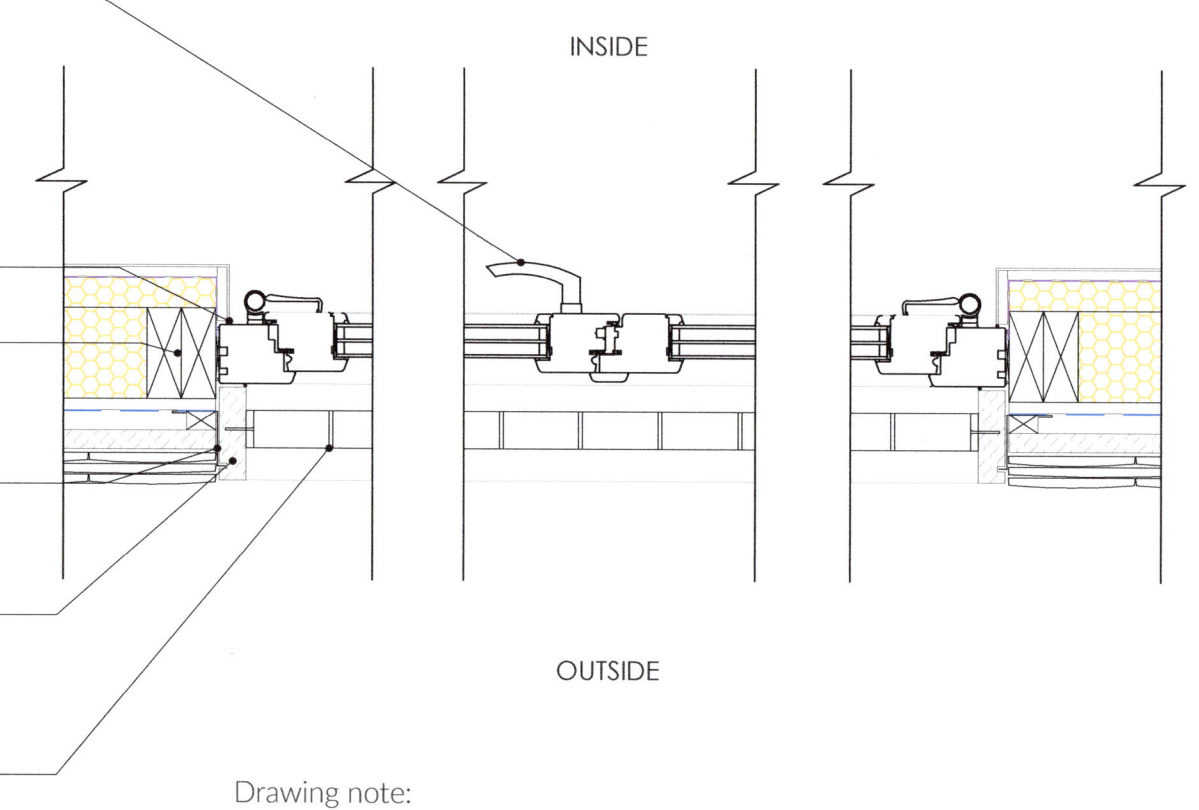

timber french doors or suitable alternative to open inwards avoiding clash with guarding and allowing for internal cleaning of windows to reduce risk under CDM regulations, note that most door manufactures allow for the omission of a handle to the outside door face
U-value not to exceed 1.4 W/m²K, G-value not to exceed 0.63 if no cross ventilation is possible

caulking / mastic seal to window board & skim junction

doubled-up timber studs as trimmers to opening to window or suitable structure to be approved by structural engineer

the reveal will typically require a code 5 vertical lead flashing or suitable non-toxic alternative were it abuts the wall finish, 150-200mm wide & terminated with a welt finish

timber external reveal shown; the exact size will vary dependant on the depth of the external reveal - other reveal finishes can be tiled, boarded or flush pointed

flat top powder coated aluminium balustrade with vertical bars, suitably fixed to structure through window cheeks laterally, no gaps should exceed 100mm and top of handrail no lower than 1100mm from FFL. alternative balustrade options include glass

INSIDE

OUTSIDE

Drawing note:
this is a typical French door jamb detail with the external wall finish shown as plain horizontal tiles; other common dormer wall finishes are uPvc or timber horizontal or vertical cladding, traditional slate, lead flashing & glazed - more modern methods are pre-formed GRP & standing seam zinc.
It is recommended that windows and doors at height should open inwards to allow for cleaning without the risk of falling, reducing the risks in use and maintenance of the building to comply with CDM regulations. a maintenance strategy, risk register and residual risk register should be updated throughout the design process to comply with CDM regulations.

2D Detail LC-15 - French door and Juliet balcony plan detail

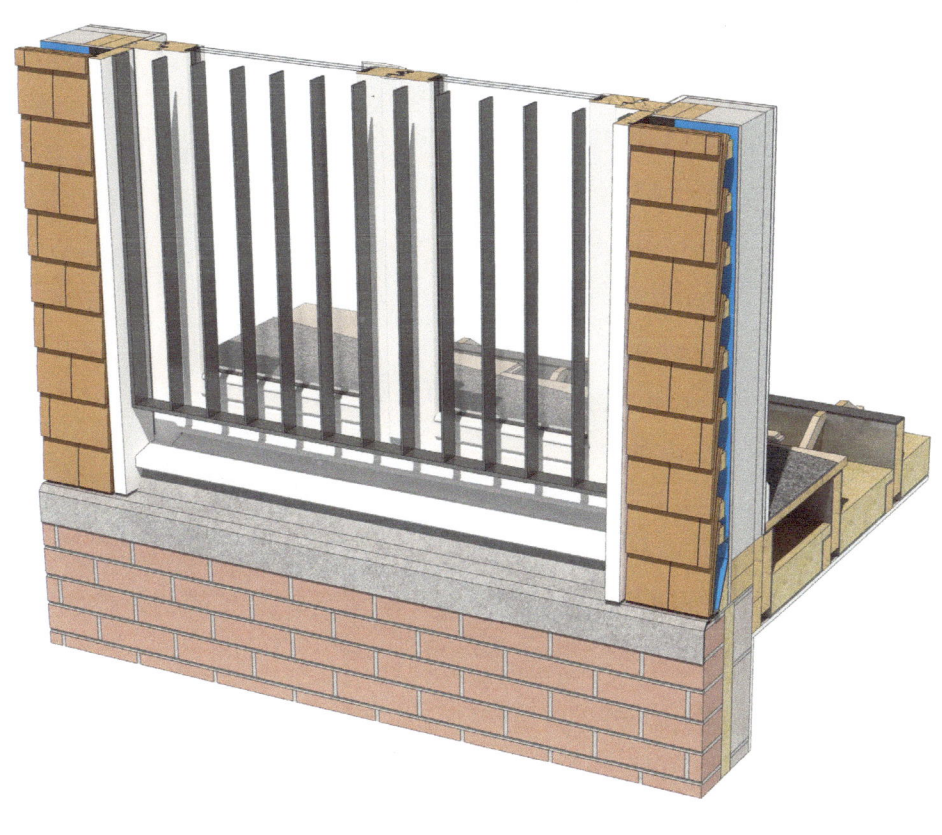

3D Detail LC-15 - French door and Juliet balcony plan detail

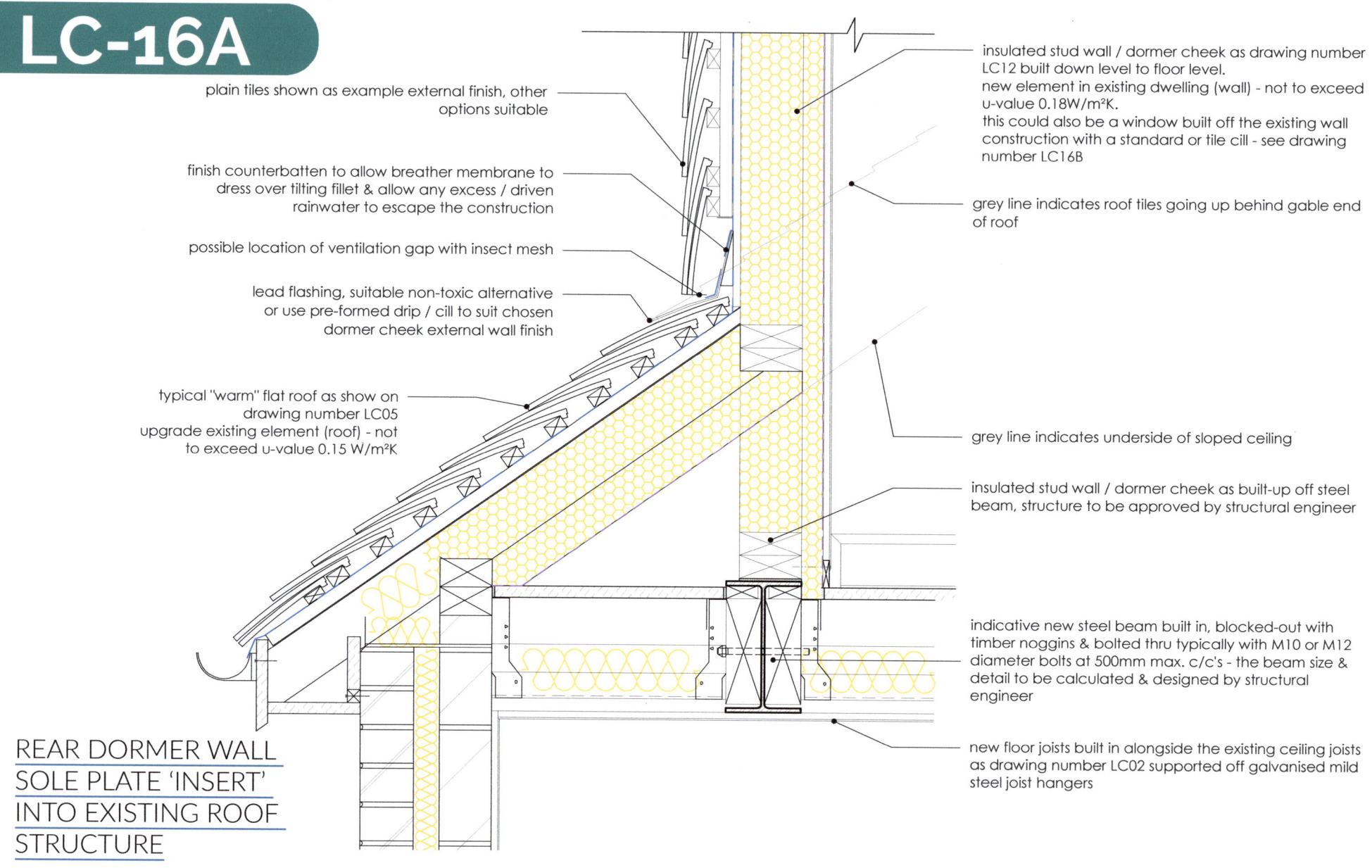

2D Detail LC-16A - Rear dormer wall sole plate 'insert' into existing roof structure

Drawing note: this is a typical rear dormer window detail were the dormer is required to be positioned up the existing roof slope as mentioned on drawing number LC14A. any new timber or steel beams will need to be carefully designed & detailed by a structural engineer to take account of imposed & super-imposed (live & dead) loads from snow / wind, roof & floor.

3D Detail LC-16A - Rear dormer wall plate 'insert' into existing roof structure

LC-16B

REAR DORMER WALL SOLE PLATE 'INSERT' INTO EXISTING ROOF STRUCTURE WITH WINDOW

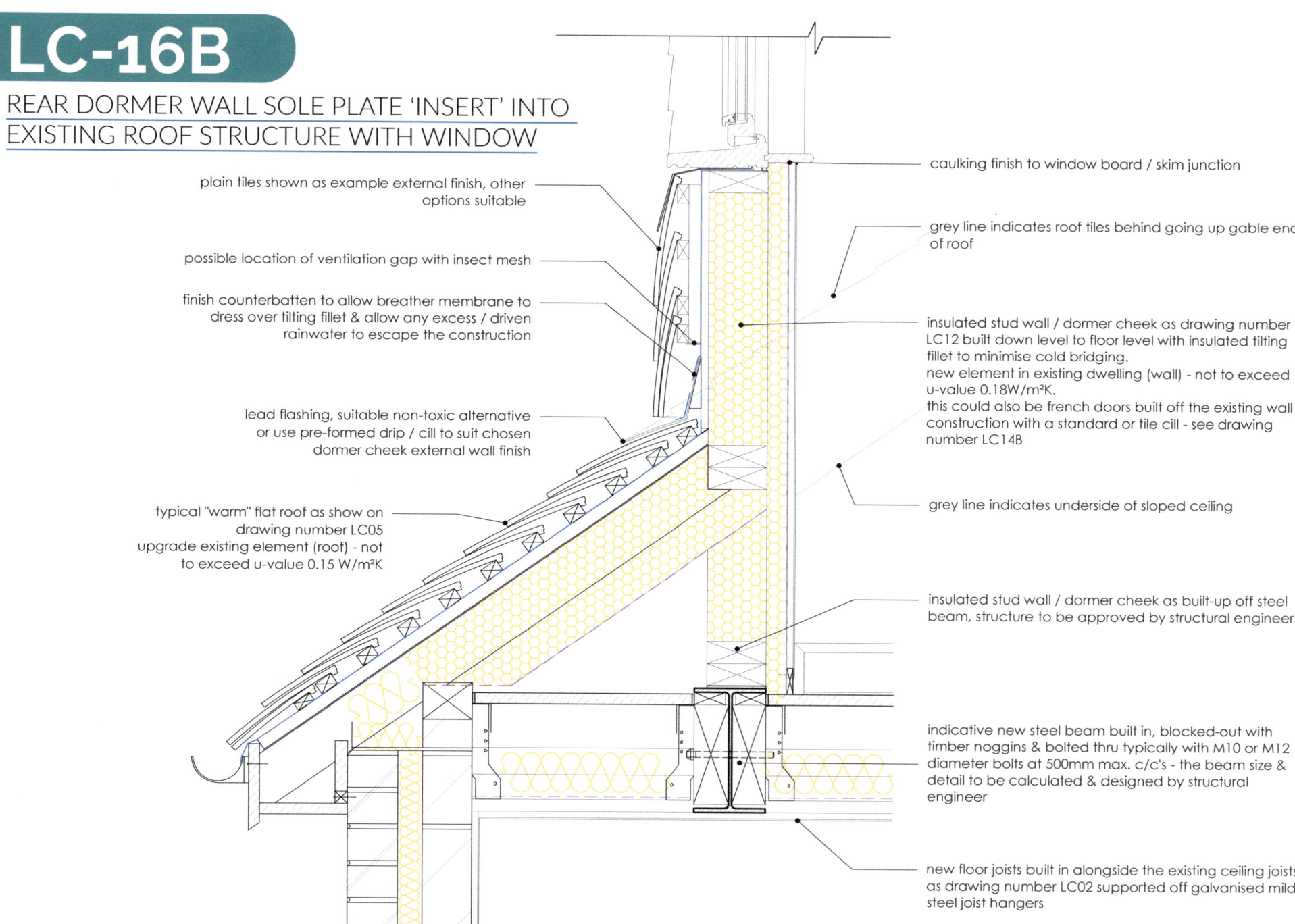

2D Detail LC-16B - Rear dormer wall sole plate 'insert' into existing roof structure with window

Drawing note: this is a typical dormer window detail were the dormer is required to be positioned up the existing roof slope as mentioned on drawing number LC14A.
any new timber or steel beams will need to be carefully designed & detailed by a structural engineer to take account of imposed & super-imposed (live & dead) loads from snow / wind, roof & floor.

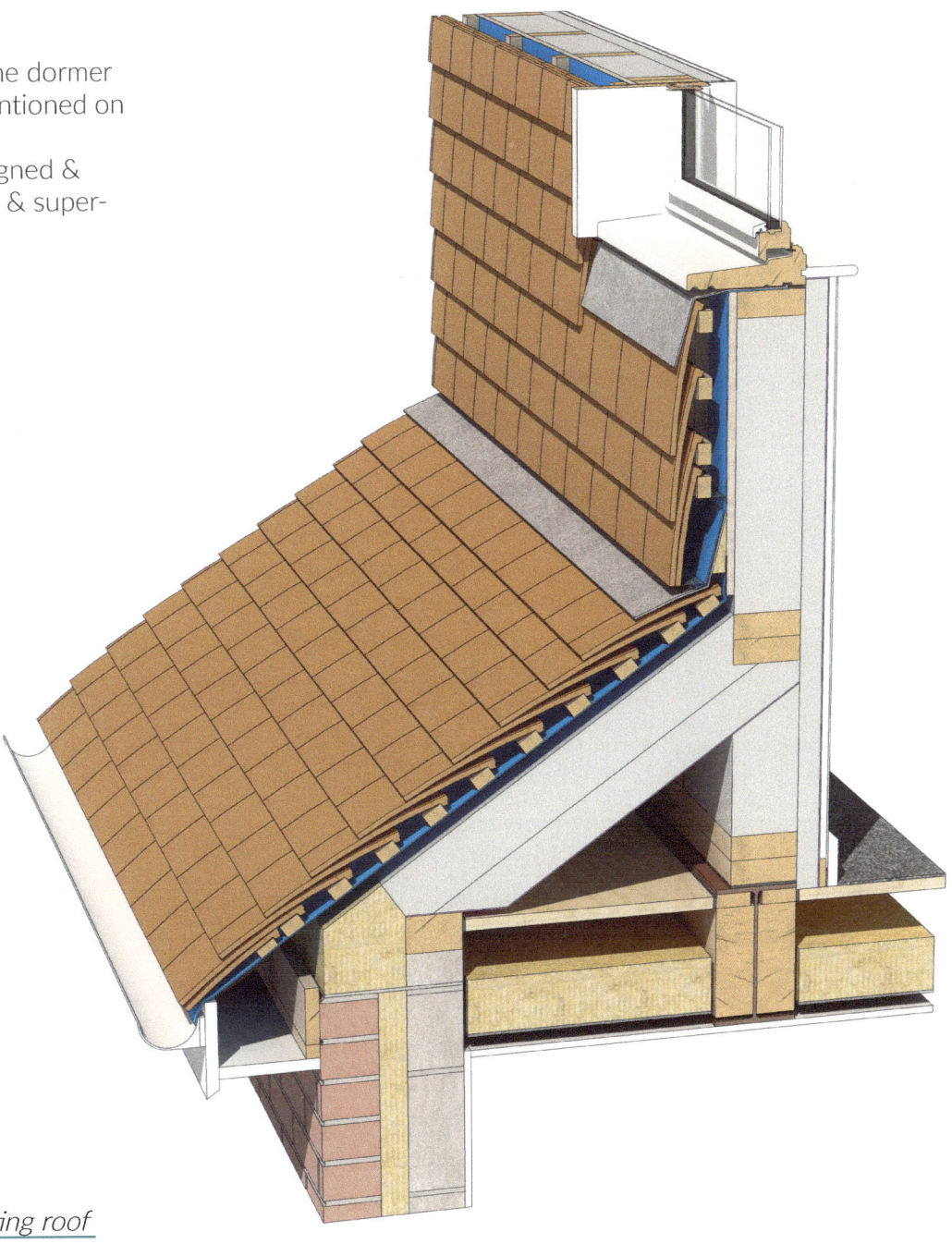

3D Detail LC-16B - Rear dormer wall plate 'insert' into existing roof structure with window

LC-17

FLAT ROOF EAVES DETAIL - WARM ROOF

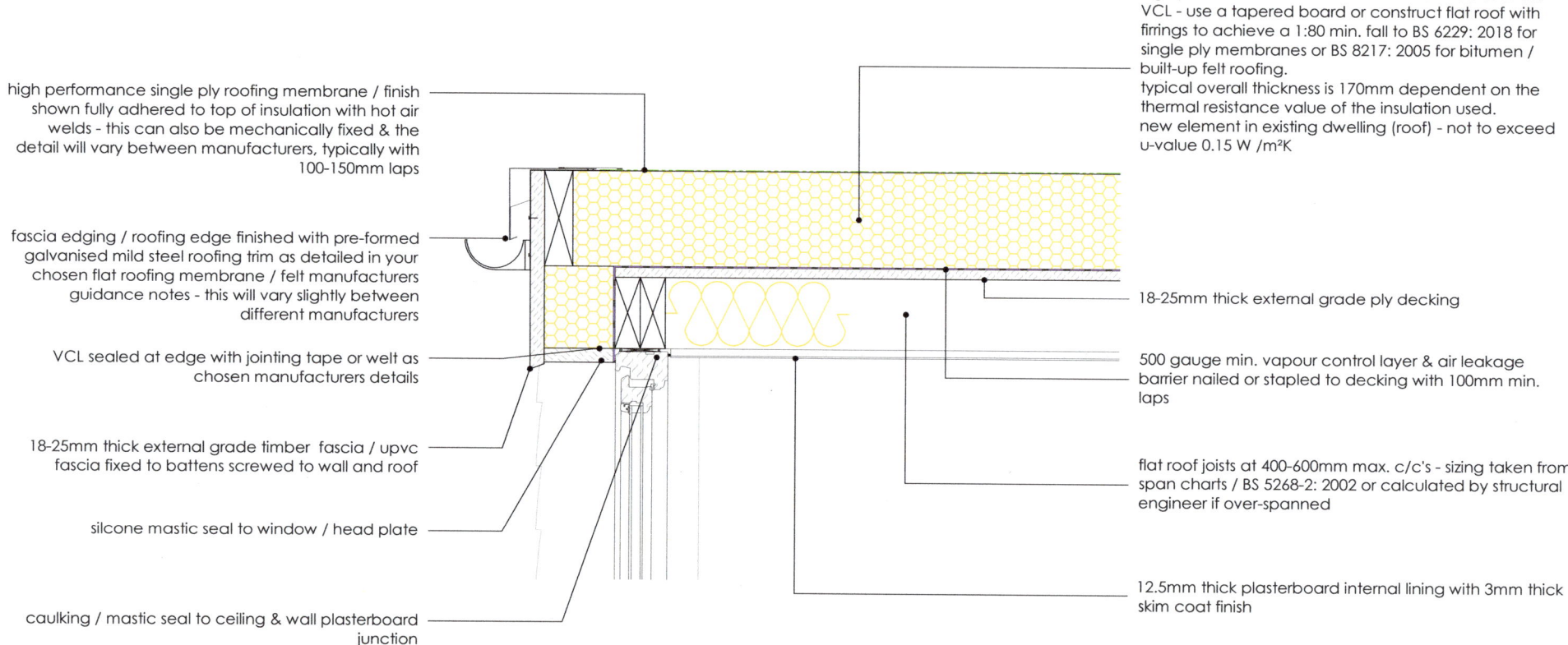

2D Detail LC-17 - Flat roof eaves detail - warm roof

Drawing note: this is a "warm" roof situation which is becoming the most common finish for flat roof extensions, a warm roof has less chance of thermal movement, condensation & cold bridging.
please note most flat roofs must be laid to a fall to avoid water pooling, check manufacturers and installers recommendations.
the window head is shown with the ceiling running through at the same level - it is also common to have a section of wall above the head to the ceiling level depending on what is the required height, minimum recommended FFL to ceiling height should be 2.3m.

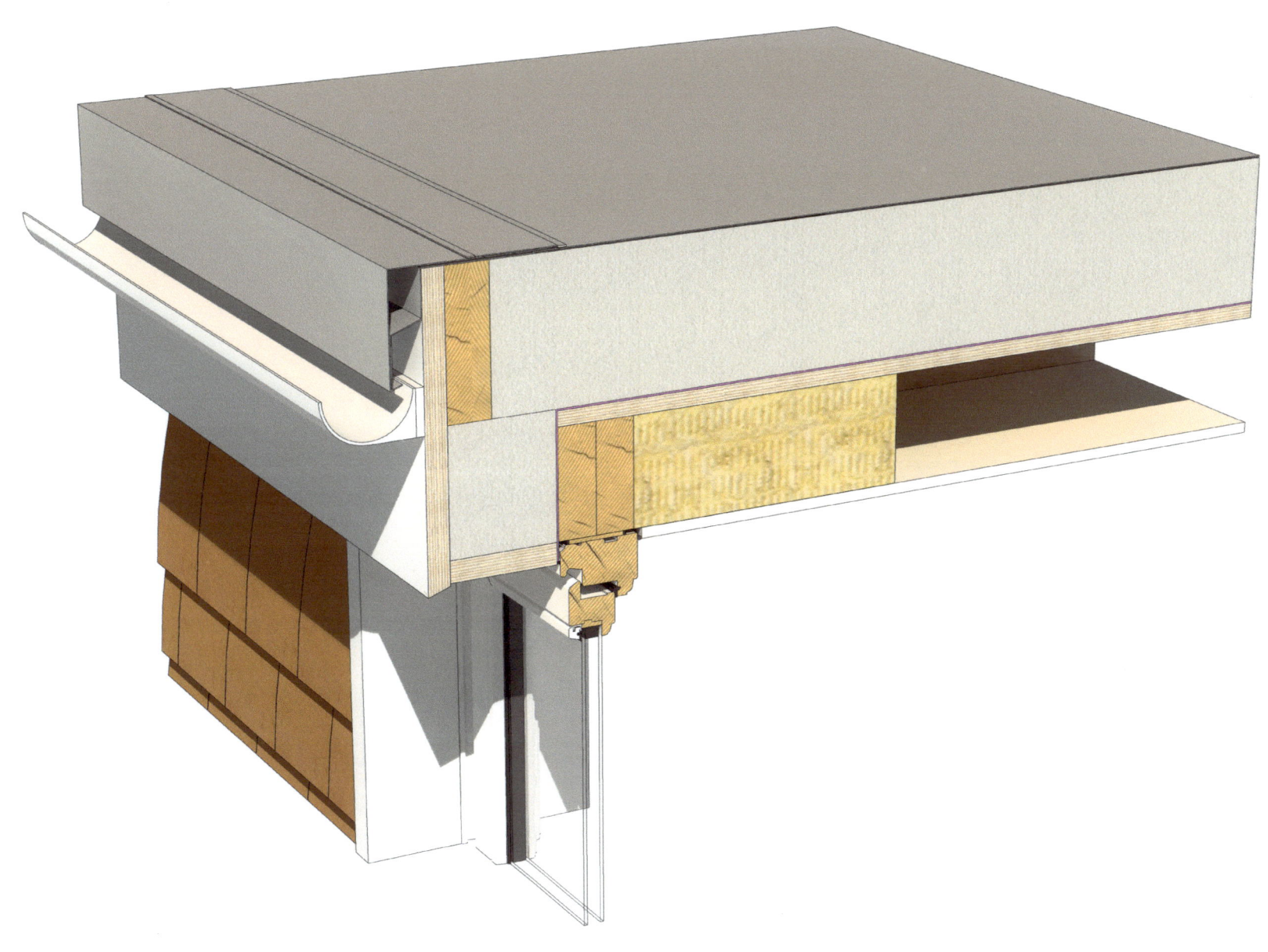

3D Detail LC-17 - Flat roof eaves detail - warm roof

LC-18

DORMER - FLAT ROOF / RIDGE ABUTMENT

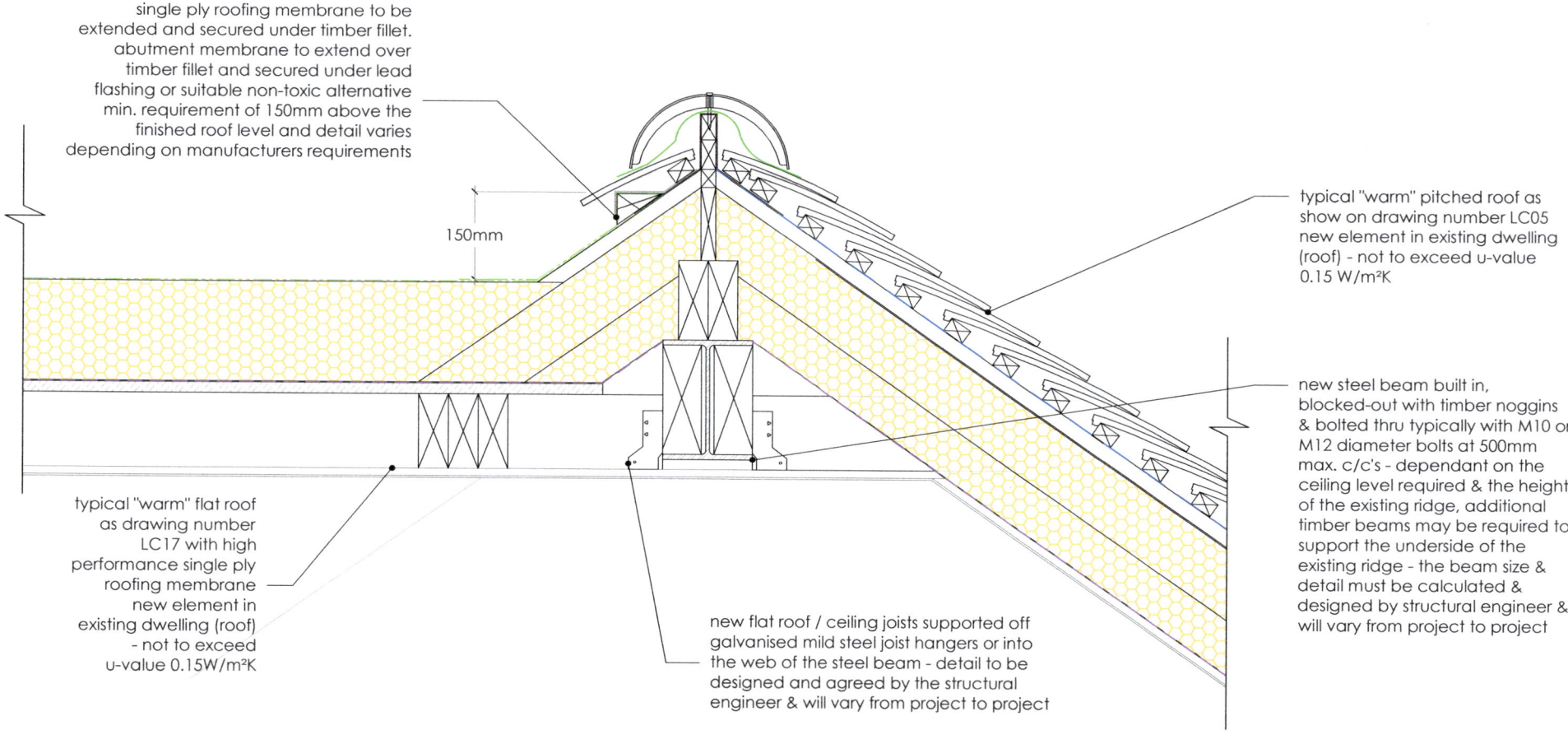

2D Detail LC-18 - Dormer - flat roof / ridge abutment

Drawing note: this is a single ply roofing membrane flat roof / ridge junction detail that is typical on many domestic loft conversions - there are many variants on this theme & they will vary depending on the height of the existing ridge & the ceiling height required for the project; sometimes the flat roof will come directly off the ridge & may require removal of the ridge board with a new ridge beam, or the new beam will be positioned directly under the existing ridge board - each project will be individually designed & calculated by a structural engineer.
ensure flashing between the new flat roof & the existing sloping roof has adequate laps to ensure it is watertight & prevents any driving rain from getting into the structure.

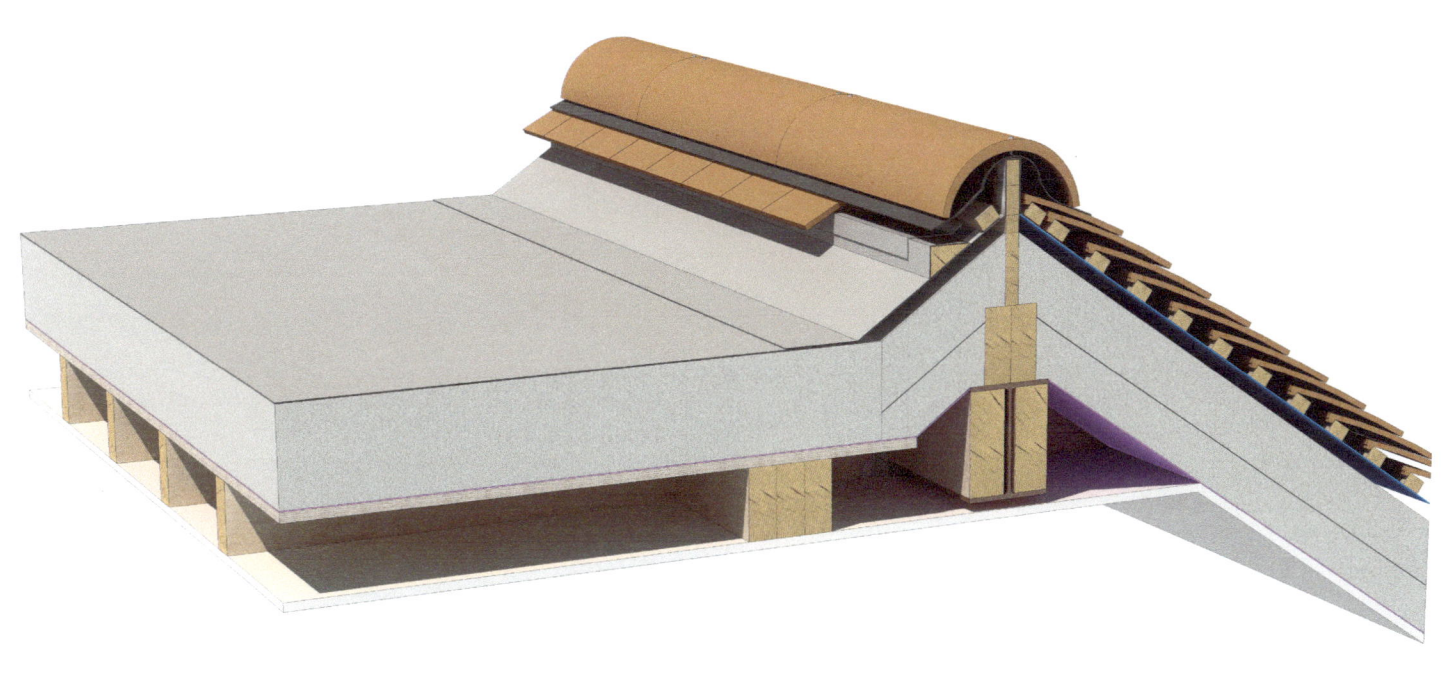
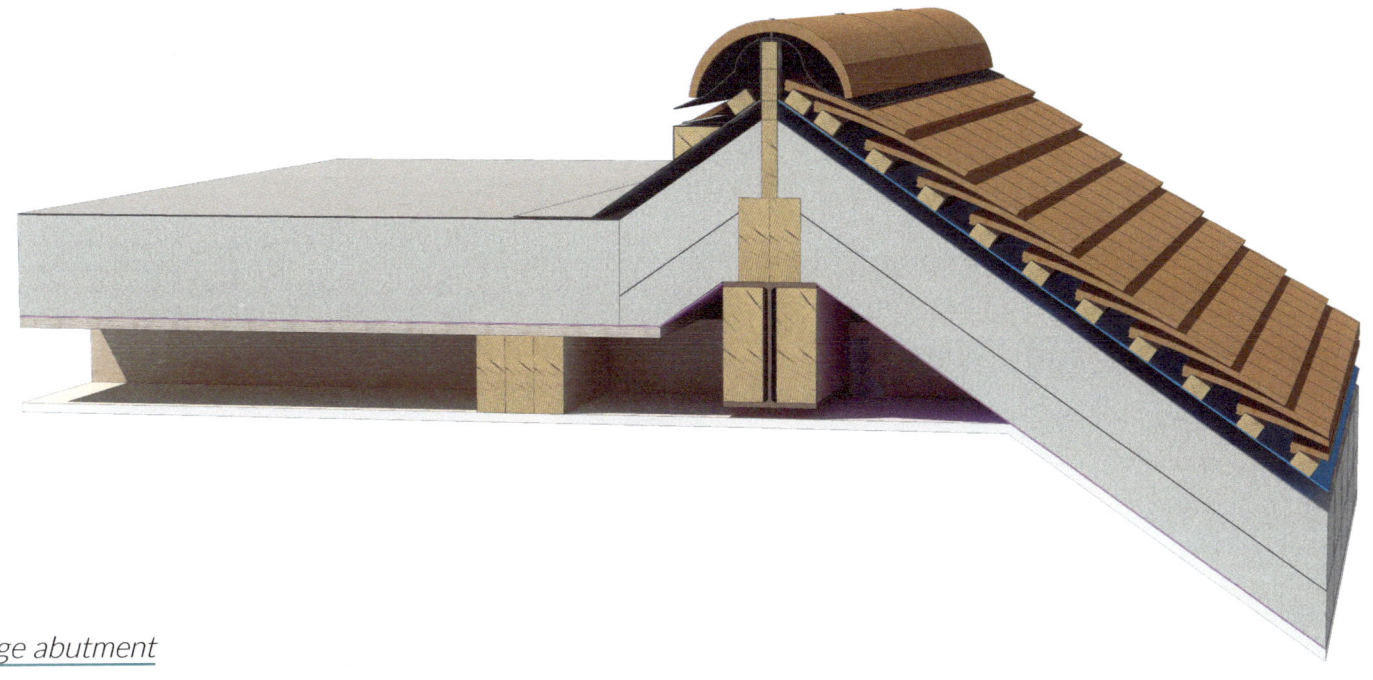

3D Detail LC-18 - Dormer - flat roof / ridge abutment

LC-19
DORMER- FLAT ROOF / EDGE ABUTMENT

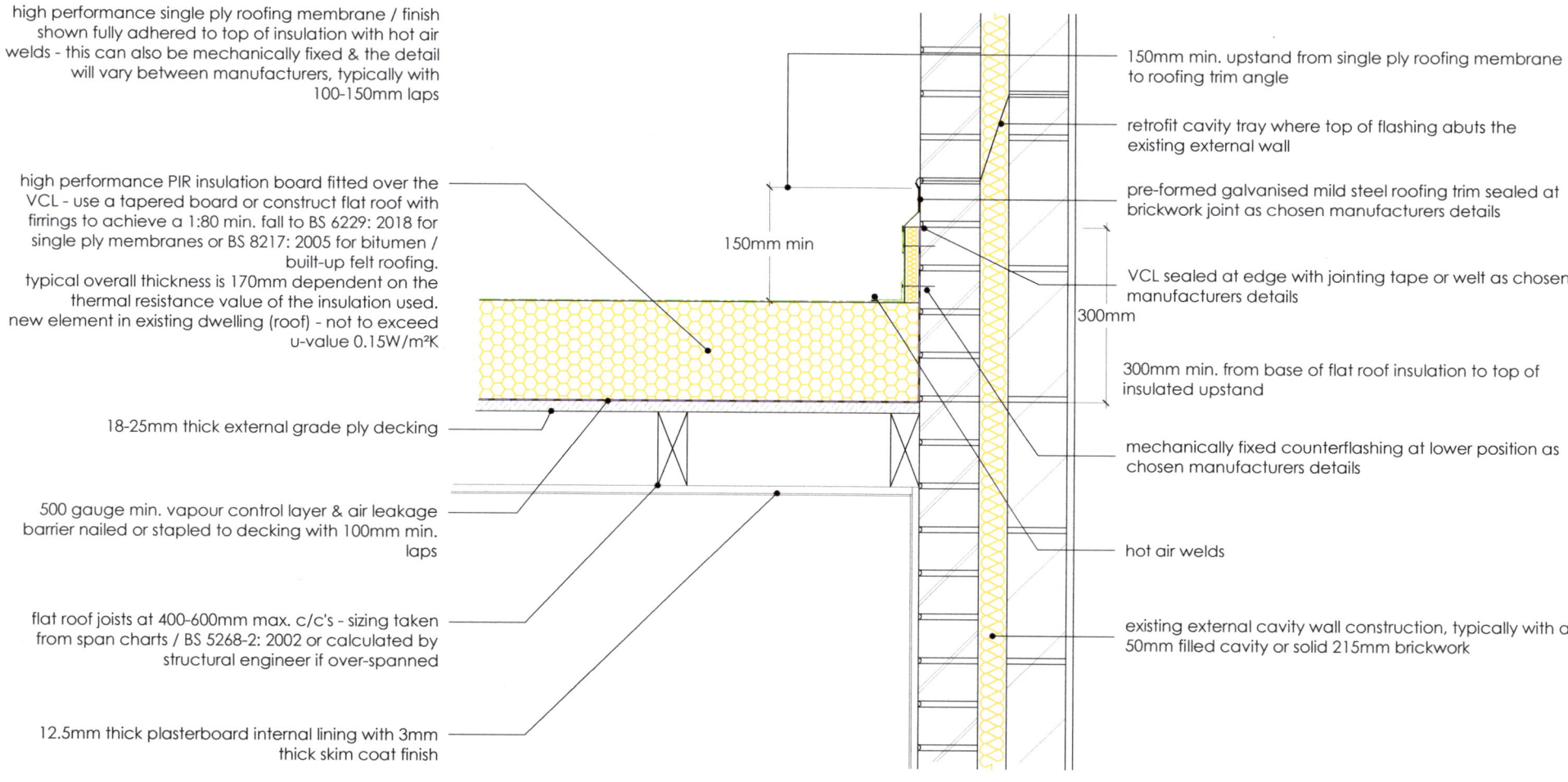

2D Detail LC-19 - Dormer - flat roof /edge abutment

Drawing note: this is a standard single ply roofing membrane flat roof / existing wall abutment detail that is typically used in urban areas were a terraced house is having a loft conversion & the adjacent properties have exposed external parapet walls, or were the loft conversion is adjacent to a higher storey building - note the thin layer of insulation to the roof / wall junction to eliminate any cold bridging effect.

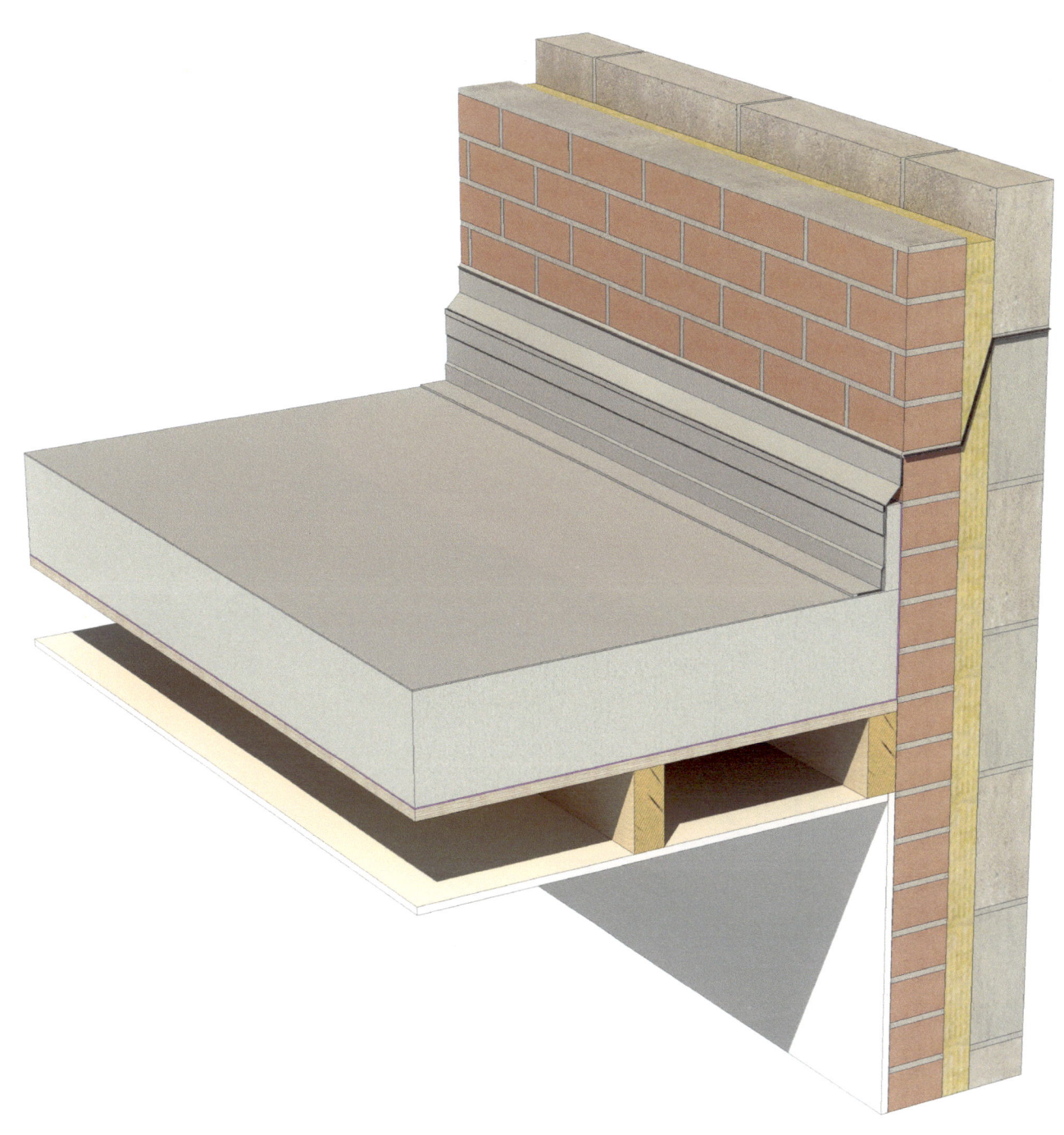

3D Detail LC-19 - Dormer - flat roof / edge abutment

Zinc Standing Seam Details

This set of standing seam details explores the more contemporary approach to a loft conversion. These details feature many of the main standing seam zinc junctions, from windows and parapets, to roof and wall junctions.

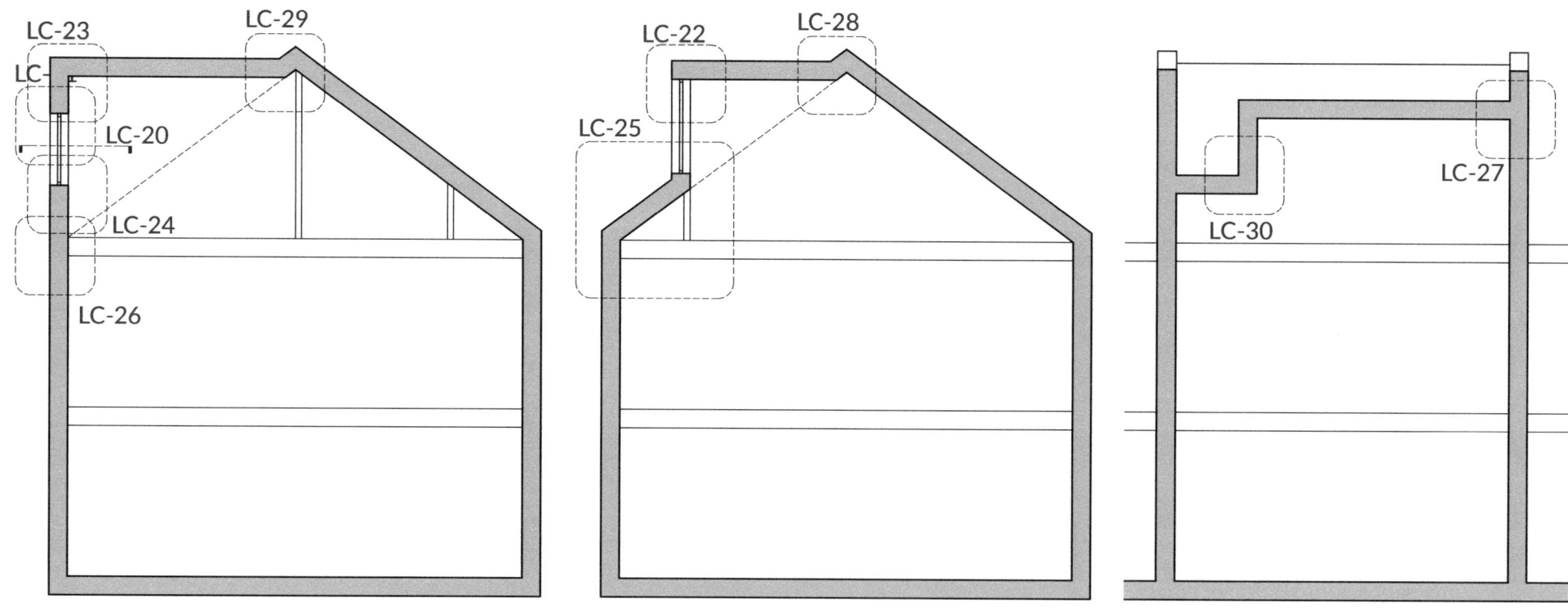

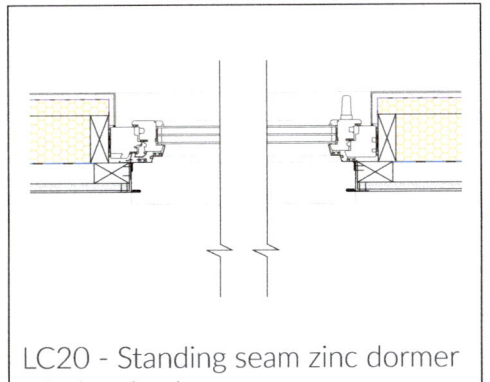
LC20 - Standing seam zinc dormer window jamb

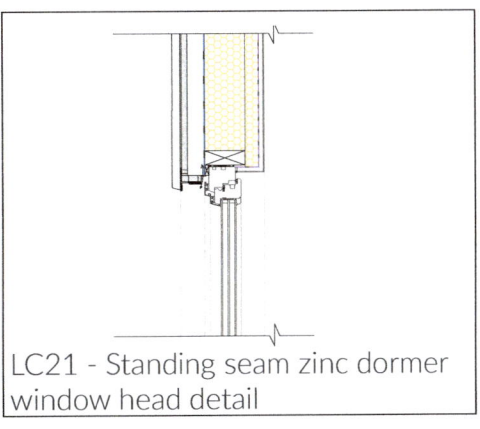
LC21 - Standing seam zinc dormer window head detail

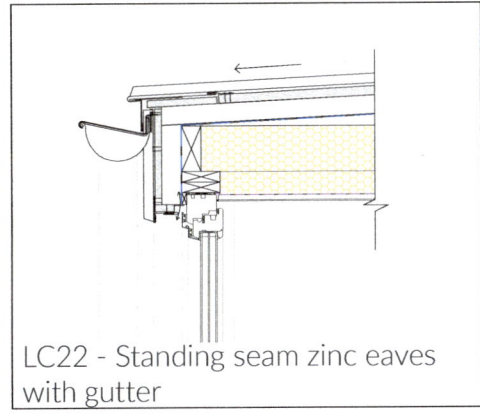
LC22 - Standing seam zinc eaves with gutter

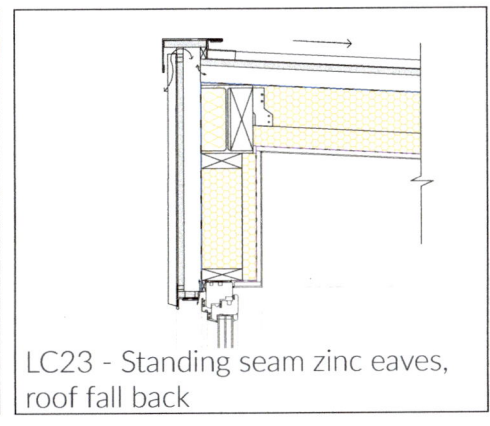
LC23 - Standing seam zinc eaves, roof fall back

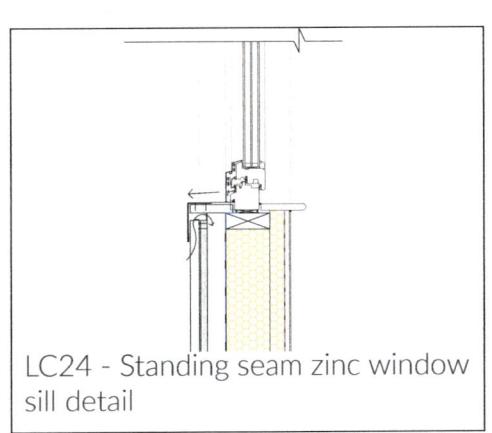
LC24 - Standing seam zinc window sill detail

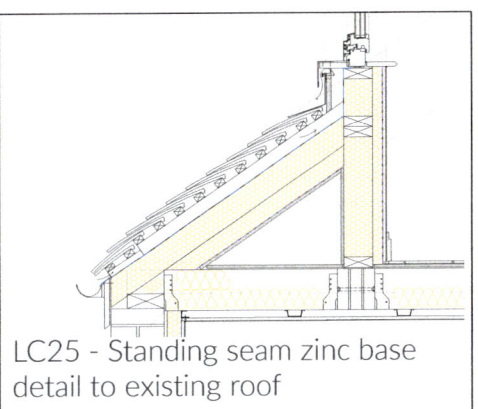
LC25 - Standing seam zinc base detail to existing roof

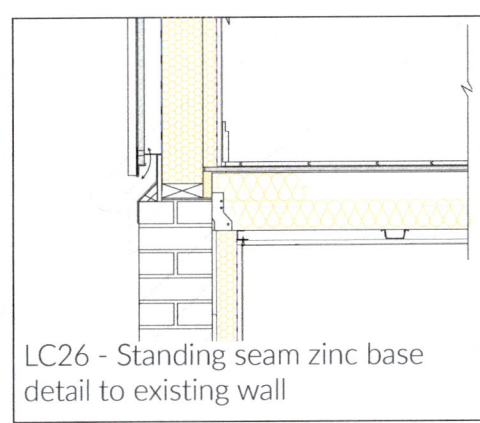
LC26 - Standing seam zinc base detail to existing wall

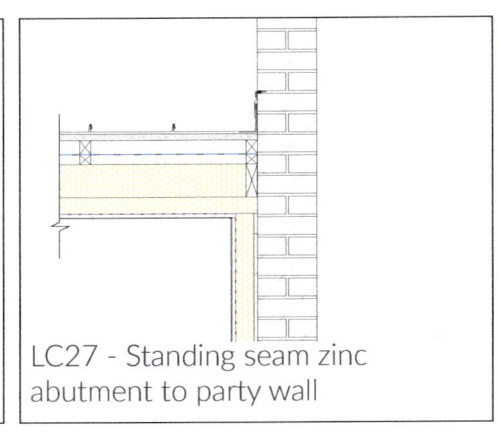
LC27 - Standing seam zinc abutment to party wall

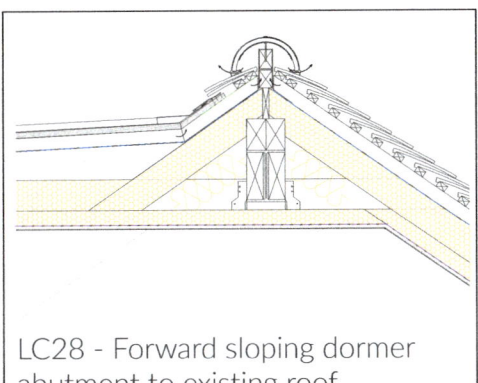
LC28 - Forward sloping dormer abutment to existing roof

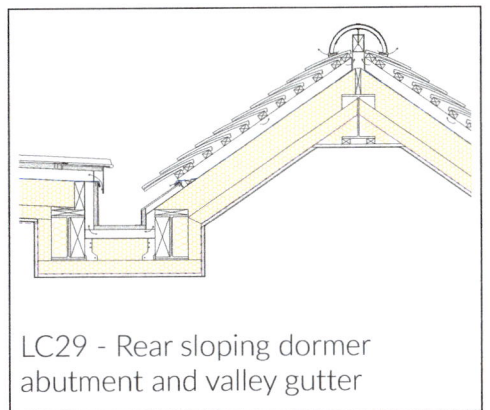
LC29 - Rear sloping dormer abutment and valley gutter

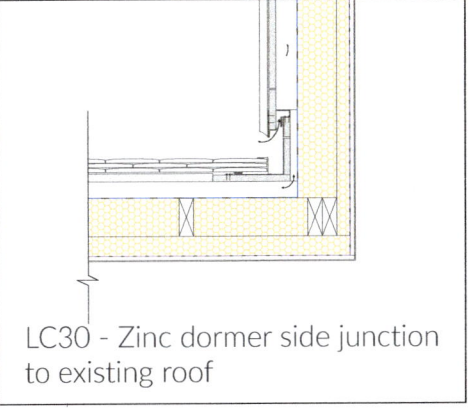
LC30 - Zinc dormer side junction to existing roof

LC-20
STANDING SEAM ZINC DORMER DETAIL - WINDOW JAMB

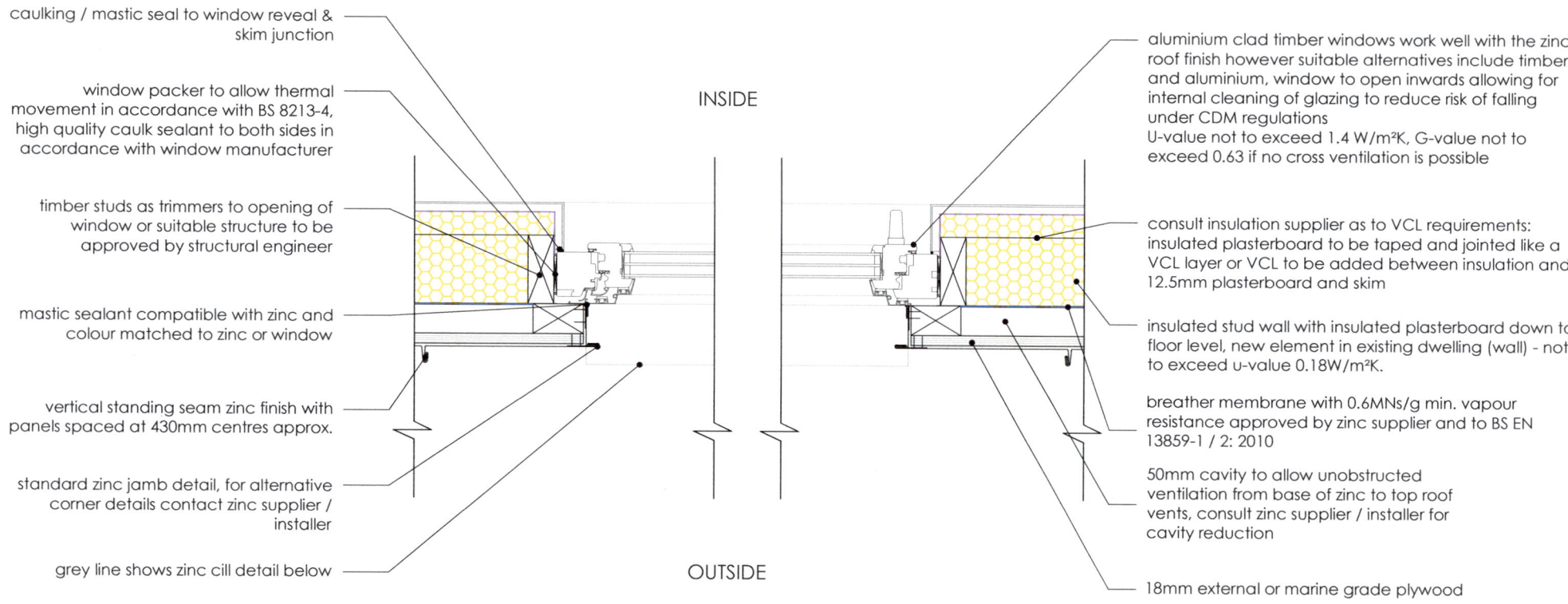

2D Detail LC-20 - Standing seam zinc dormer detail - window jamb

Drawing note: this is a typical vertical standing seam window jamb detail, alternative zinc setting out includes horizontal standing seam, interlocking panels, overlapping panels, flat lock panels, composite panels, wave profiles and zinc tiles.
it is recommended that windows and doors at height should open inwards to allow for cleaning without the risk of falling, reducing the risks in use and maintenance of the building to comply with CDM regulations. a maintenance strategy, risk register and residual risk register should be updated throughout the design process to comply with CDM regulations.

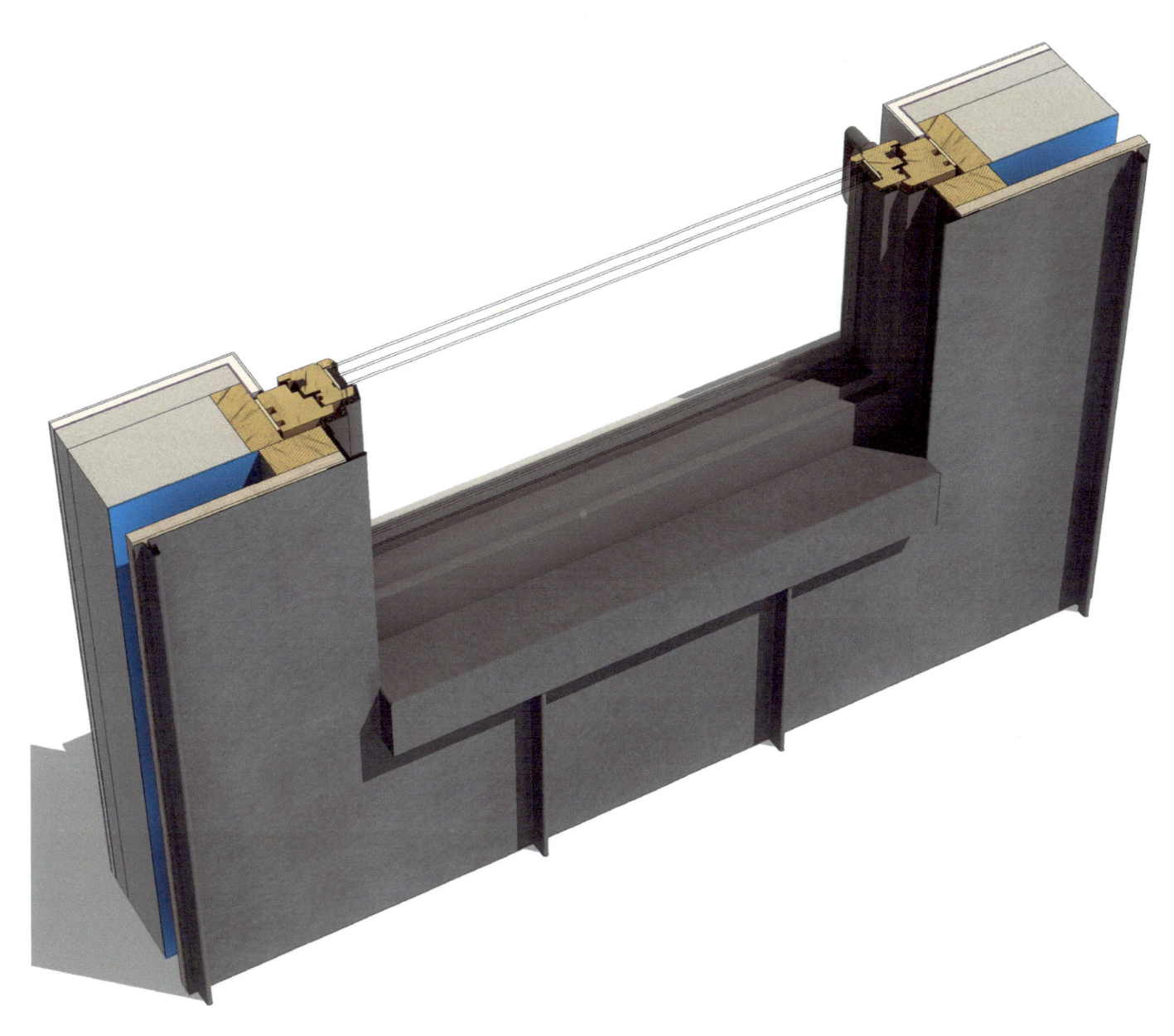

3D Detail LC-20 - Standing seam zinc dormer detail - window jamb

LC-21

STANDING SEAM ZINC DORMER DETAIL - WINDOW HEAD

Left-side annotations:
- 50mm cavity to allow unobstructed ventilation from base of zinc to top roof vents, consult zinc supplier / installer for cavity reduction
- 18mm external or marine grade plywood
- timber stud header to opening of window or suitable structure to be approved by structural engineer
- ventilation gap with insect mesh
- vertical standing seam zinc finish with panels spaced at 430mm centres approx.
- standard zinc head detail, for alternative corner details contact zinc supplier / installer
- grey line shows zinc window reveal to sides

Right-side annotations:
- consult insulation supplier as to VCL requirements: insulated plasterboard to be taped and jointed like a VCL layer or VCL to be added between insulation and 12.5mm plasterboard and skim
- insulated stud wall with insulated plasterboard down to floor level, new element in existing dwelling (wall) - not to exceed u-value 0.18W/m²K.
- breather membrane with 0.6MNs/g min. vapour resistance approved by zinc supplier and to BS EN 13859-1 / 2: 2010
- caulking / mastic seal to window reveal & skim junction
- window packer to allow thermal movement in accordance with BS 8213-4, high quality caulk sealant to both sides in accordance with window manufacturer
- aluminium clad timber windows work well with the zinc roof finish however suitable alternatives include timber and aluminium, window to open inwards allowing for internal cleaning of glazing to reduce risk of falling under CDM regulations
  U-value not to exceed 1.4 W/m²K, G-value not to exceed 0.63 if no cross ventilation is possible

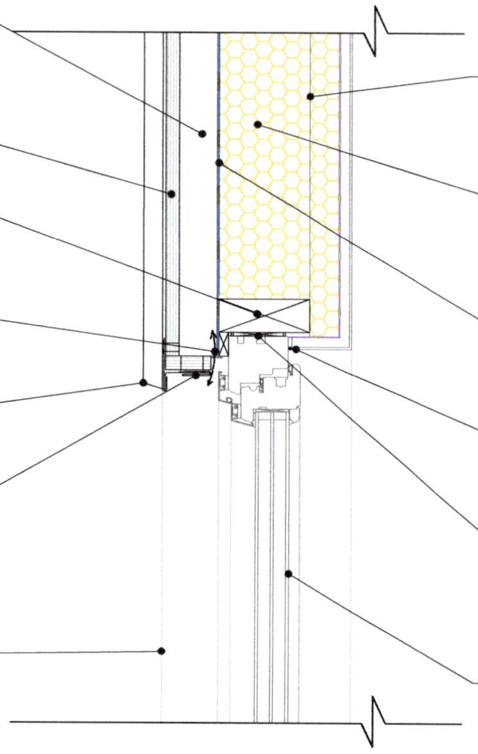

2D Detail LC-21 - Standing seam zinc dormer detail - window head

Drawing note:
this is a typical vertical standing seam window head detail, alternative zinc setting out includes horizontal standing seam, interlocking panels, overlapping panels, flat lock panels, composite panels, wave profiles and zinc tiles. it is recommended that windows and doors at height should open inwards to allow for cleaning without the risk of falling, reducing the risks in use and maintenance of the building to comply with CDM regulations. a maintenance strategy, risk register and residual risk register should be updated throughout the design process to comply with CDM regulations.

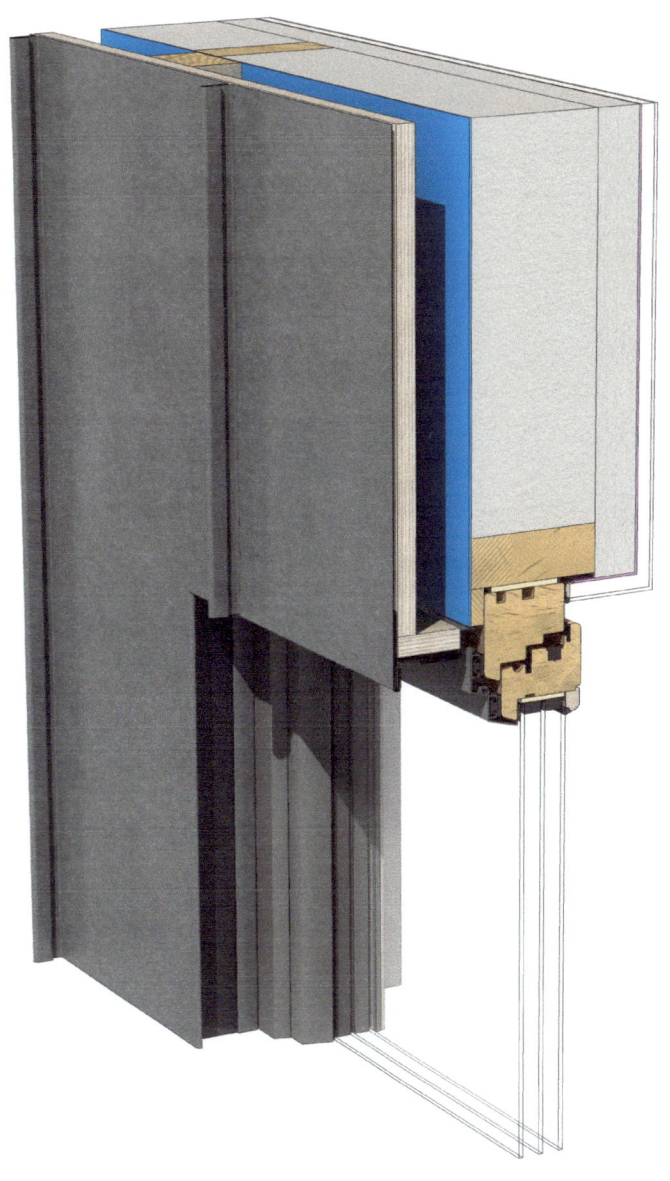

3D Detail LC-21 - Standing seam zinc dormer detail - window head

LC-22

STANDING SEAM ZINC DORMER EAVES DETAIL - FALL TO FORWARD GUTTER

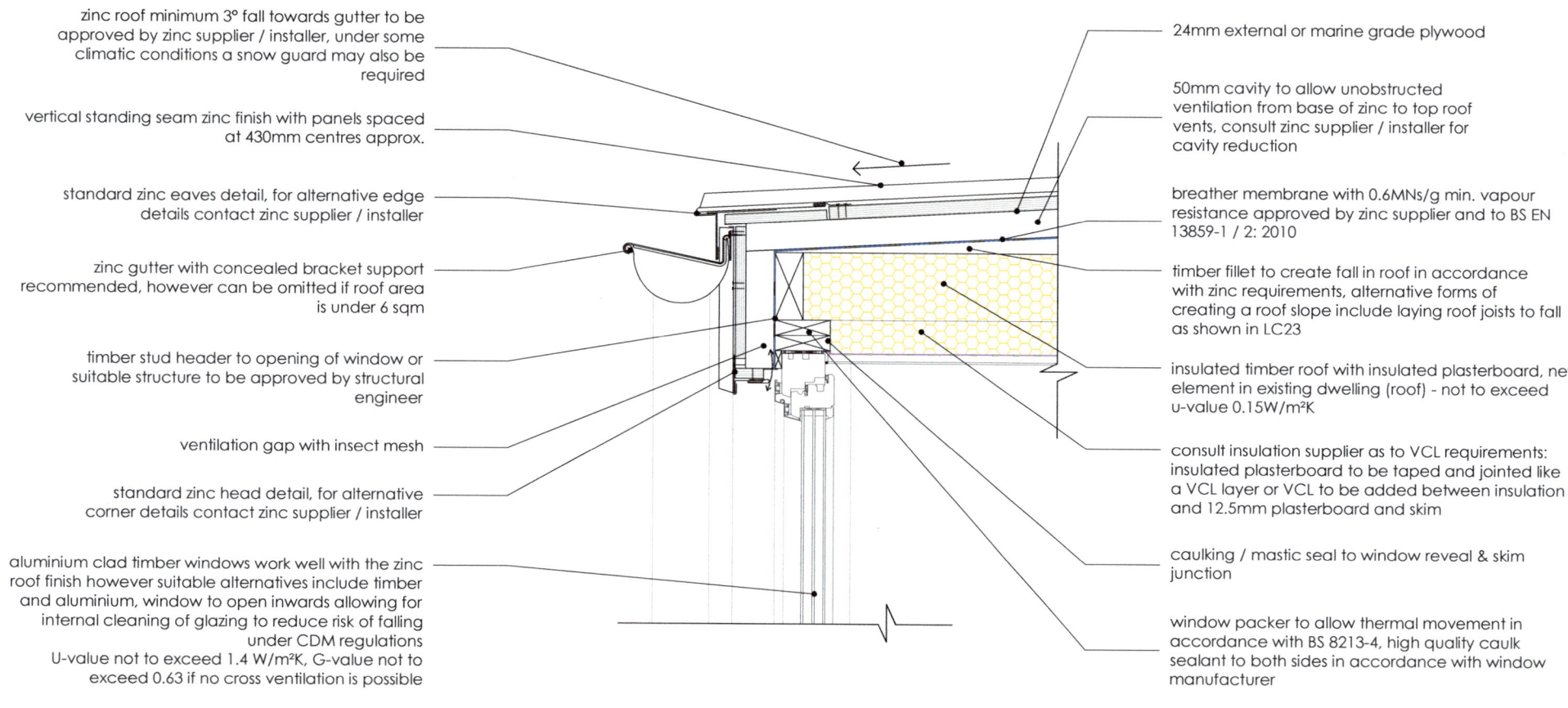

Labels (left side):
- zinc roof minimum 3° fall towards gutter to be approved by zinc supplier / installer, under some climatic conditions a snow guard may also be required
- vertical standing seam zinc finish with panels spaced at 430mm centres approx.
- standard zinc eaves detail, for alternative edge details contact zinc supplier / installer
- zinc gutter with concealed bracket support recommended, however can be omitted if roof area is under 6 sqm
- timber stud header to opening of window or suitable structure to be approved by structural engineer
- ventilation gap with insect mesh
- standard zinc head detail, for alternative corner details contact zinc supplier / installer
- aluminium clad timber windows work well with the zinc roof finish however suitable alternatives include timber and aluminium, window to open inwards allowing for internal cleaning of glazing to reduce risk of falling under CDM regulations U-value not to exceed 1.4 W/m²K, G-value not to exceed 0.63 if no cross ventilation is possible

Labels (right side):
- 24mm external or marine grade plywood
- 50mm cavity to allow unobstructed ventilation from base of zinc to top roof vents, consult zinc supplier / installer for cavity reduction
- breather membrane with 0.6MNs/g min. vapour resistance approved by zinc supplier and to BS EN 13859-1 / 2: 2010
- timber fillet to create fall in roof in accordance with zinc requirements, alternative forms of creating a roof slope include laying roof joists to fall as shown in LC23
- insulated timber roof with insulated plasterboard, new element in existing dwelling (roof) - not to exceed u-value 0.15W/m²K
- consult insulation supplier as to VCL requirements: insulated plasterboard to be taped and jointed like a VCL layer or VCL to be added between insulation and 12.5mm plasterboard and skim
- caulking / mastic seal to window reveal & skim junction
- window packer to allow thermal movement in accordance with BS 8213-4, high quality caulk sealant to both sides in accordance with window manufacturer

2D Detail LC-22 - Standing seam zinc dormer eaves detail - fall to forward gutter

Drawing note: this is a typical vertical standing seam window head detail with a flush ceiling finish, alternative zinc setting out includes horizontal standing seam, interlocking panels, overlapping panels, flat lock panels, composite panels, wave profiles and zinc tiles.
it is recommended that windows and doors at height should open inwards to allow for cleaning without the risk of falling, reducing the risks in use and maintenance of the building to comply with CDM regulations. a maintenance strategy, risk register and residual risk register should be updated throughout the design process to comply with CDM regulations. see LC28 for junction with existing roof detail.

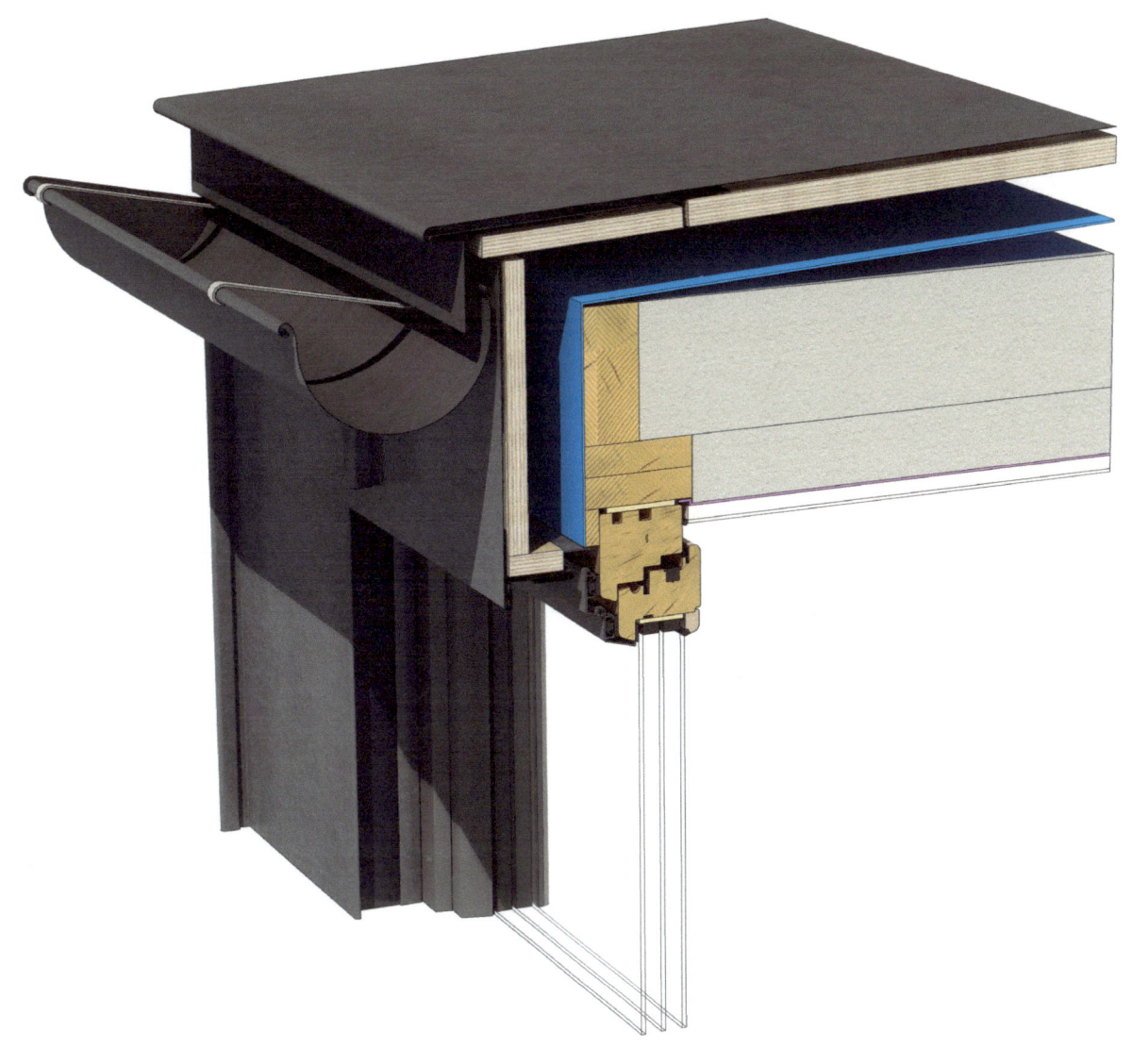

3D Detail LC-22 - Standing seam zinc dormer eaves detail - fall to forward gutter

LC-23

STANDING SEAM ZINC DORMER EAVES DETAIL - FALL BACK TO EXISTING ROOF

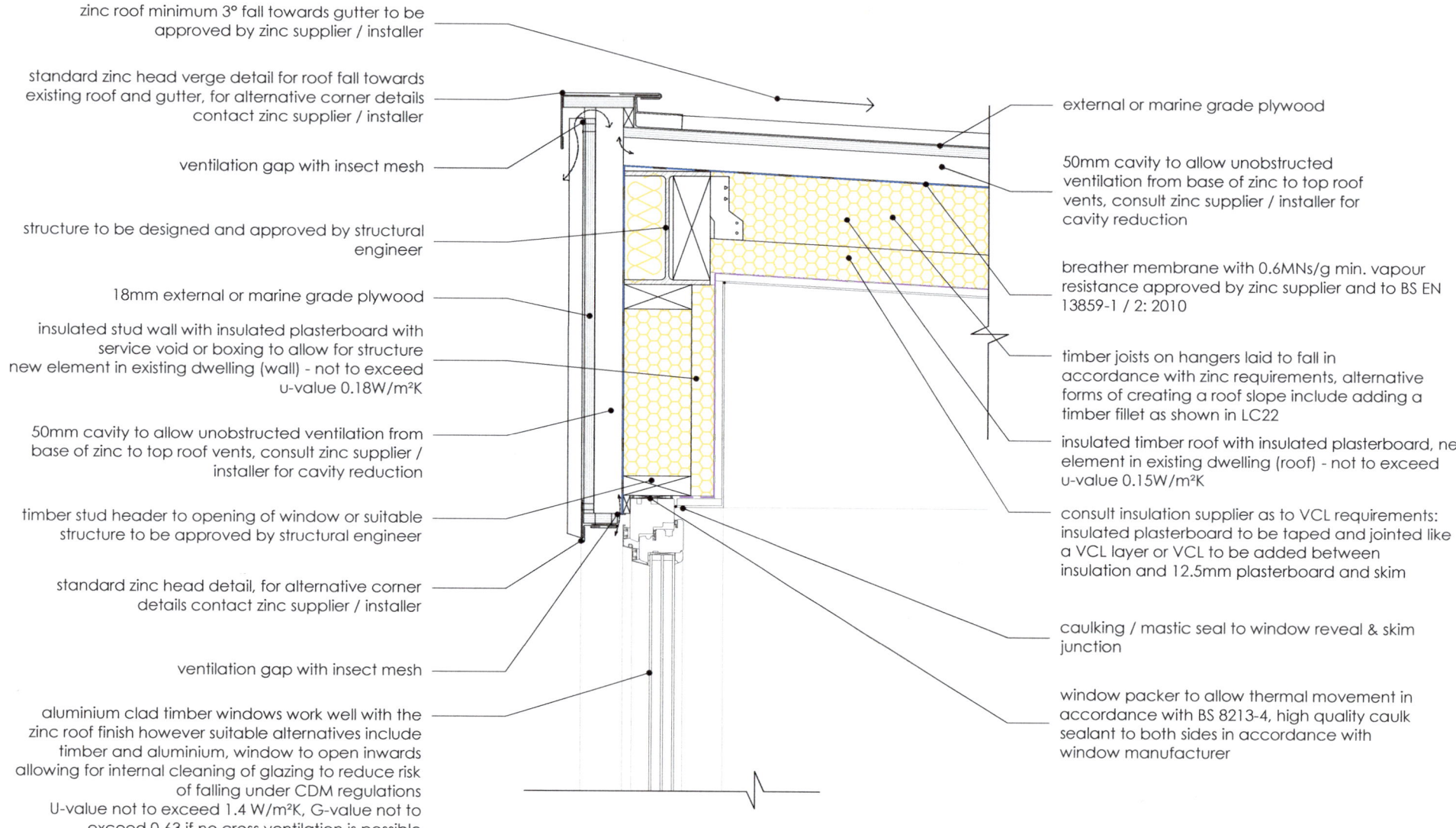

- zinc roof minimum 3° fall towards gutter to be approved by zinc supplier / installer
- standard zinc head verge detail for roof fall towards existing roof and gutter, for alternative corner details contact zinc supplier / installer
- ventilation gap with insect mesh
- structure to be designed and approved by structural engineer
- 18mm external or marine grade plywood
- insulated stud wall with insulated plasterboard with service void or boxing to allow for structure new element in existing dwelling (wall) - not to exceed u-value 0.18W/m²K
- 50mm cavity to allow unobstructed ventilation from base of zinc to top roof vents, consult zinc supplier / installer for cavity reduction
- timber stud header to opening of window or suitable structure to be approved by structural engineer
- standard zinc head detail, for alternative corner details contact zinc supplier / installer
- ventilation gap with insect mesh
- aluminium clad timber windows work well with the zinc roof finish however suitable alternatives include timber and aluminium, window to open inwards allowing for internal cleaning of glazing to reduce risk of falling under CDM regulations U-value not to exceed 1.4 W/m²K, G-value not to exceed 0.63 if no cross ventilation is possible

- external or marine grade plywood
- 50mm cavity to allow unobstructed ventilation from base of zinc to top roof vents, consult zinc supplier / installer for cavity reduction
- breather membrane with 0.6MNs/g min. vapour resistance approved by zinc supplier and to BS EN 13859-1 / 2: 2010
- timber joists on hangers laid to fall in accordance with zinc requirements, alternative forms of creating a roof slope include adding a timber fillet as shown in LC22
- insulated timber roof with insulated plasterboard, new element in existing dwelling (roof) - not to exceed u-value 0.15W/m²K
- consult insulation supplier as to VCL requirements: insulated plasterboard to be taped and jointed like a VCL layer or VCL to be added between insulation and 12.5mm plasterboard and skim
- caulking / mastic seal to window reveal & skim junction
- window packer to allow thermal movement in accordance with BS 8213-4, high quality caulk sealant to both sides in accordance with window manufacturer

2D Detail LC-23 - Standing seam zinc dormer eaves detail - fall back to existing roof

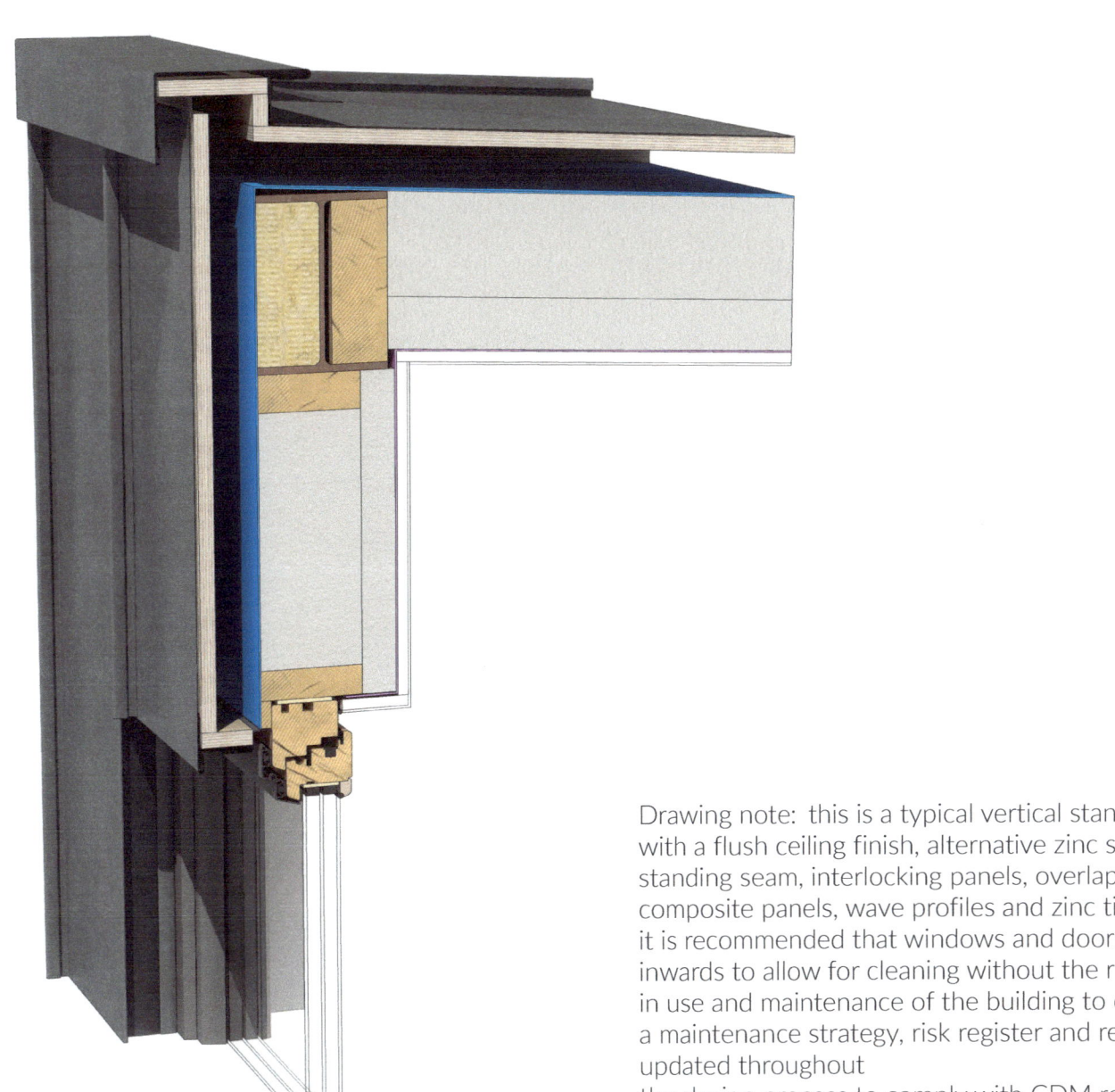

Drawing note: this is a typical vertical standing seam window head detail with a flush ceiling finish, alternative zinc setting out includes horizontal standing seam, interlocking panels, overlapping panels, flat lock panels, composite panels, wave profiles and zinc tiles.
it is recommended that windows and doors at height should open inwards to allow for cleaning without the risk of falling, reducing the risks in use and maintenance of the building to comply with CDM regulations.
a maintenance strategy, risk register and residual risk register should be updated throughout
the design process to comply with CDM regulations.
see LC29 for junction with existing roof detail and inset gutter detail.

3D Detail LC-23 - Standing seam zinc dormer eaves detail - fall back to existing roof

LC-24

STANDING SEAM ZINC DETAIL - WINDOW CILL

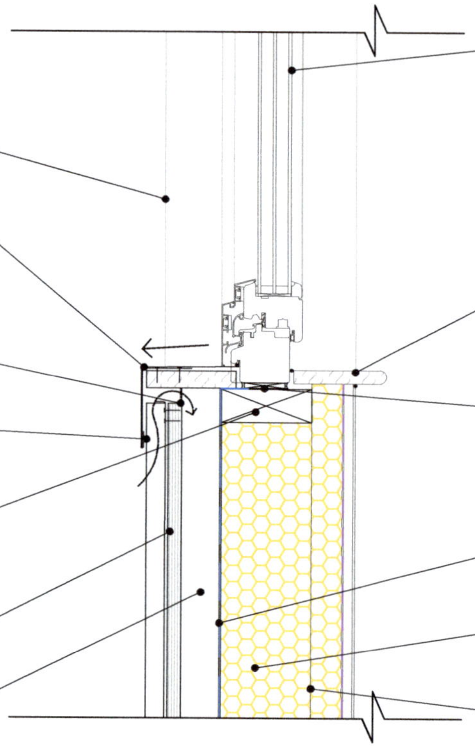

grey line shows zinc window reveal to sides
standard zinc cill detail to fall away window, for alternative corner details contact zinc supplier / installer
ventilation gap with insect mesh
vertical standing seam zinc finish with panels spaced at 430mm centres approx.
timber base to opening of window or suitable structure to be approved by structural engineer
18mm external or marine grade plywood
50mm cavity to allow unobstructed ventilation from base of zinc to top roof vents, consult zinc supplier / installer for cavity reduction
aluminium clad timber windows work well with the zinc roof finish however suitable alternatives include timber and aluminium, window to open inwards allowing for internal cleaning of galzing to reduce risk of falling under CDM regulations
U-value not to exceed 1.4 W/m²K, G-value not to exceed 0.63 if no cross ventilation is possible
internal timber cill with caulking / mastic seal to window junction
window packer to allow thermal movement in accordance with BS 8213-4, high quality caulk sealant to both sides in accordance with window manufacturer
breather membrane with 0.6MNs/g min. vapour resistance approved by zinc supplier and to BS EN 13859-1 / 2: 2010
insulated stud wall with insulated plasterboard down to floor level, new element in existing dwelling (wall) - not to exceed u-value 0.18W/m²K
consult insulation supplier as to VCL requirements: insulated plasterboard to be taped and jointed like a VCL layer or VCL to be added between insulation and 12.5mm plasterboard and skim

2D Detail LC-24 - Standing seam zinc detail - window cill

Drawing note: this is a typical vertical standing seam window cill detail, alternative zinc setting out includes horizontal standing seam, interlocking panels, overlapping panels, flat lock panels, composite panels, wave profiles and zinc tiles.
it is recommended that windows and doors at height should open inwards to allow for cleaning without the risk of falling, reducing the risks in use and maintenance of the building to comply with CDM regulations. a maintenance strategy, risk register and residual risk register should be updated throughout the design process to comply with CDM regulations.

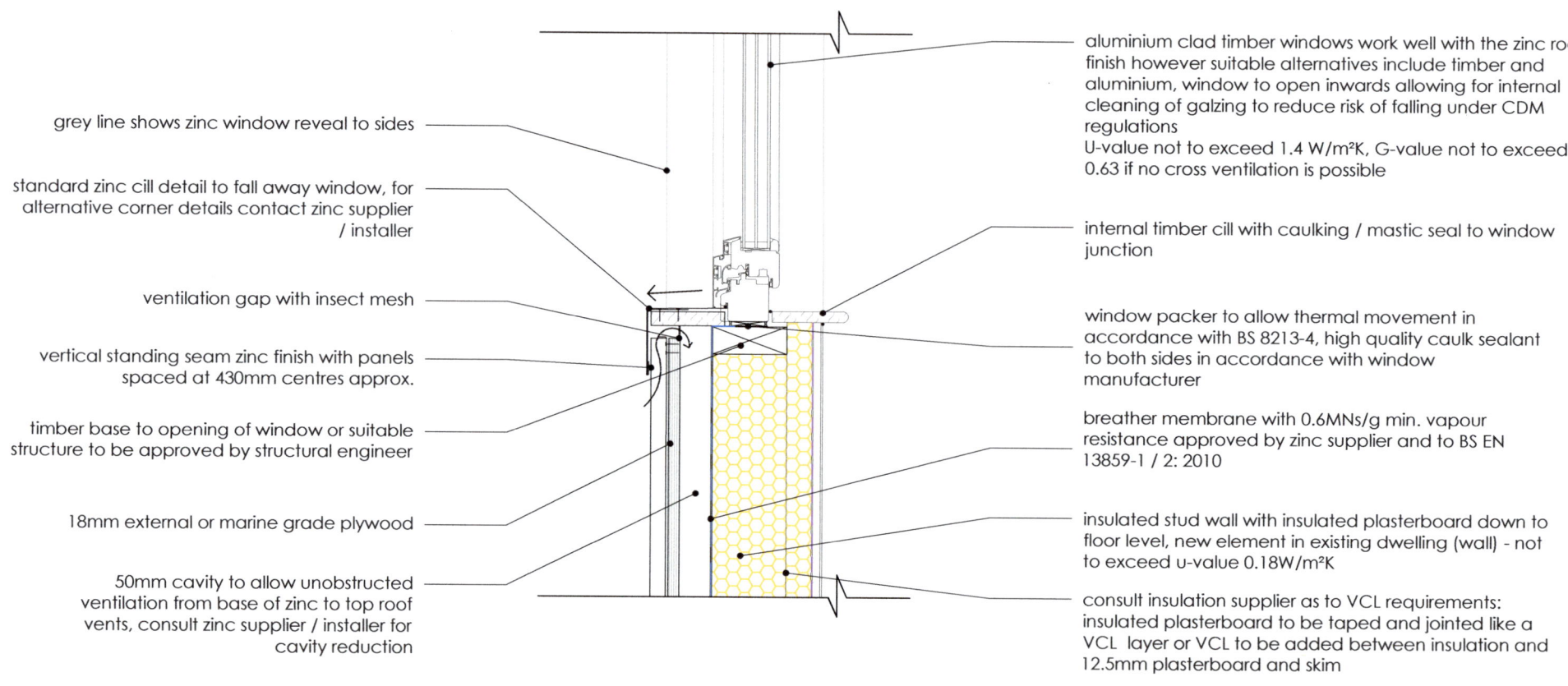

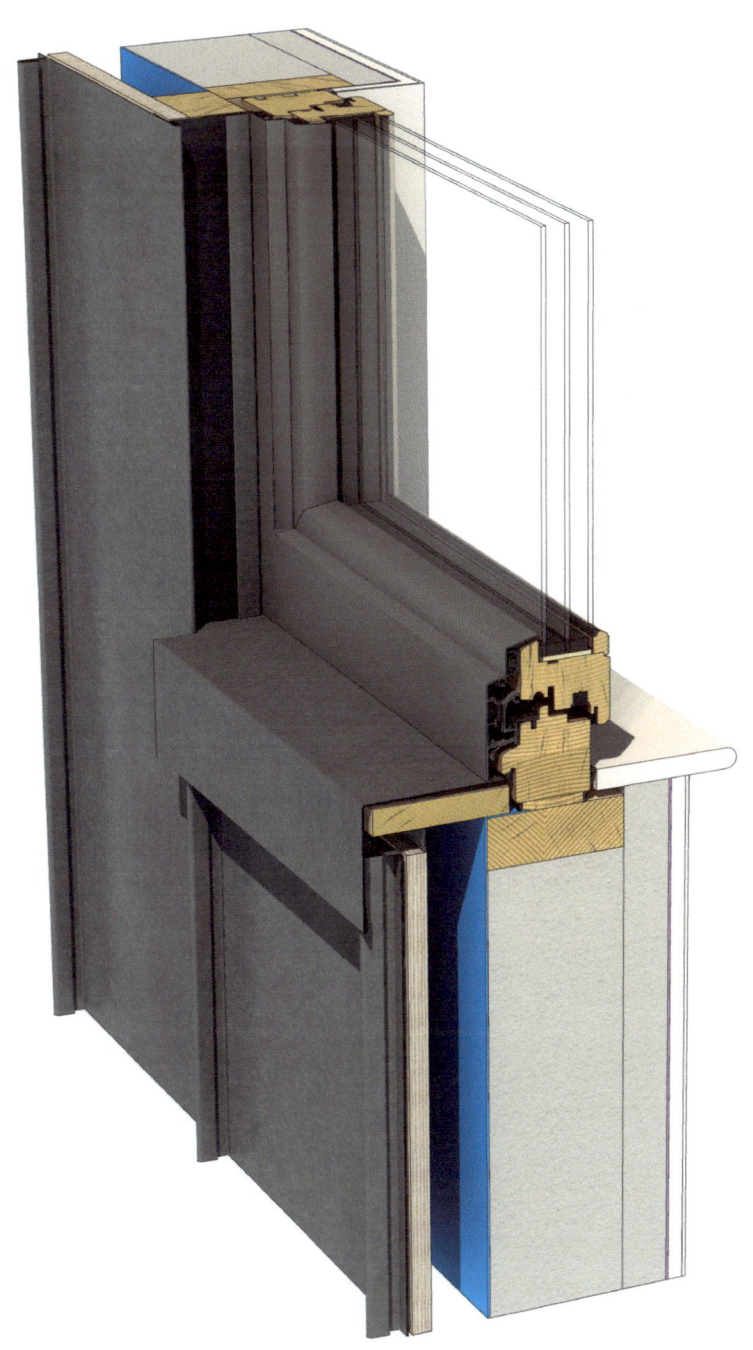

3D Detail LC-24 - Standing seam zinc detail - window cill

LC-25
STANDING SEAM ZINC BASE DETAIL - TO EXISTING ROOF

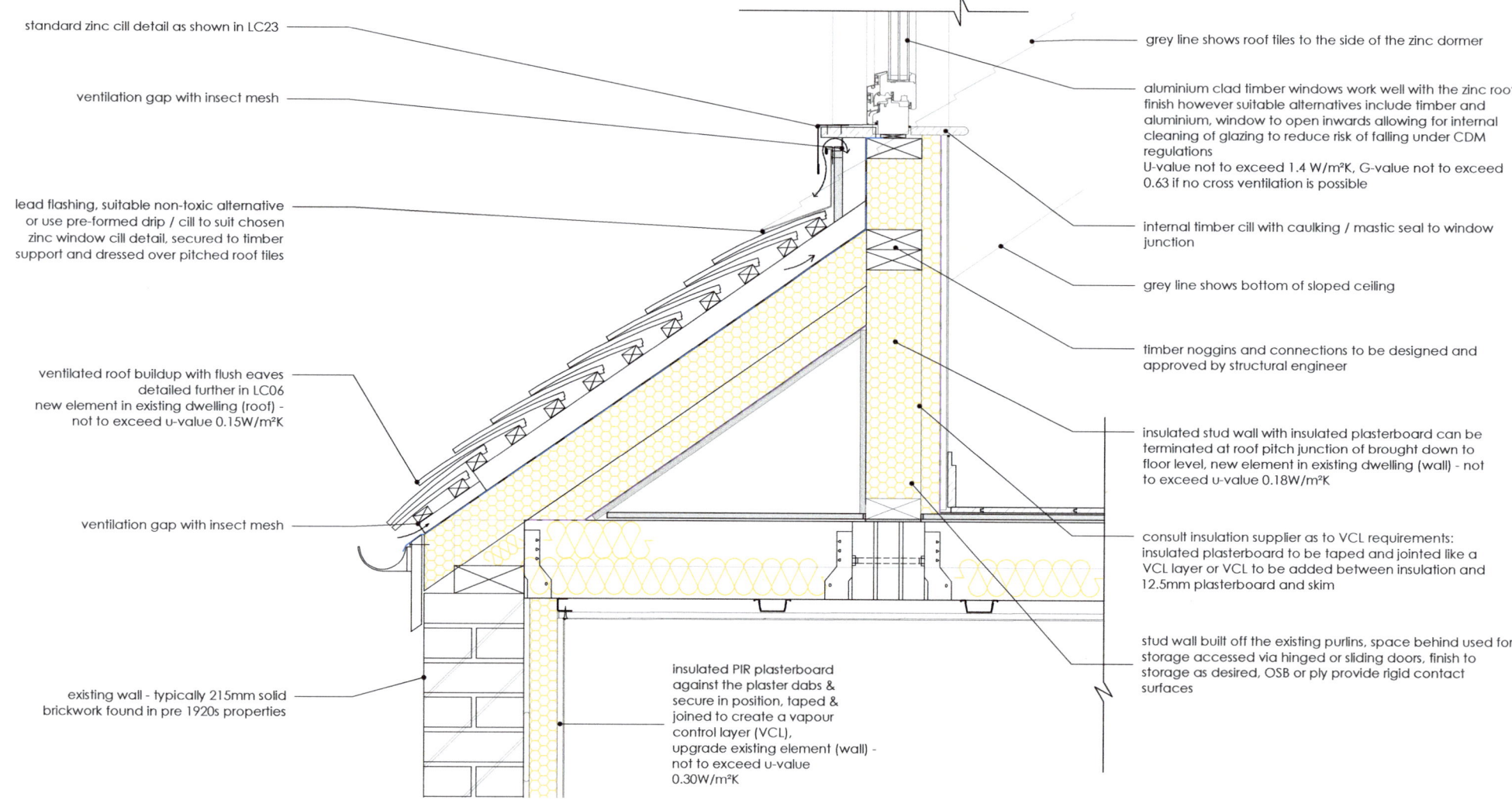

2D Detail LC-25 - Standing seam zinc base detail - to existing roof

Drawing note: this is a typical dormer window detail were the dormer is required to be positioned up the existing roof slope as mentioned on drawing number LC16. any new timber or steel beams will need to be carefully designed & detailed by a structural engineer to take account of imposed & super-imposed (live & dead) loads from snow / wind, roof & floor.

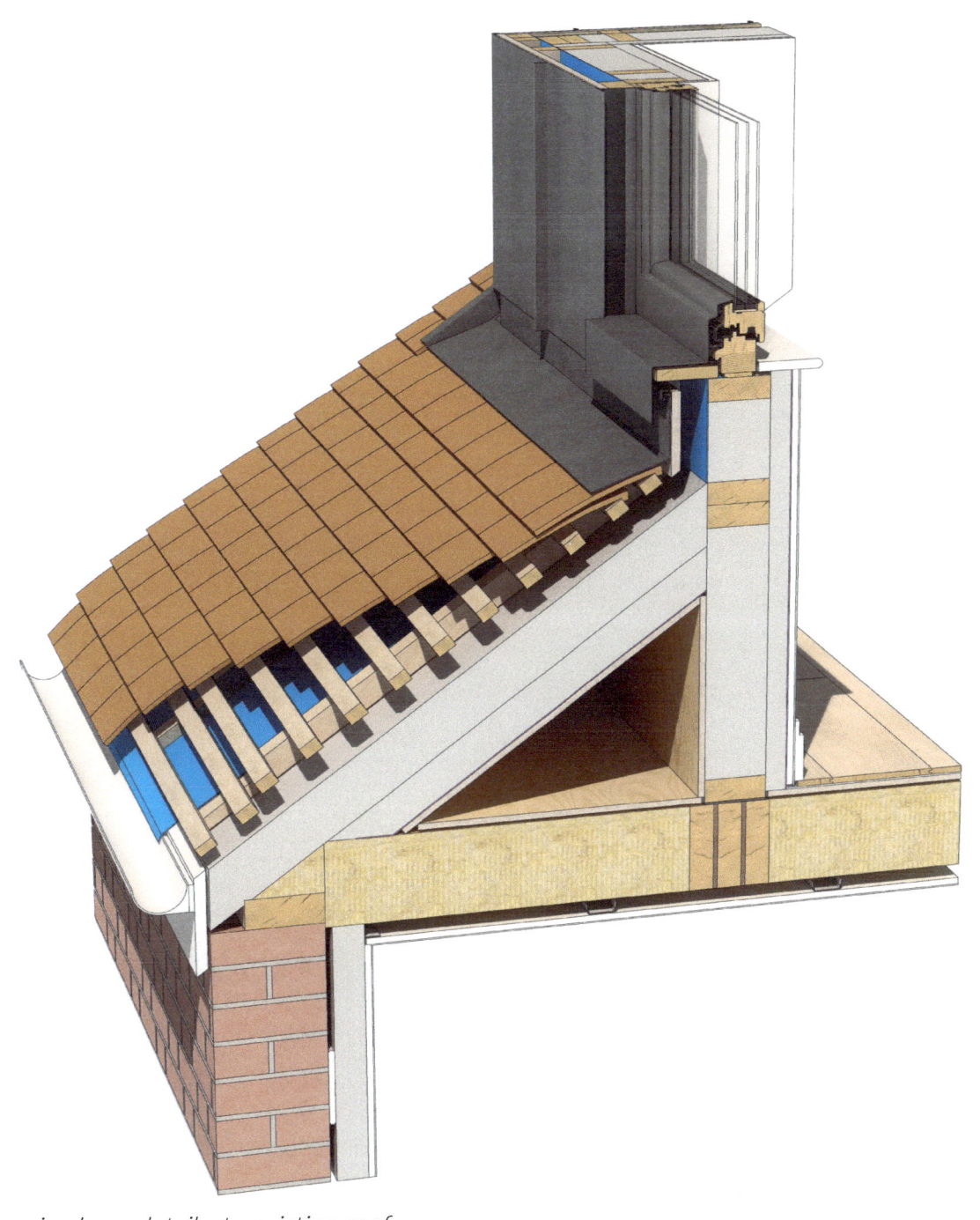

3D Detail LC-25 - Standing seam zinc base detail - to existing roof

LC-26

STANDING SEAM ZINC BASE DETAIL - TO EXISTING WALL

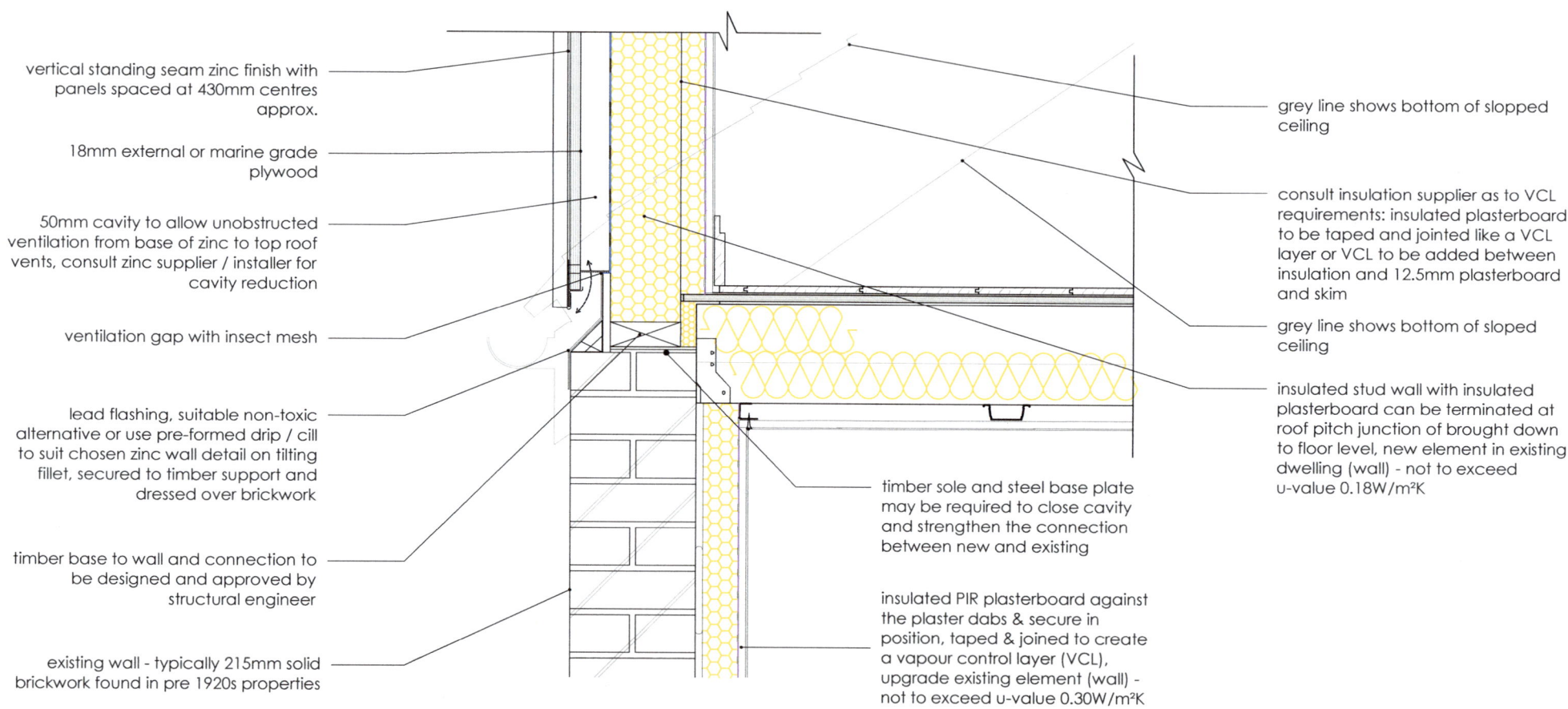

2D Detail LC-26 - Standing seam zinc base detail - to existing wall

Drawing note: this is a typical dormer window sole plate detail that is aligned with the inside face of the existing external wall (note that planning restrictions in your local area may require the dormer to be positioned further up a roof slope rather than off the existing external wall to appear more like an "insert" in the roof structure rather than an "extension" to it - see drawing number LC25 for details). any new timber or steel beams will need to be carefully designed & detailed by a structural engineer to take account of imposed & super-imposed (live & dead) loads from snow / wind, roof & floor.

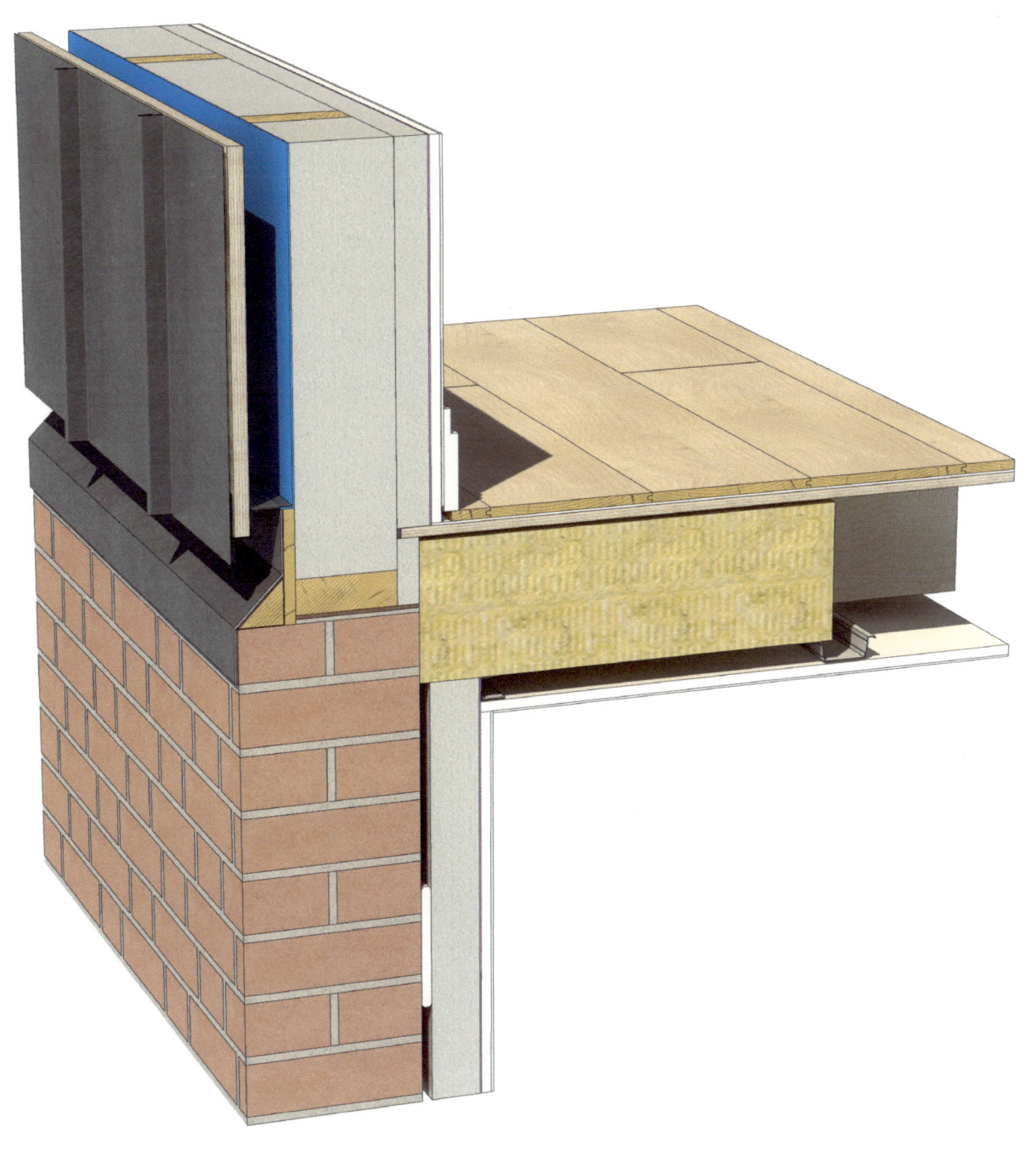

3D Detail LC-26 - Standing seam zinc base detail - to existing wall

LC-27

STANDING SEAM ZINC DORMER ABUTMENT DETAIL - TO PARTY WALL

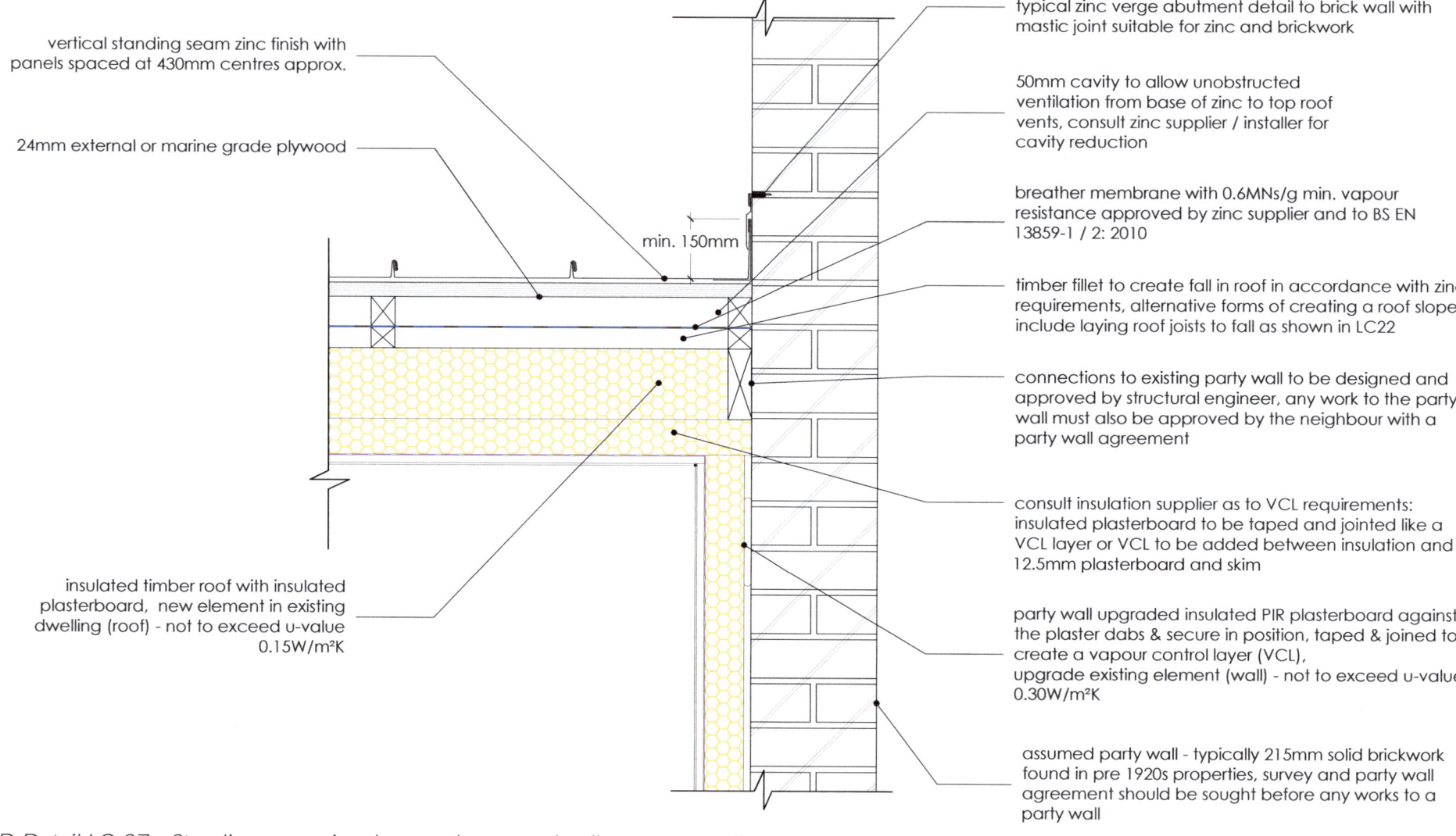

2D Detail LC-27 - Standing seam zinc dormer abutment detail - to party wall

Drawing note: this is a standard ventilated zinc roof / existing wall abutment detail that is typically used in urban areas were a terraced house is having a loft conversion & the adjacent properties have exposed external parapet walls, or were the loft conversion is adjacent to a higher storey building. Any work to a party wall must be approved by the neighbour with a party wall agreement.

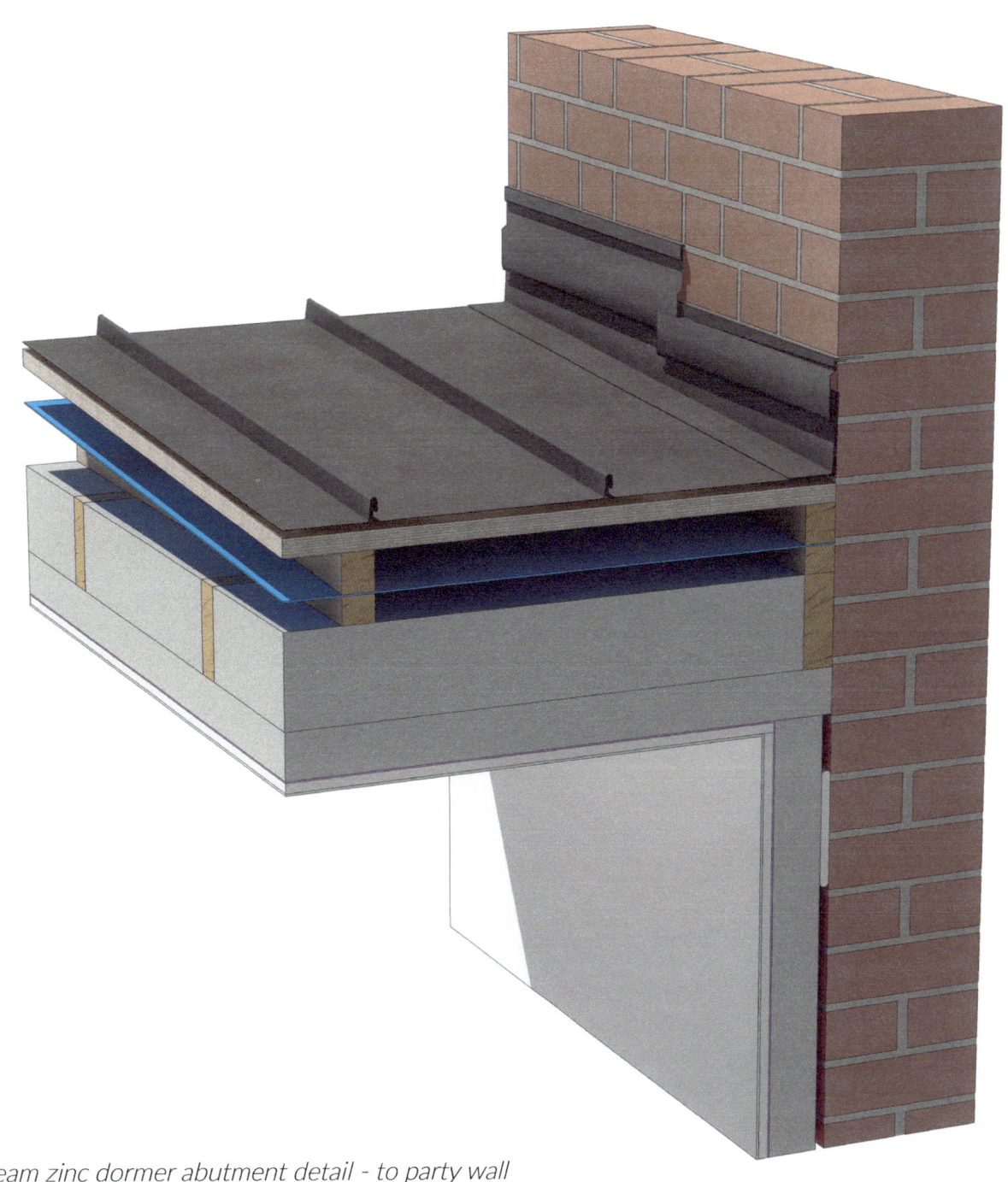

3D Detail LC-27 - Standing seam zinc dormer abutment detail - to party wall

LC-28

FORWARD SLOPING DORMER - RIDGE ABUTMENT TO EXISTING ROOF

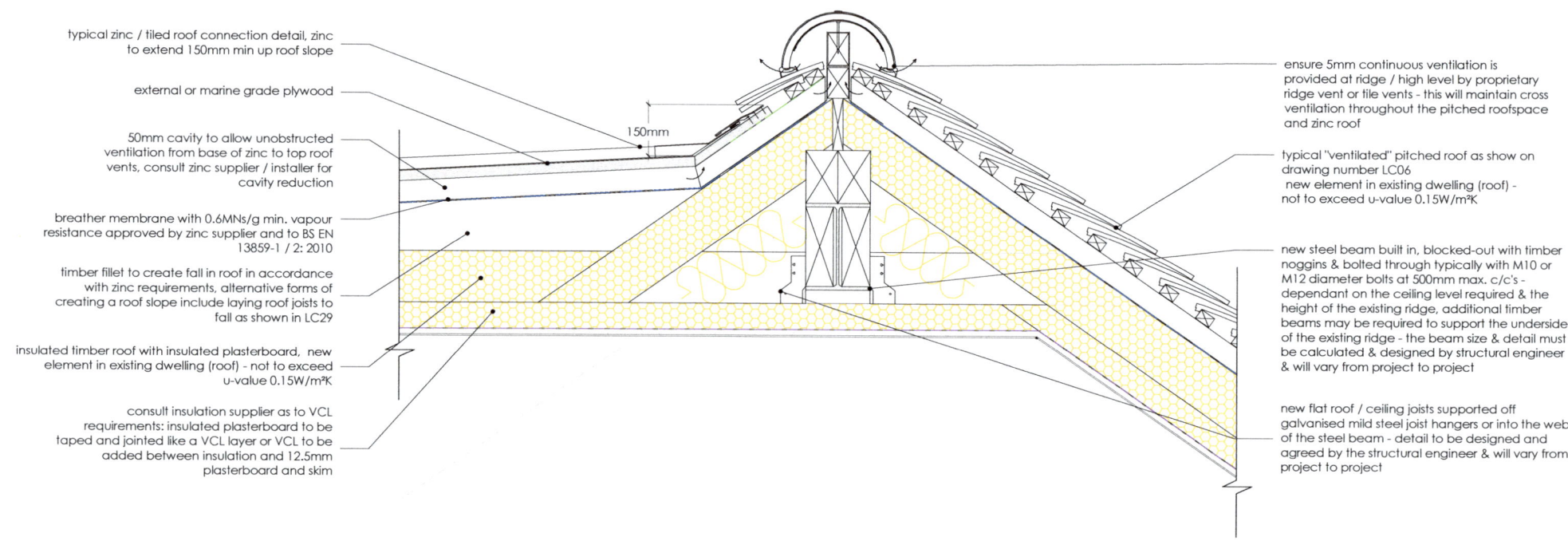

2D Detail LC-28 - Forward sloping dormer - ridge abutment to existing roof

Drawing note: this is a zinc dormer roof / ridge junction detail where the zinc falls away from the existing roof - there are many variants on this theme & they will vary depending on the height of the existing ridge, planning regulation & the ceiling height required for the project. An alternative example, LC29 shows the zinc roof falling towards the existing roof with a box gutter detail. If designing a barrel vaulted or pitched dormer, water can be evacuated laterally. ensure flashing between the new flat roof & the existing sloping roof has adequate laps to ensure it is watertight & prevents any driving rain from getting into the structure. each project must be individually designed & calculated by a structural engineer.

3D Detail LC-28 - Forward sloping dormer - ridge abutment to existing roof

LC-29

REAR SLOPING DORMER - RIDGE ABUTMENT AND VALLEY GUTTER TO EXISTING ROOF

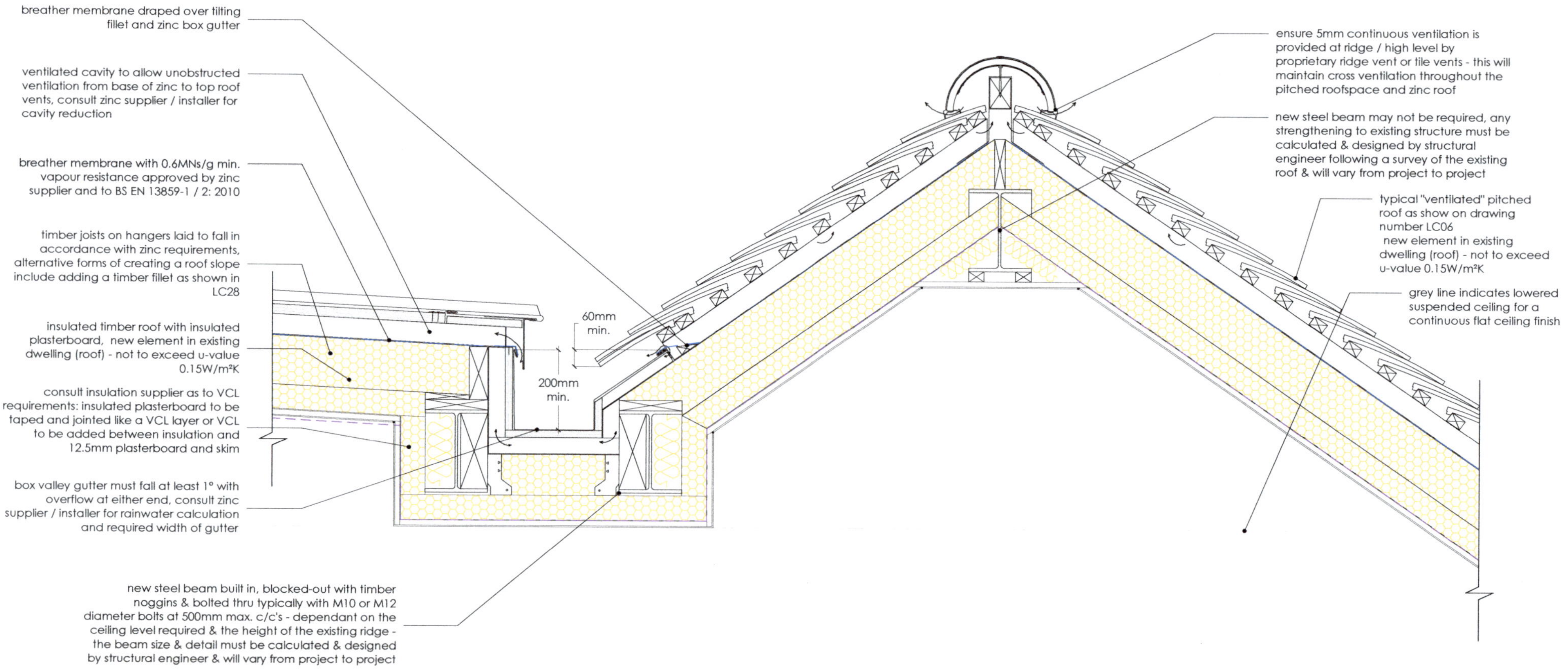

2D Detail LC-29 - Rear sloping dormer - ridge abutment and valley gutter to existing roof

Drawing note: this is a zinc dormer roof / ridge junction detail where the zinc falls towards the existing roof - there are many variations on this theme & they will vary depending on the height of the existing ridge, planning regulation & the ceiling height required for the project. An alternative example, LC28 shows the zinc roof falling away from the existing roof. If designing a barrel vaulted or pitched dormer, water can be evacuated laterally. ensure overlaps between the zinc box gutter comply with supplier / installer recommendations to ensure it is watertight & prevents water due to driving rain and blocked gutters from getting into the structure. each project must be individually designed & calculated by a structural engineer, structure is shown indicatively of where it may be required.

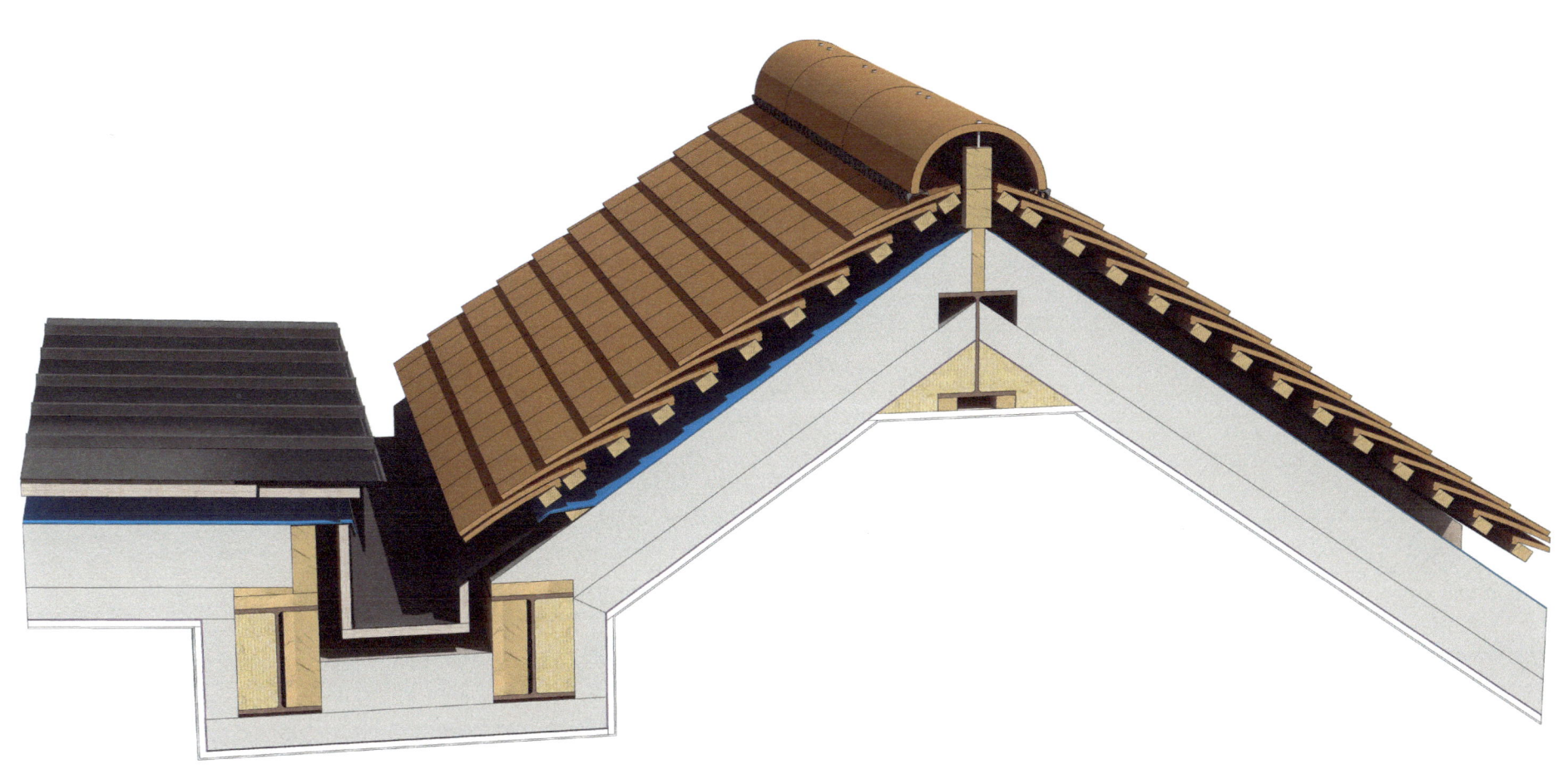

3D Detail LC-29 - Rear sloping dormer - ridge abutment and valley gutter to existing roof

LC-30
ZINC DORMER - SIDE JUNCTION TO EXISTING ROOF

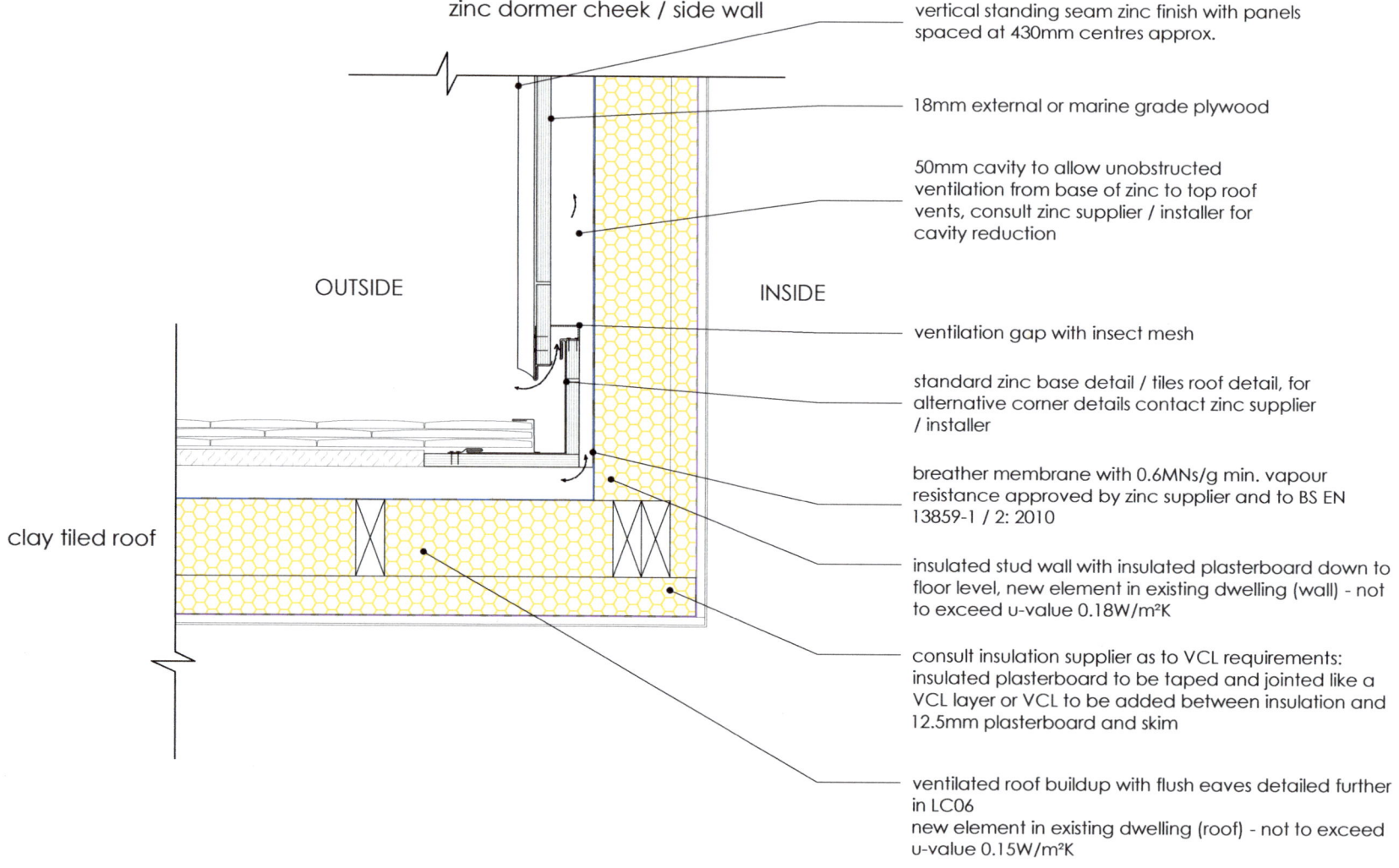

2D Detail LC-30 - Zinc dormer - side junction to existing roof

Drawing note: this is a standard ventilated zinc roof / existing clay roof abutment detail that is typically seen at the side of the dormer wall when the dormer does not reach the party walls.

any new timber or steel beams will need to be carefully designed & detailed by a structural engineer to take account of imposed & super-imposed (live & dead) loads from snow / wind, roof & floor.

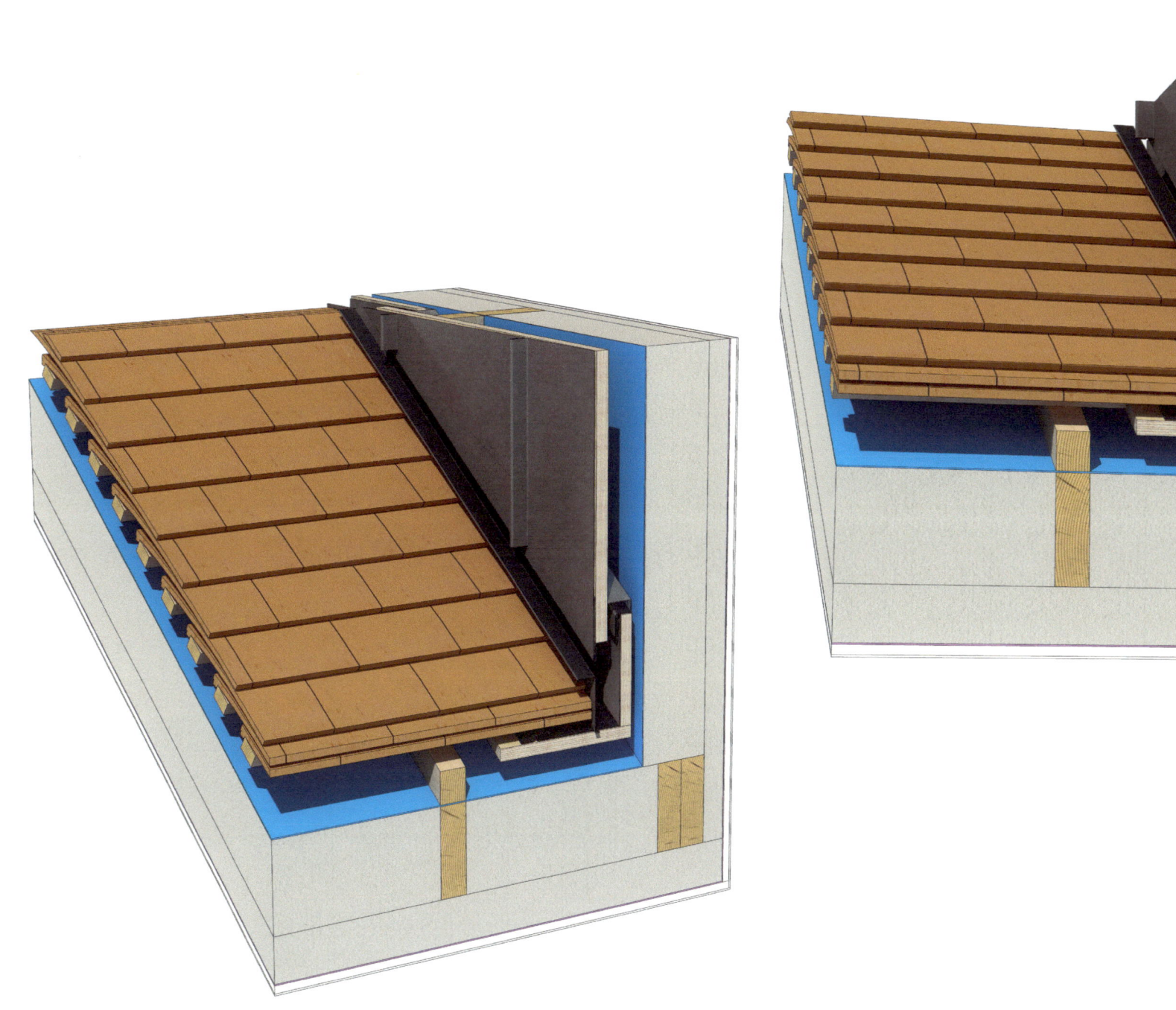

3D Detail LC-30 - Zinc dormer - side junction to existing roof

Faceted Zinc Dormer Details

This set of details includes a more contemporary approach to a flat roof dormer. The faceted zinc dormer is shown in both plan and section, with window details and corner options.

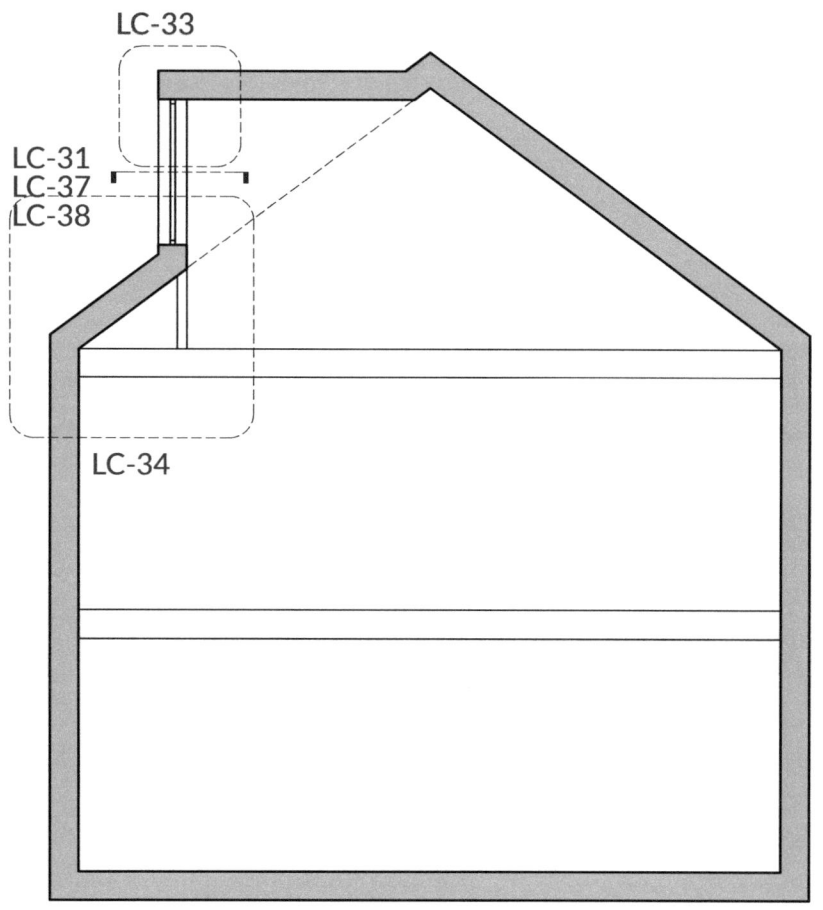
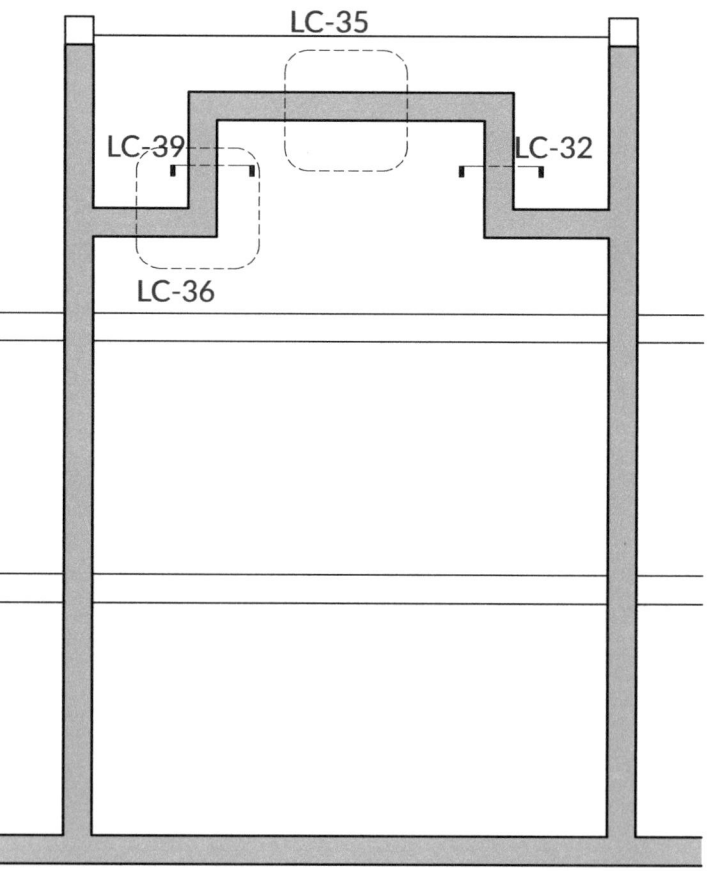

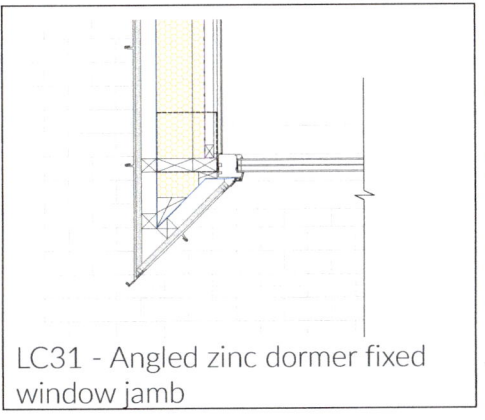
LC31 - Angled zinc dormer fixed window jamb

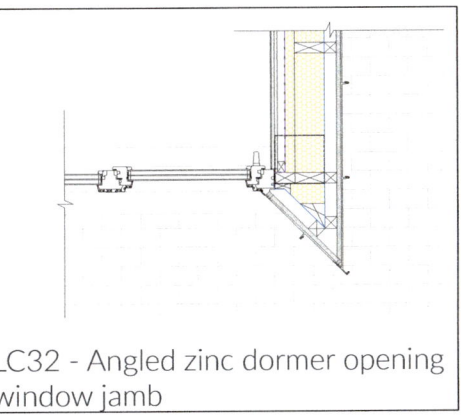
LC32 - Angled zinc dormer opening window jamb

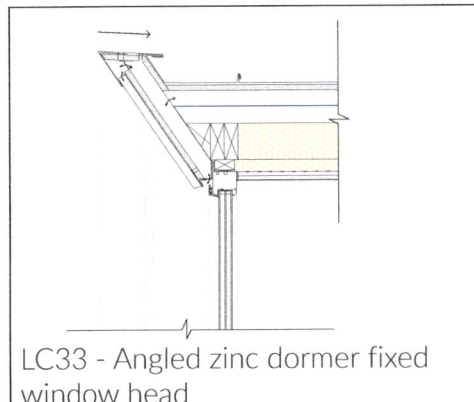
LC33 - Angled zinc dormer fixed window head

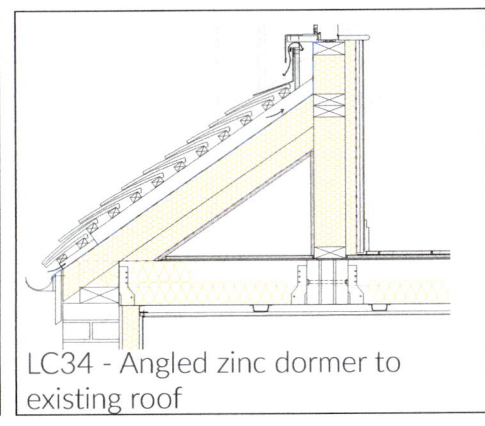
LC34 - Angled zinc dormer to existing roof

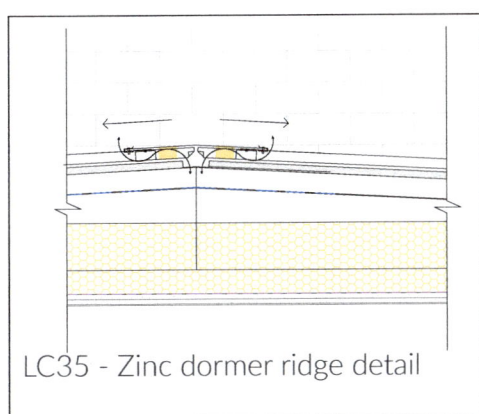
LC35 - Zinc dormer ridge detail

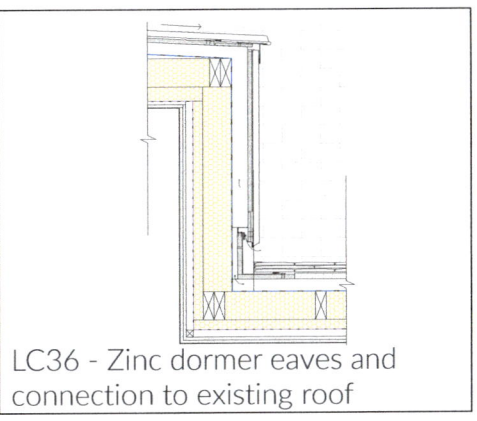
LC36 - Zinc dormer eaves and connection to existing roof

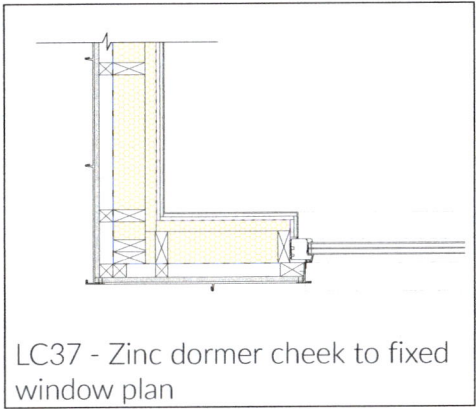
LC37 - Zinc dormer cheek to fixed window plan

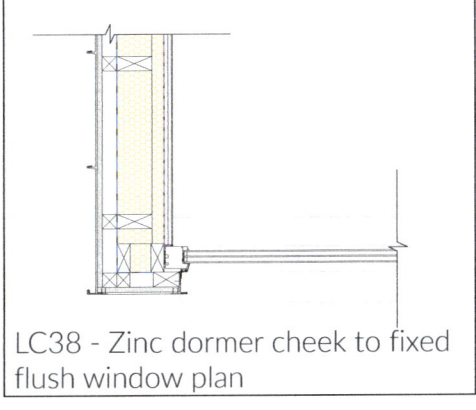
LC38 - Zinc dormer cheek to fixed flush window plan

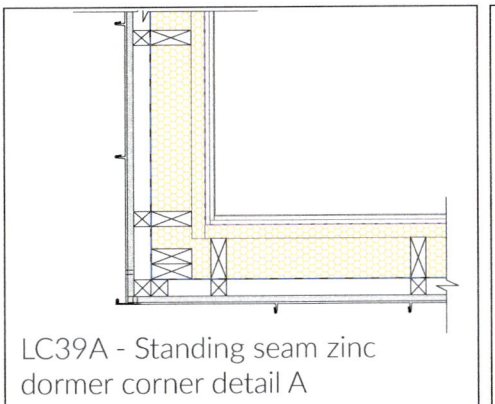
LC39A - Standing seam zinc dormer corner detail A

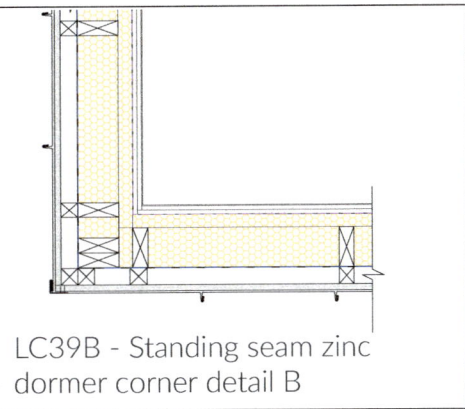
LC39B - Standing seam zinc dormer corner detail B

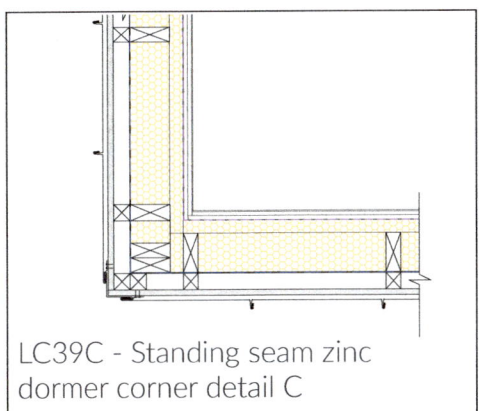
LC39C - Standing seam zinc dormer corner detail C

LC-31

STANDING SEAM ANGLED ZINC DORMER DETAIL - FIXED WINDOW JAMB

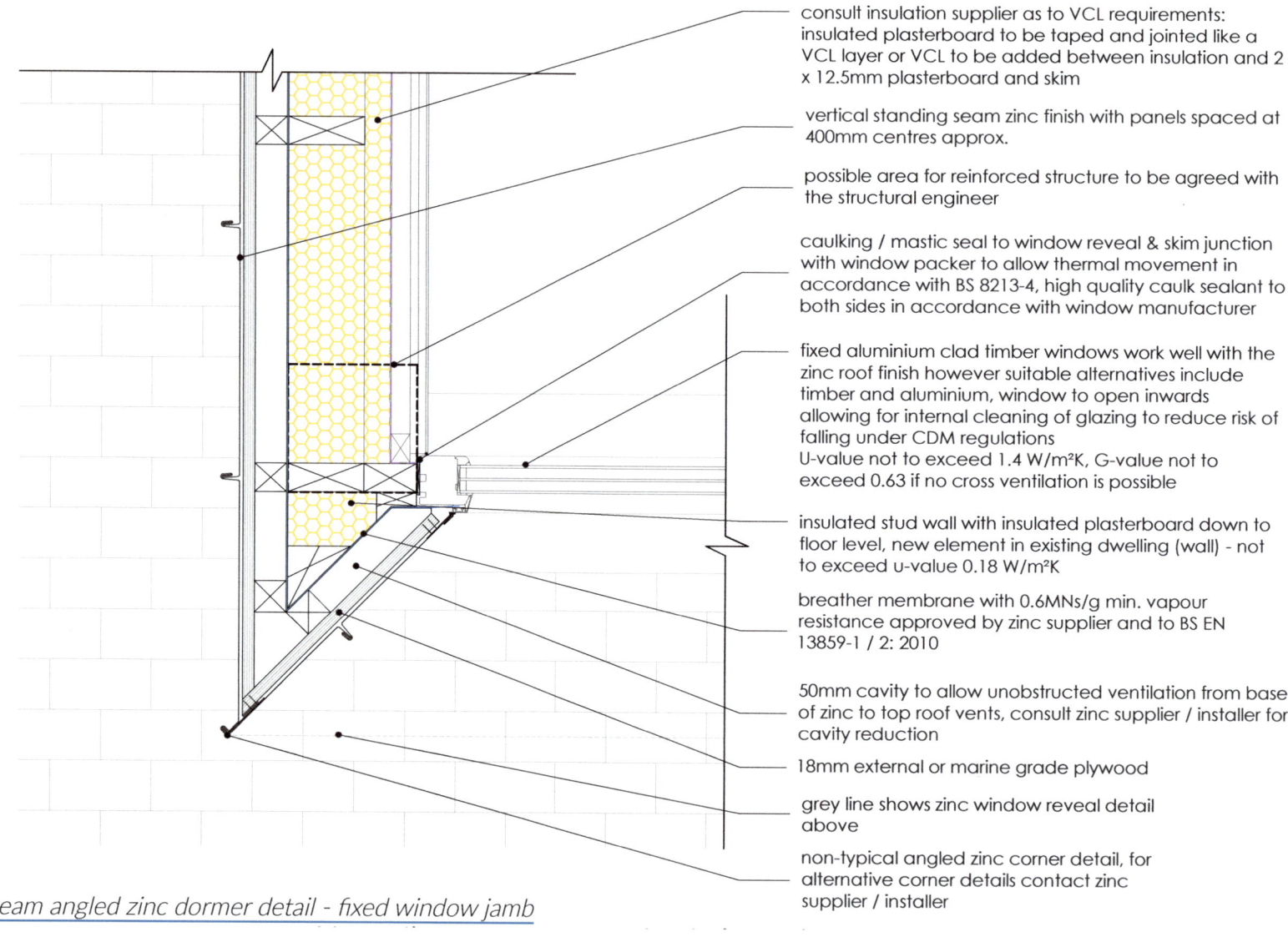

- consult insulation supplier as to VCL requirements: insulated plasterboard to be taped and jointed like a VCL layer or VCL to be added between insulation and 2 x 12.5mm plasterboard and skim
- vertical standing seam zinc finish with panels spaced at 400mm centres approx.
- possible area for reinforced structure to be agreed with the structural engineer
- caulking / mastic seal to window reveal & skim junction with window packer to allow thermal movement in accordance with BS 8213-4, high quality caulk sealant to both sides in accordance with window manufacturer
- fixed aluminium clad timber windows work well with the zinc roof finish however suitable alternatives include timber and aluminium, window to open inwards allowing for internal cleaning of glazing to reduce risk of falling under CDM regulations
U-value not to exceed 1.4 W/m²K, G-value not to exceed 0.63 if no cross ventilation is possible
- insulated stud wall with insulated plasterboard down to floor level, new element in existing dwelling (wall) - not to exceed u-value 0.18 W/m²K
- breather membrane with 0.6MNs/g min. vapour resistance approved by zinc supplier and to BS EN 13859-1 / 2: 2010
- 50mm cavity to allow unobstructed ventilation from base of zinc to top roof vents, consult zinc supplier / installer for cavity reduction
- 18mm external or marine grade plywood
- grey line shows zinc window reveal detail above
- non-typical angled zinc corner detail, for alternative corner details contact zinc supplier / installer

2D Detail LC-31 - Standing seam angled zinc dormer detail - fixed window jamb

Drawing note: this is an non-typical angled zinc standing seam window jamb detail, all details should be approved by the zinc manufacturer / installer, structural engineer and building control officer.
wall thickness and angle may be dependant on the structural solution and u-value requirements.

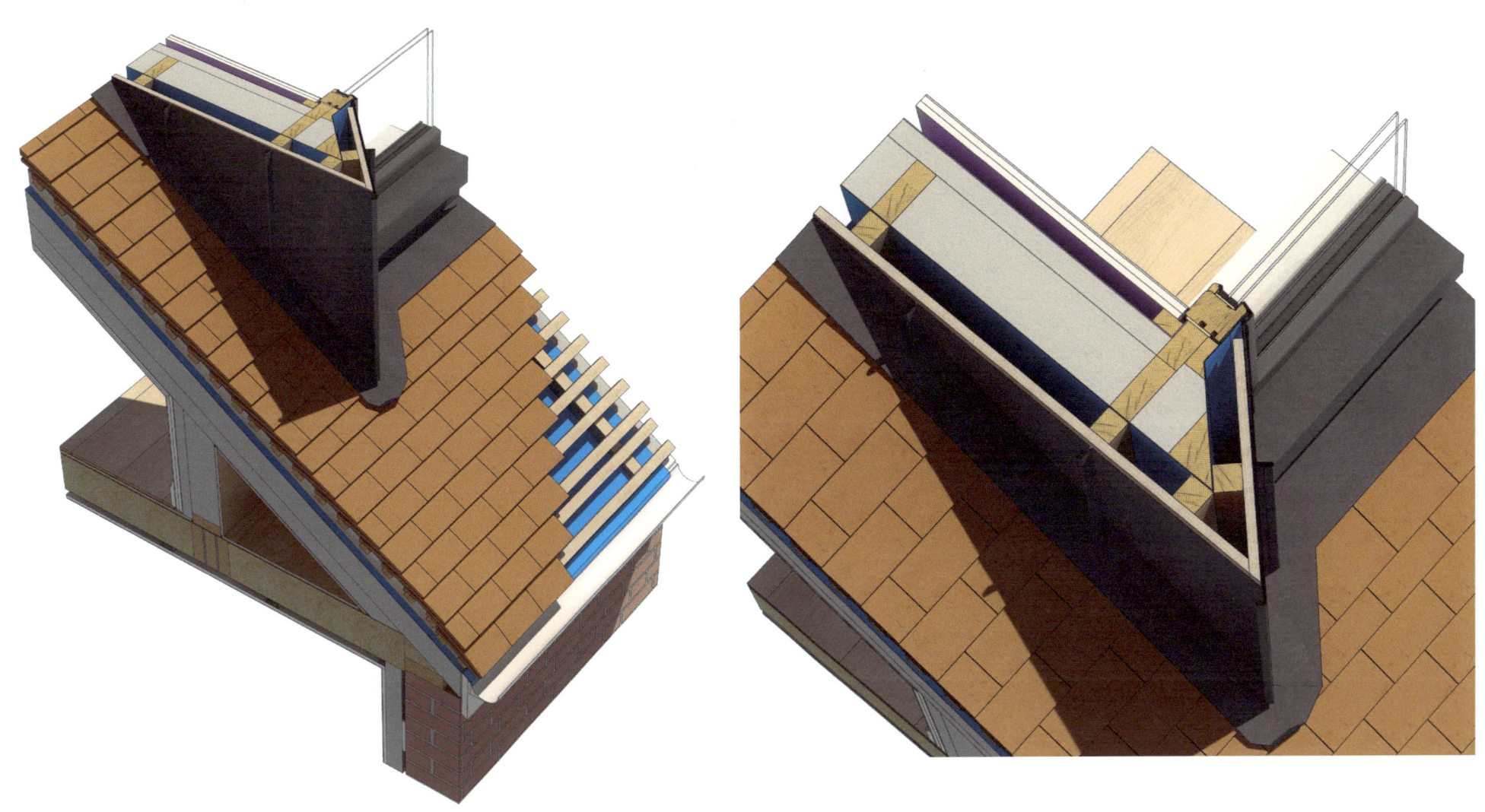

3D Detail LC-31 - Standing seam angled zinc dormer detail - fixed window jamb

LC-32

STANDING SEAM ANGLED ZINC DORMER DETAIL - OPENING WINDOW JAMB

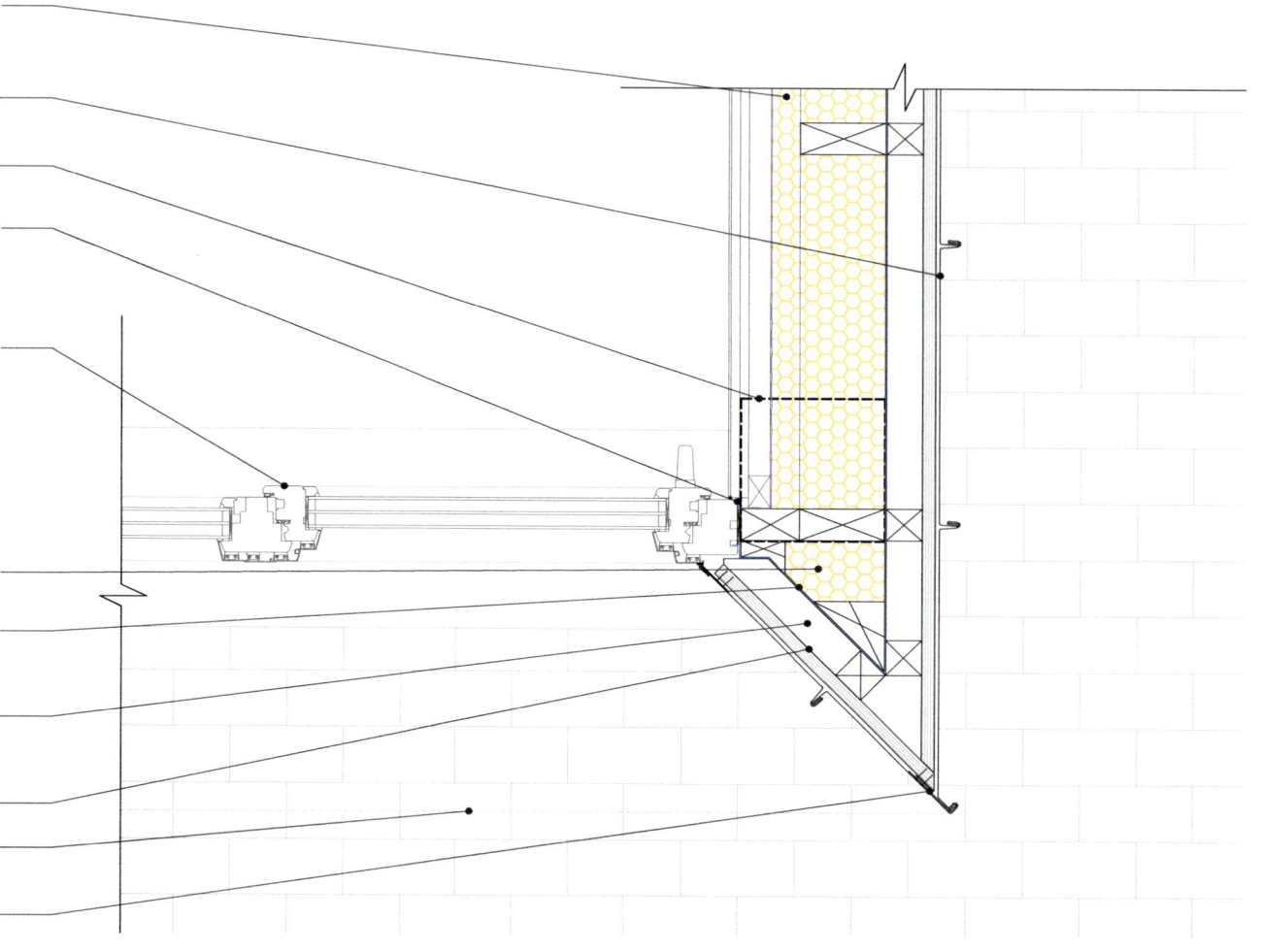

- consult insulation supplier as to VCL requirements: insulated plasterboard to be taped and jointed like a VCL layer or VCL to be added between insulation and 2 x 12.5mm plasterboard and skim

- vertical standing seam zinc finish with panels spaced at 400mm centres approx.

- possible area for reinforced structure to be agreed with the structural engineer

- caulking / mastic seal to window reveal & skim junction with window packer to allow thermal movement in accordance with BS 8213-4, high quality caulk sealant to both sides in accordance with window manufacturer

- fixed to opening aluminium clad timber windows work well with the zinc roof finish however suitable alternatives include timber and aluminium, window to open inwards allowing for internal cleaning of glazing to reduce risk of falling under CDM regulations U-value not to exceed 1.4 W/m²K, G-value not to exceed 0.63 if no cross ventilation is possible

- insulated stud wall with insulated plasterboard down to floor level, new element in existing dwelling (wall) - not to exceed u-value 0.18 W/m²K

- breather membrane with 0.6MNs/g min. vapour resistance approved by zinc supplier and to BS EN 13859-1 / 2: 2010

- 50mm cavity to allow unobstructed ventilation from base of zinc to top roof vents, consult zinc supplier / installer for cavity reduction

- 18mm external or marine grade plywood

- grey line shows zinc window reveal detail above

- non-typical angled zinc corner detail, for alternative corner details contact zinc supplier / installer

2D Detail LC-32 - Standing seam angled zinc dormer detail - opening window jamb

Drawing note: this is an non-typical angled zinc standing seam window jamb detail, all details should be approved by the zinc manufacturer / installer, structural engineer and building control officer. it is recommended that windows and doors at height should open inwards to allow for cleaning without the risk of falling, reducing the risks in use and maintenance of the building to comply with CDM regulations. a maintenance strategy, risk register and residual risk register should be updated throughout the design process to comply with CDM regulations. wall thickness and angle may be dependant on the structural solution and u-value requirements.

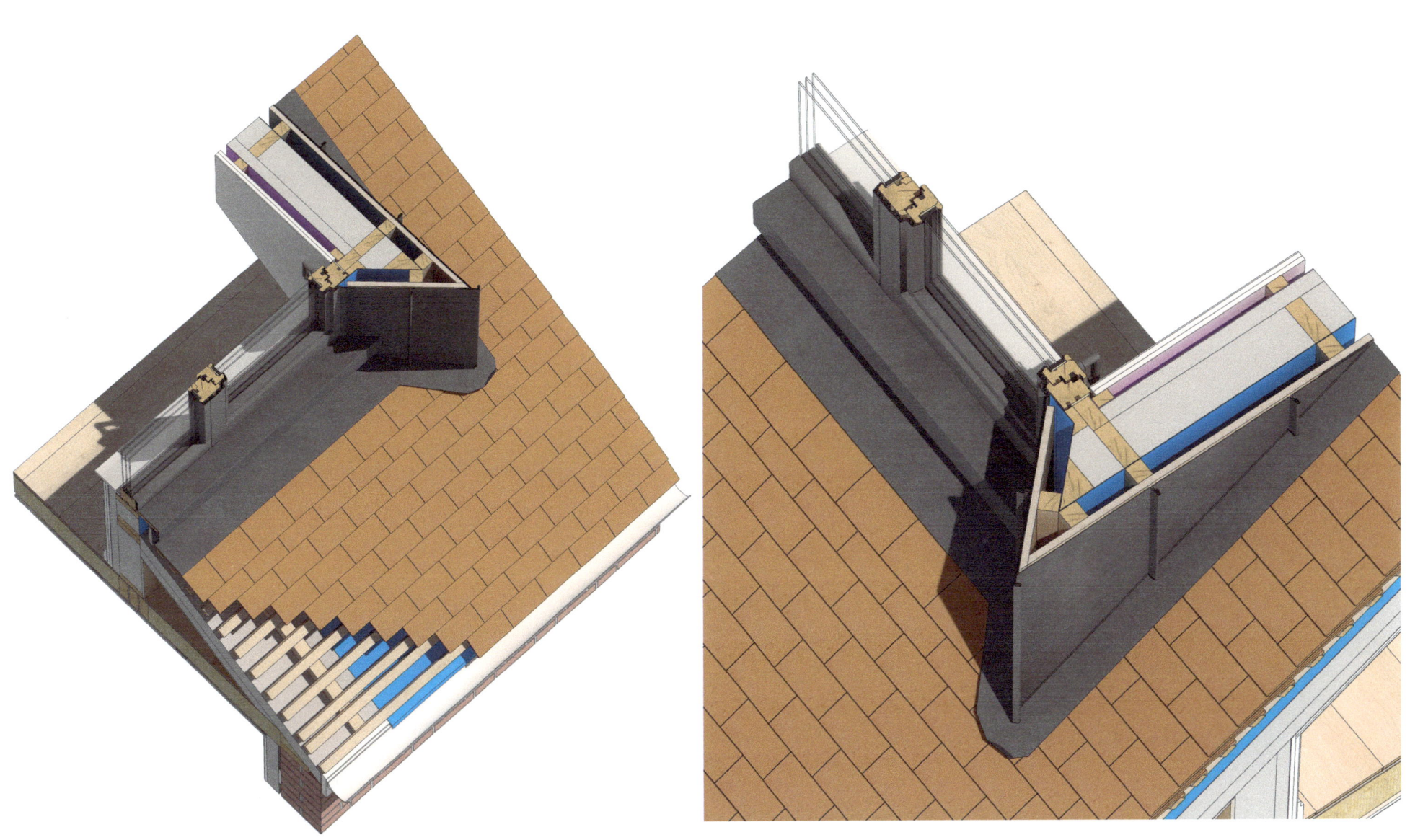

3D Detail LC-32 - Standing seam angled zinc dormer detail - opening window jamb

LC-33

STANDING SEAM ANGLED ZINC DORMER DETAIL - FIXED WINDOW HEAD

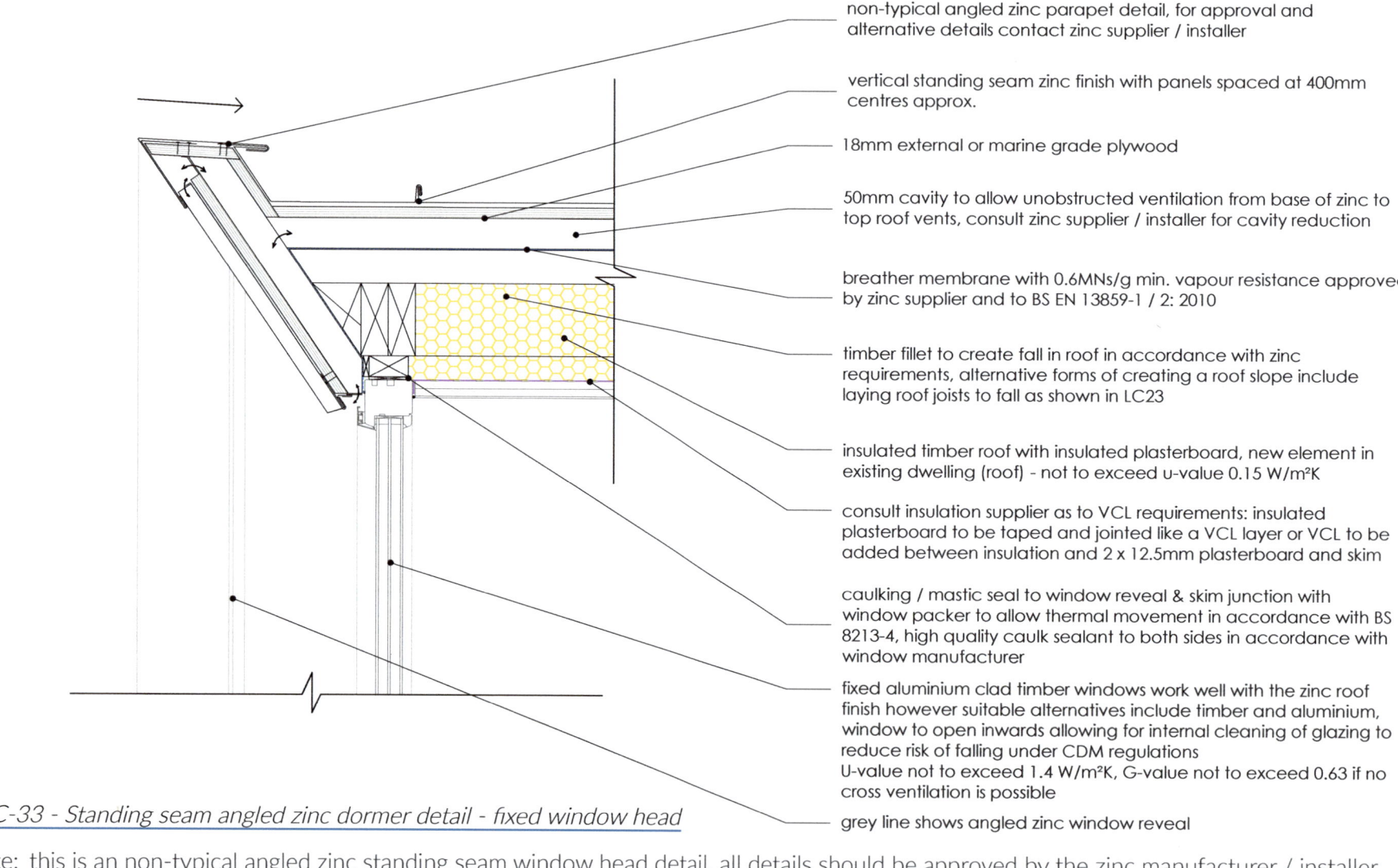

- non-typical angled zinc parapet detail, for approval and alternative details contact zinc supplier / installer
- vertical standing seam zinc finish with panels spaced at 400mm centres approx.
- 18mm external or marine grade plywood
- 50mm cavity to allow unobstructed ventilation from base of zinc to top roof vents, consult zinc supplier / installer for cavity reduction
- breather membrane with 0.6MNs/g min. vapour resistance approved by zinc supplier and to BS EN 13859-1 / 2: 2010
- timber fillet to create fall in roof in accordance with zinc requirements, alternative forms of creating a roof slope include laying roof joists to fall as shown in LC23
- insulated timber roof with insulated plasterboard, new element in existing dwelling (roof) - not to exceed u-value 0.15 W/m²K
- consult insulation supplier as to VCL requirements: insulated plasterboard to be taped and jointed like a VCL layer or VCL to be added between insulation and 2 x 12.5mm plasterboard and skim
- caulking / mastic seal to window reveal & skim junction with window packer to allow thermal movement in accordance with BS 8213-4, high quality caulk sealant to both sides in accordance with window manufacturer
- fixed aluminium clad timber windows work well with the zinc roof finish however suitable alternatives include timber and aluminium, window to open inwards allowing for internal cleaning of glazing to reduce risk of falling under CDM regulations
U-value not to exceed 1.4 W/m²K, G-value not to exceed 0.63 if no cross ventilation is possible
- grey line shows angled zinc window reveal

2D Detail LC-33 - Standing seam angled zinc dormer detail - fixed window head

Drawing note: this is an non-typical angled zinc standing seam window head detail, all details should be approved by the zinc manufacturer / installer, structural engineer and building control officer. it is recommended that windows and doors at height should open inwards to allow for cleaning without the risk of falling, reducing the risks in use and maintenance of the building to comply with CDM regulations. a maintenance strategy, risk register and residual risk register should be updated throughout the design process to comply with CDM regulations.
wall thickness and angle may be dependant on the structural solution and u-value requirements.

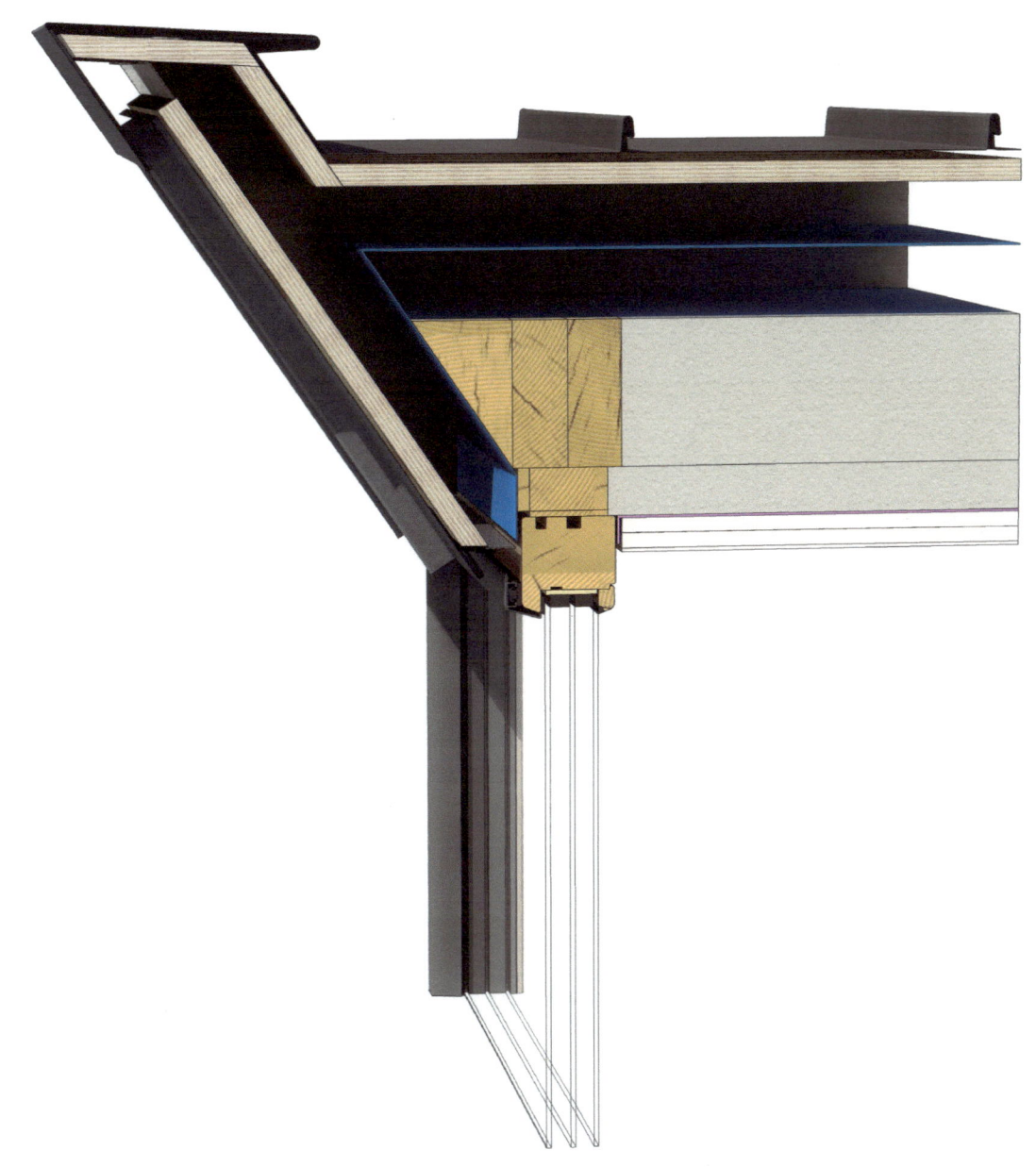

3D Detail LC-33 - Standing seam angled zinc dormer detail - fixed window head

LC-34
STANDING SEAM ANGLED ZINC WINDOW DETAIL - TO EXISTING ROOF

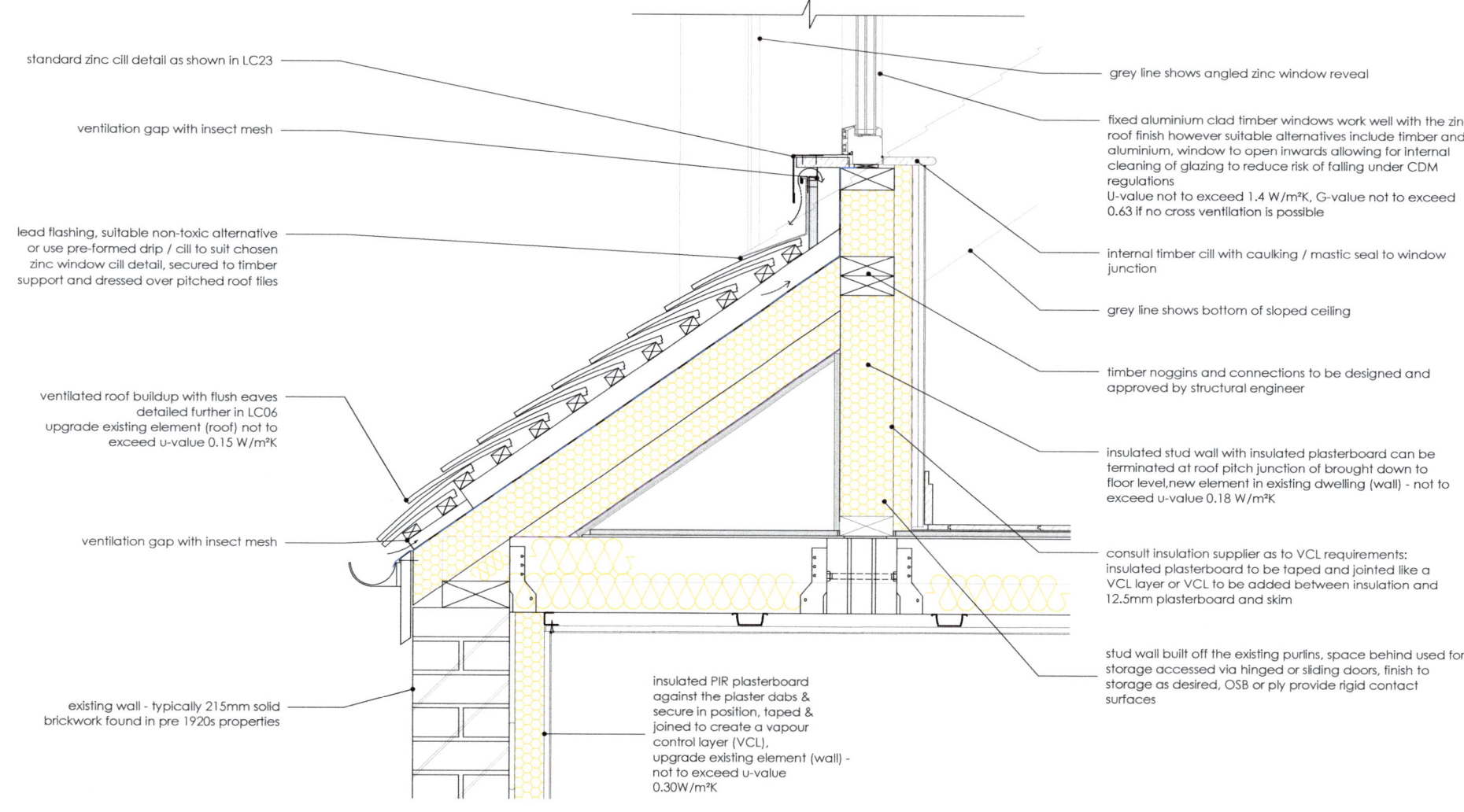

2D Detail LC-34 - Standing seam angled zinc window detail - to existing roof

Drawing note: this is an non-typical angled zinc standing seam window base detail, all details should be approved by the zinc manufacturer / installer, structural engineer and building control officer.
any new timber or steel beams will need to be carefully designed & detailed by a structural engineer to take account of imposed & super-imposed (live & dead) loads from snow / wind, roof & floor.

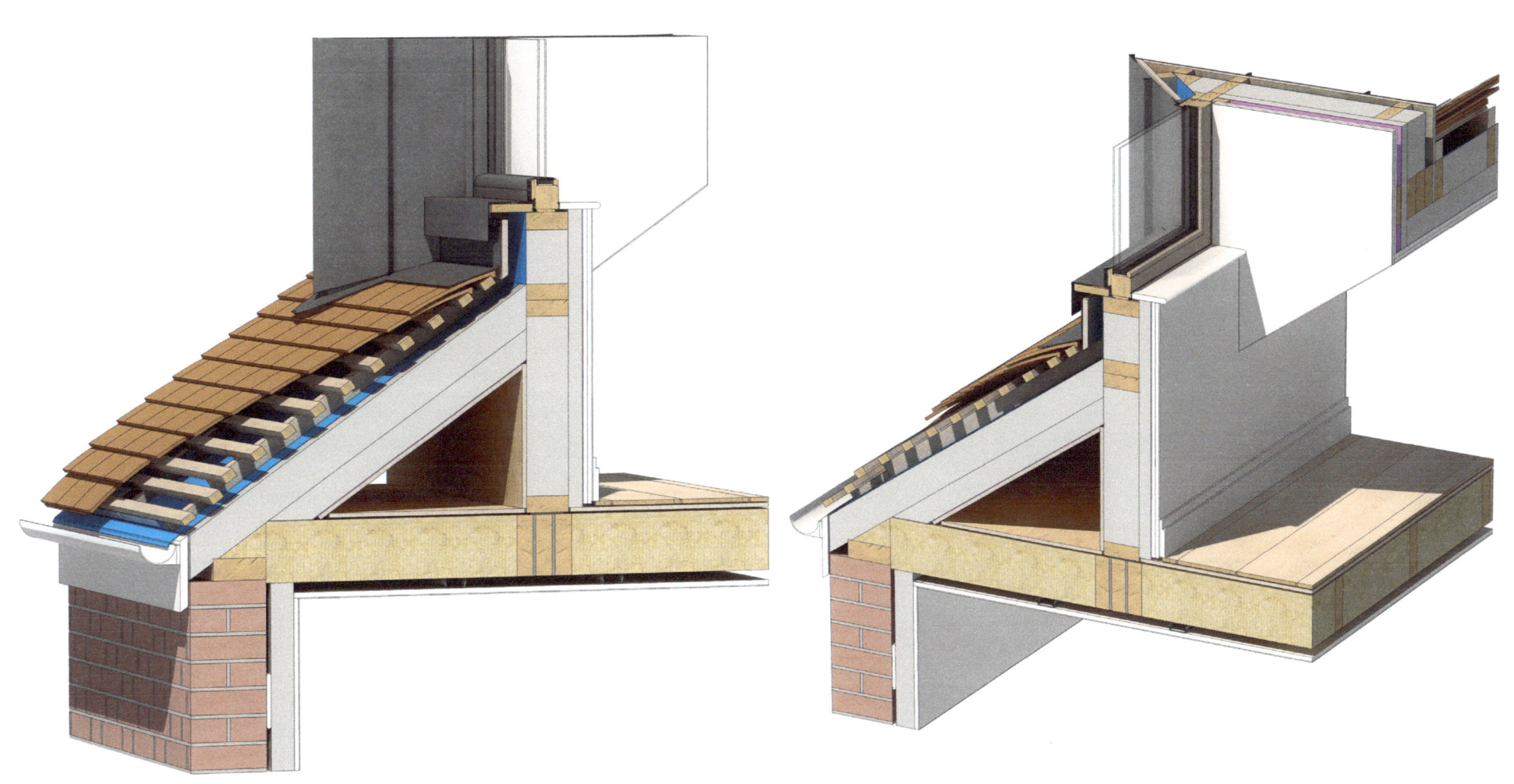

3D Detail LC-34 - Standing seam angled zinc window detail - to existing roof

LC-35
STANDING SEAM ZINC DORMER DETAIL - RIDGE VENT

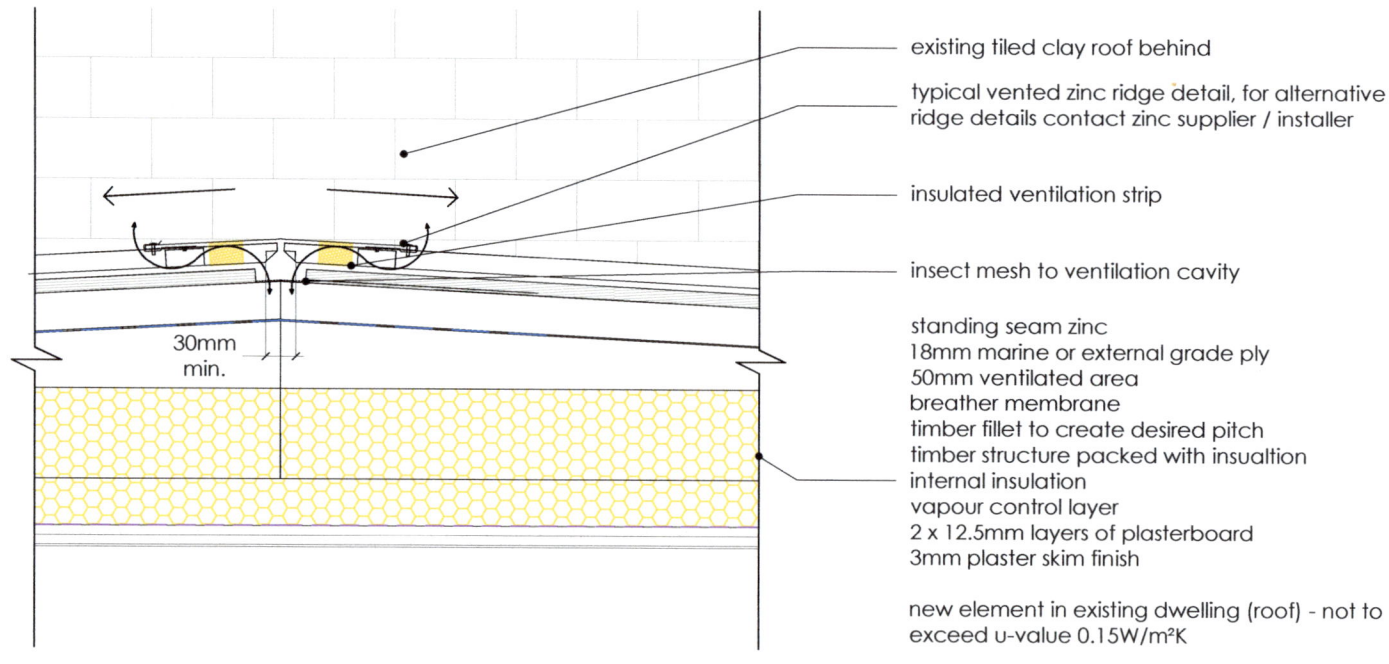

2D Detail LC-35 - Standing seam zinc dormer detail - ridge vent

Drawing note: this is a typical zinc standing seam ridge vent detail, alternative zinc setting out includes horizontal standing seam, interlocking panels, overlapping panels, flat lock panels, composite panels, wave profiles and zinc tiles.
wall thickness and angle may be dependant on the structural solution and u-value requirements.

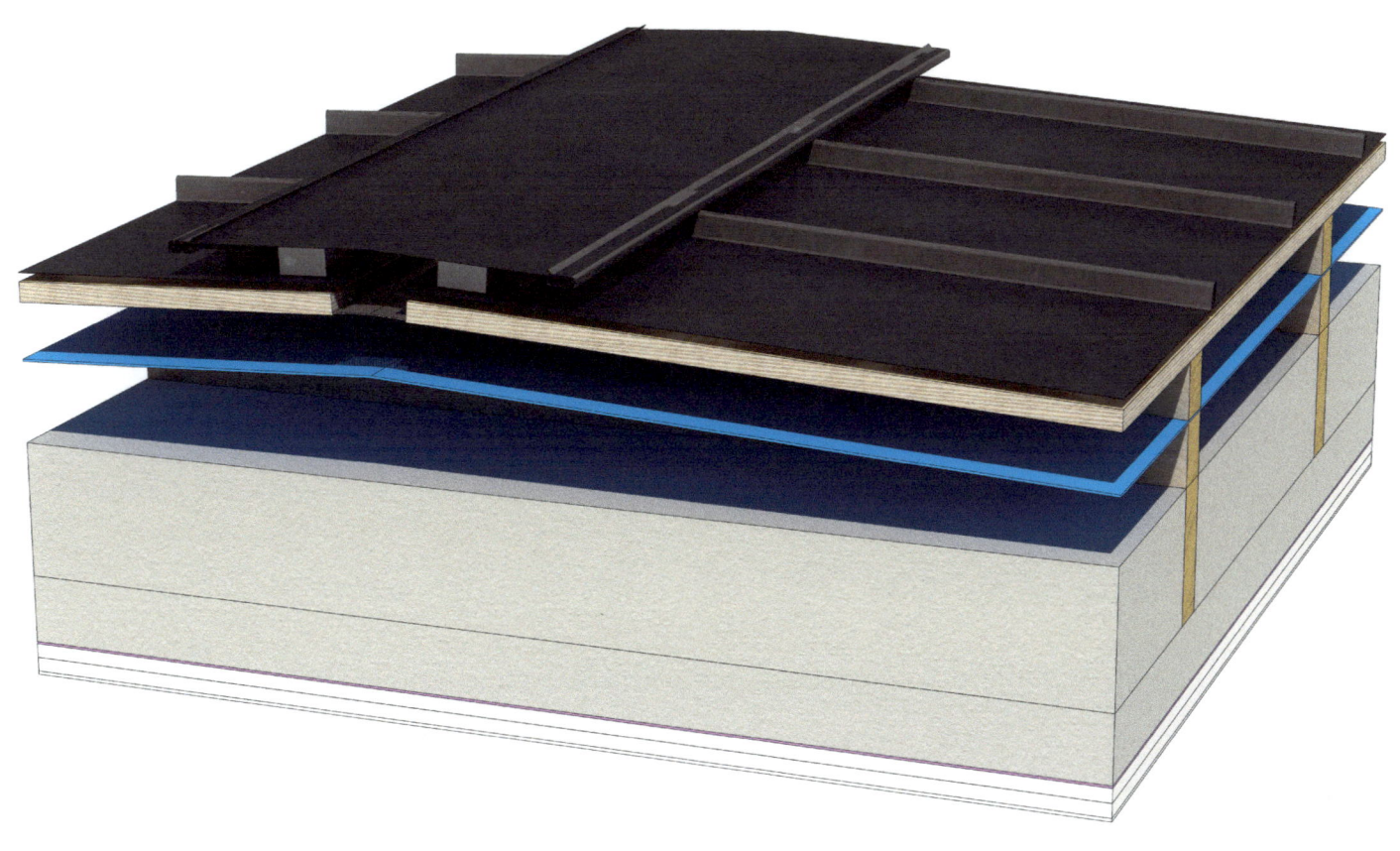

3D Detail LC-35 - Standing seam zinc dormer detail - ridge vent

LC-36

STANDING SEAM ZINC DORMER DETAIL - EAVES AND CONNECTION TO EXISTING ROOF

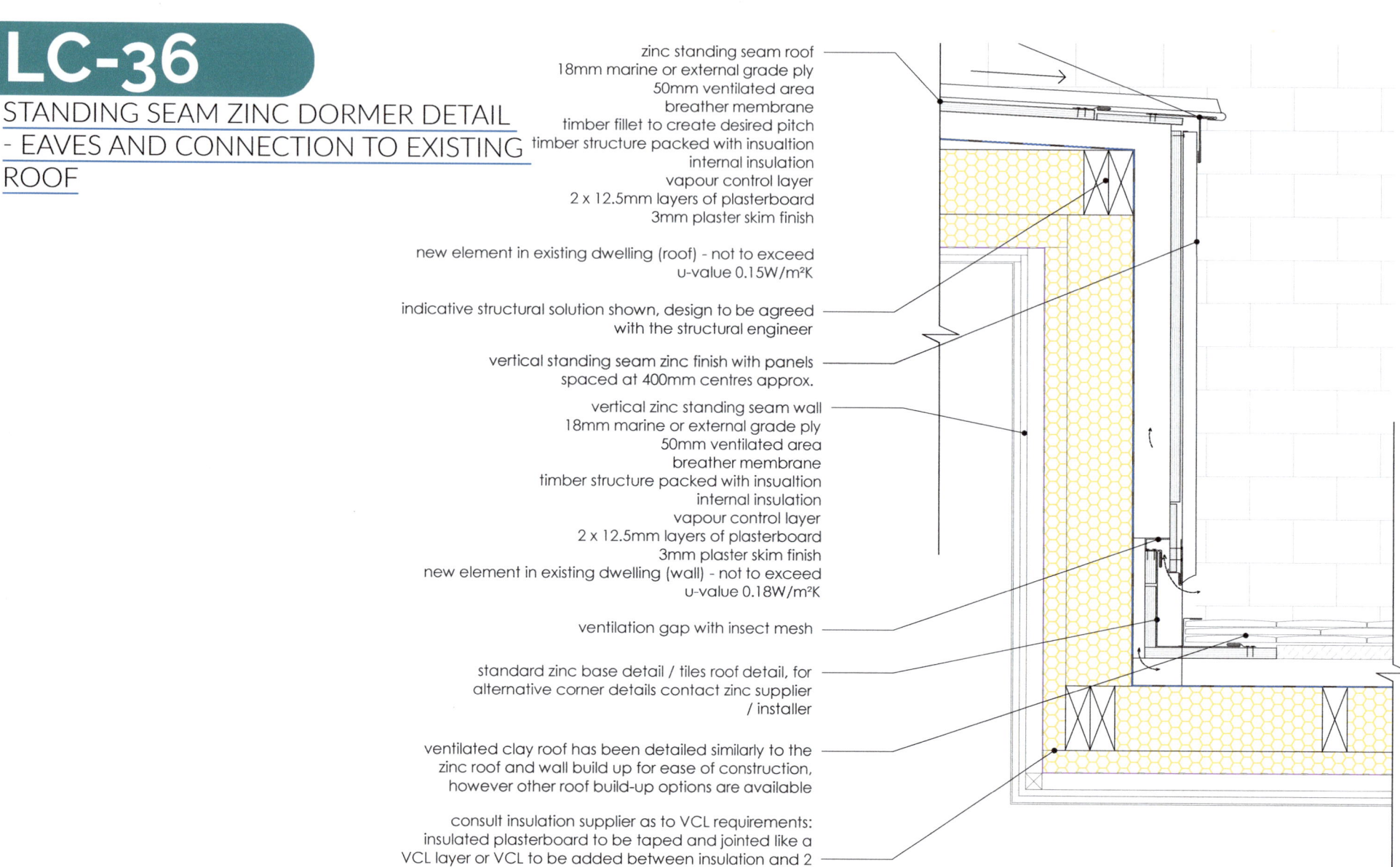

zinc standing seam roof
18mm marine or external grade ply
50mm ventilated area
breather membrane
timber fillet to create desired pitch
timber structure packed with insualtion
internal insulation
vapour control layer
2 x 12.5mm layers of plasterboard
3mm plaster skim finish

new element in existing dwelling (roof) - not to exceed u-value 0.15W/m²K

indicative structural solution shown, design to be agreed with the structural engineer

vertical standing seam zinc finish with panels spaced at 400mm centres approx.

vertical zinc standing seam wall
18mm marine or external grade ply
50mm ventilated area
breather membrane
timber structure packed with insualtion
internal insulation
vapour control layer
2 x 12.5mm layers of plasterboard
3mm plaster skim finish
new element in existing dwelling (wall) - not to exceed u-value 0.18W/m²K

ventilation gap with insect mesh

standard zinc base detail / tiles roof detail, for alternative corner details contact zinc supplier / installer

ventilated clay roof has been detailed similarly to the zinc roof and wall build up for ease of construction, however other roof build-up options are available

consult insulation supplier as to VCL requirements: insulated plasterboard to be taped and jointed like a VCL layer or VCL to be added between insulation and 2 x 12.5mm plasterboard and skim

2D Detail LC-36 - Standing seam zinc dormer detail - eaves and connection to existing roof

Drawing note: this is a standard ventilated zinc roof eaves corner and existing clay roof abutment detail that is typically seen at the side of the dormer wall when the dormer does not reach the party walls.
any new timber or steel beams will need to be carefully designed & detailed by a structural engineer to take account of imposed & super-imposed (live & dead) loads from snow / wind, roof & floor

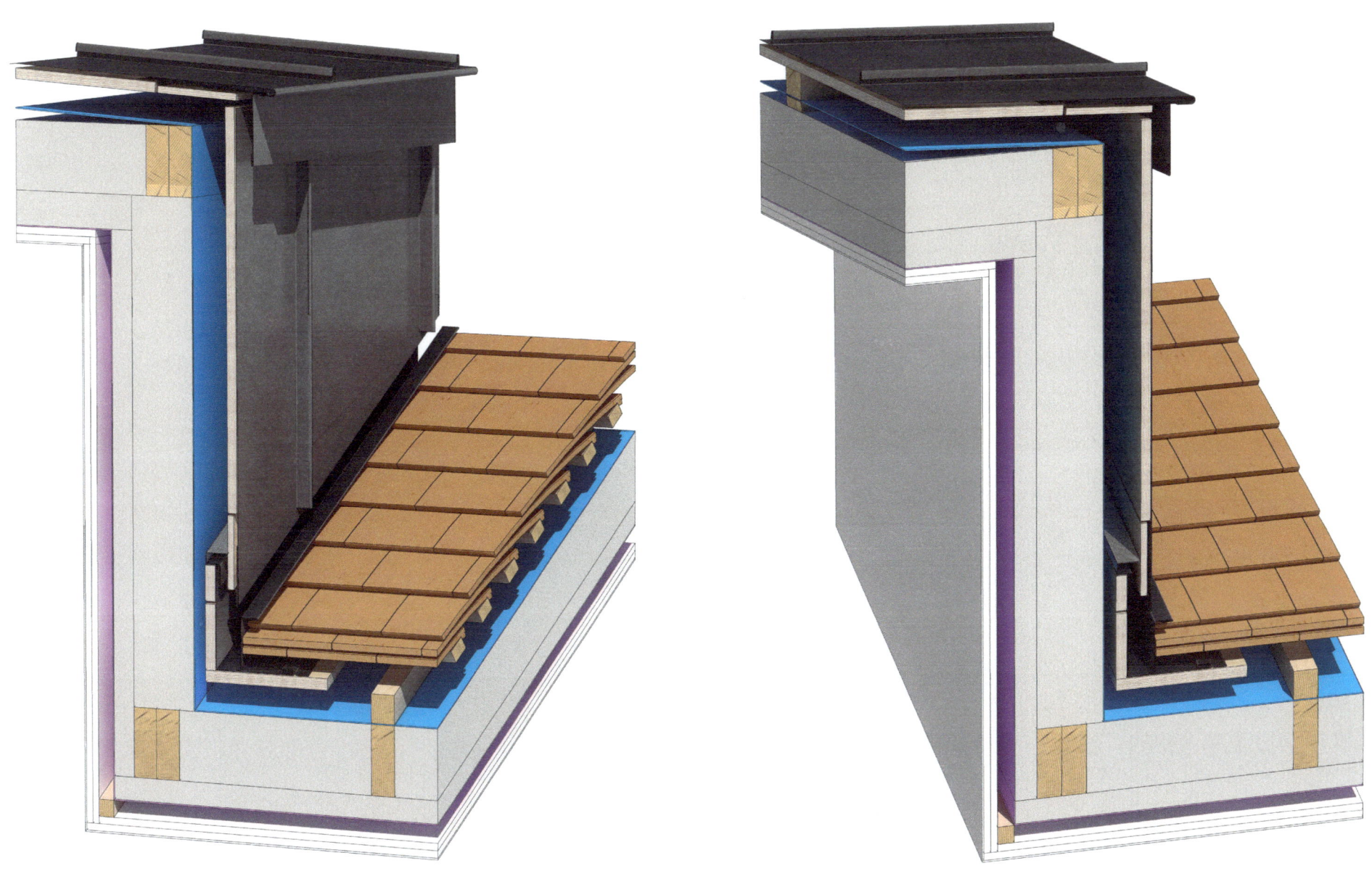

3D Detail LC-36 - Standing seam zinc dormer detail - eaves and connection to existing roof

LC-37
STANDING SEAM ZINC DORMER CHEEK TO WINDOW PLAN DETAIL - FIXED WINDOW

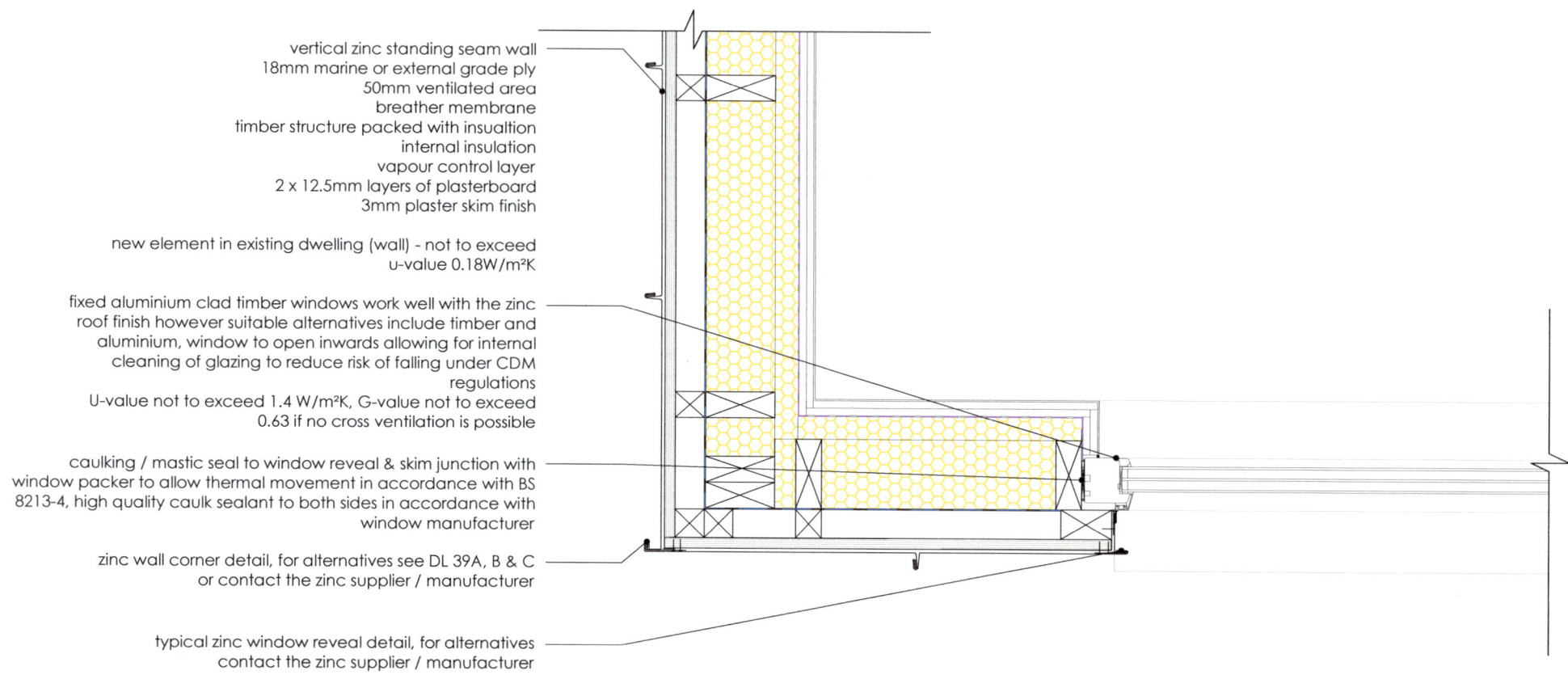

2D Detail LC-37 - Standing seam zinc dormer cheek to window plan detail - fixed window

Drawing note: this is a standard ventilated zinc wall corner plan and fixed window detail, alternative zinc setting out includes horizontal standing seam, interlocking panels, overlapping panels, flat lock panels, composite panels, wave profiles and zinc tiles.
any new timber or steel columns will need to be carefully designed & detailed by a structural engineer to take account of imposed & super-imposed (live & dead) loads from snow / wind, roof & floor

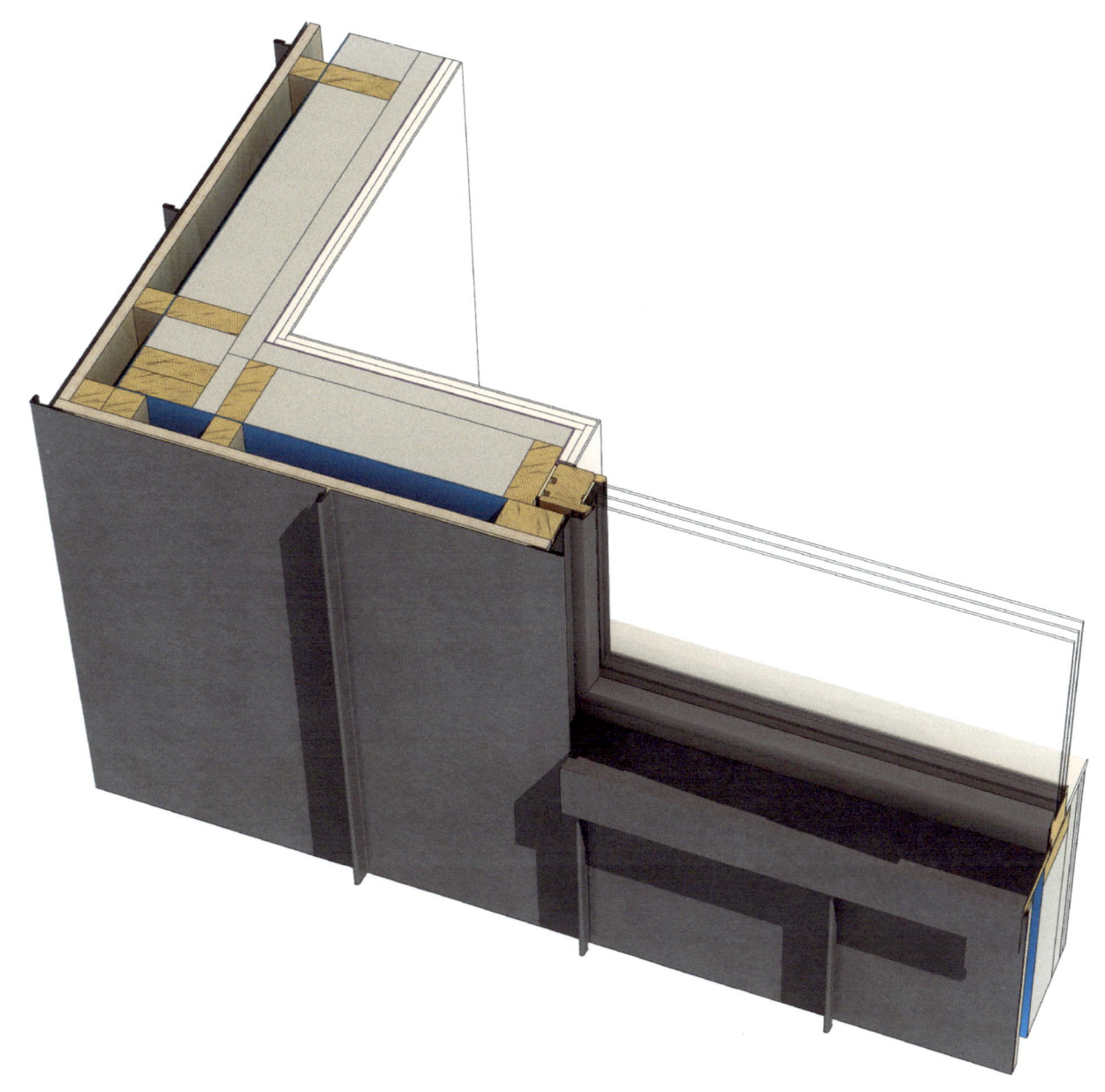

3D Detail LC-37 - Standing seam zinc dormer cheek to window plan detail - fixed window

LC-38
STANDING SEAM ZINC DORMER CHEEK TO FLUSH WINDOW PLAN DETAIL - FIXED WINDOW

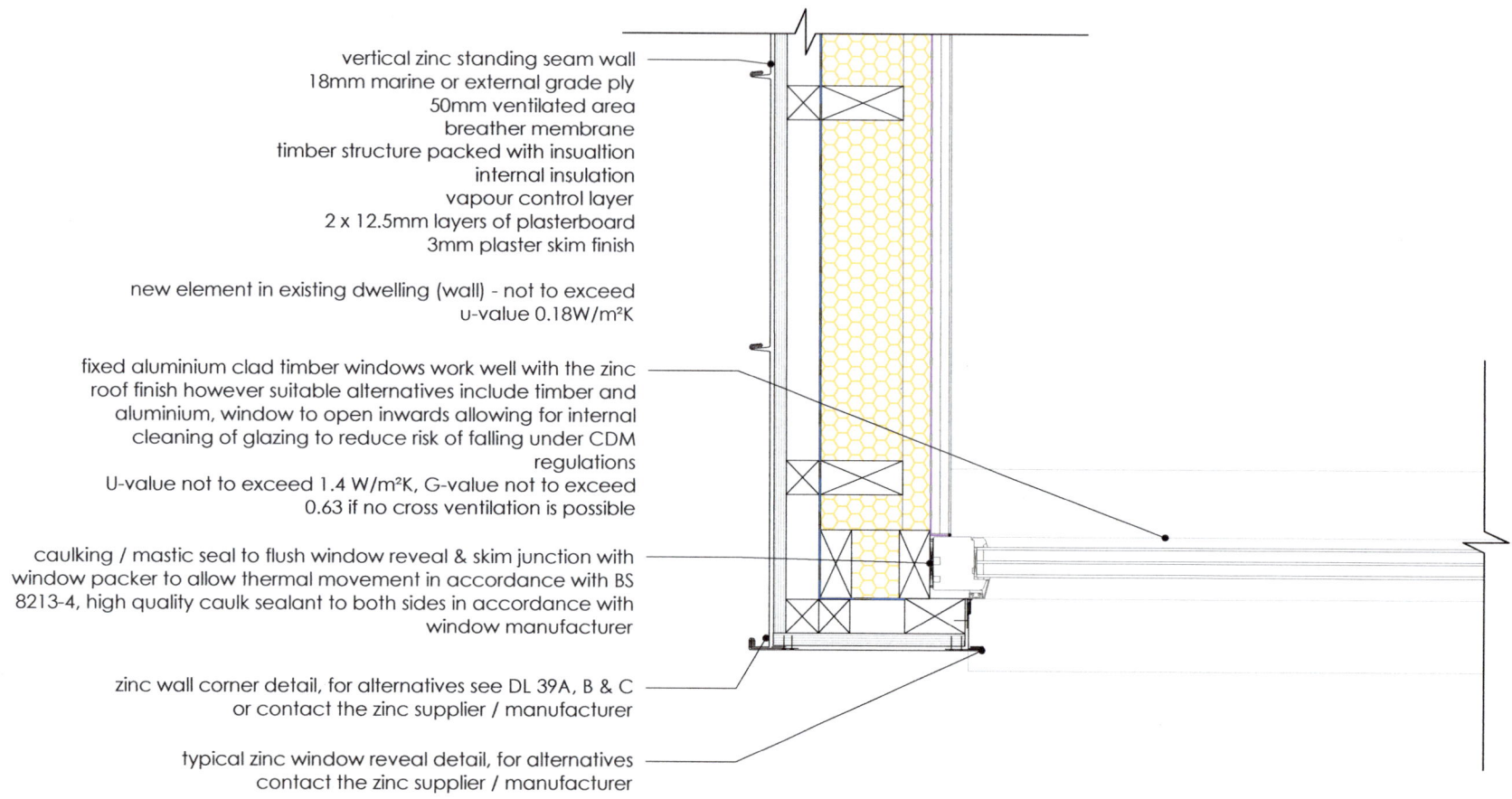

vertical zinc standing seam wall
18mm marine or external grade ply
50mm ventilated area
breather membrane
timber structure packed with insualtion
internal insulation
vapour control layer
2 x 12.5mm layers of plasterboard
3mm plaster skim finish

new element in existing dwelling (wall) - not to exceed u-value 0.18W/m²K

fixed aluminium clad timber windows work well with the zinc roof finish however suitable alternatives include timber and aluminium, window to open inwards allowing for internal cleaning of glazing to reduce risk of falling under CDM regulations
U-value not to exceed 1.4 W/m²K, G-value not to exceed 0.63 if no cross ventilation is possible

caulking / mastic seal to flush window reveal & skim junction with window packer to allow thermal movement in accordance with BS 8213-4, high quality caulk sealant to both sides in accordance with window manufacturer

zinc wall corner detail, for alternatives see DL 39A, B & C or contact the zinc supplier / manufacturer

typical zinc window reveal detail, for alternatives contact the zinc supplier / manufacturer

2D Detail LC-38 - Standing seam zinc dormer cheek to flush window plan detail - fixed window

Drawing note: this is a standard ventilated zinc wall corner plan and flush fixed window detail, alternative zinc setting out includes horizontal standing seam, interlocking panels, overlapping panels, flat lock panels, composite panels, wave profiles and zinc tiles.
any new timber or steel columns will need to be carefully designed & detailed by a structural engineer to take account of imposed & super-imposed (live & dead) loads from snow / wind, roof & floor

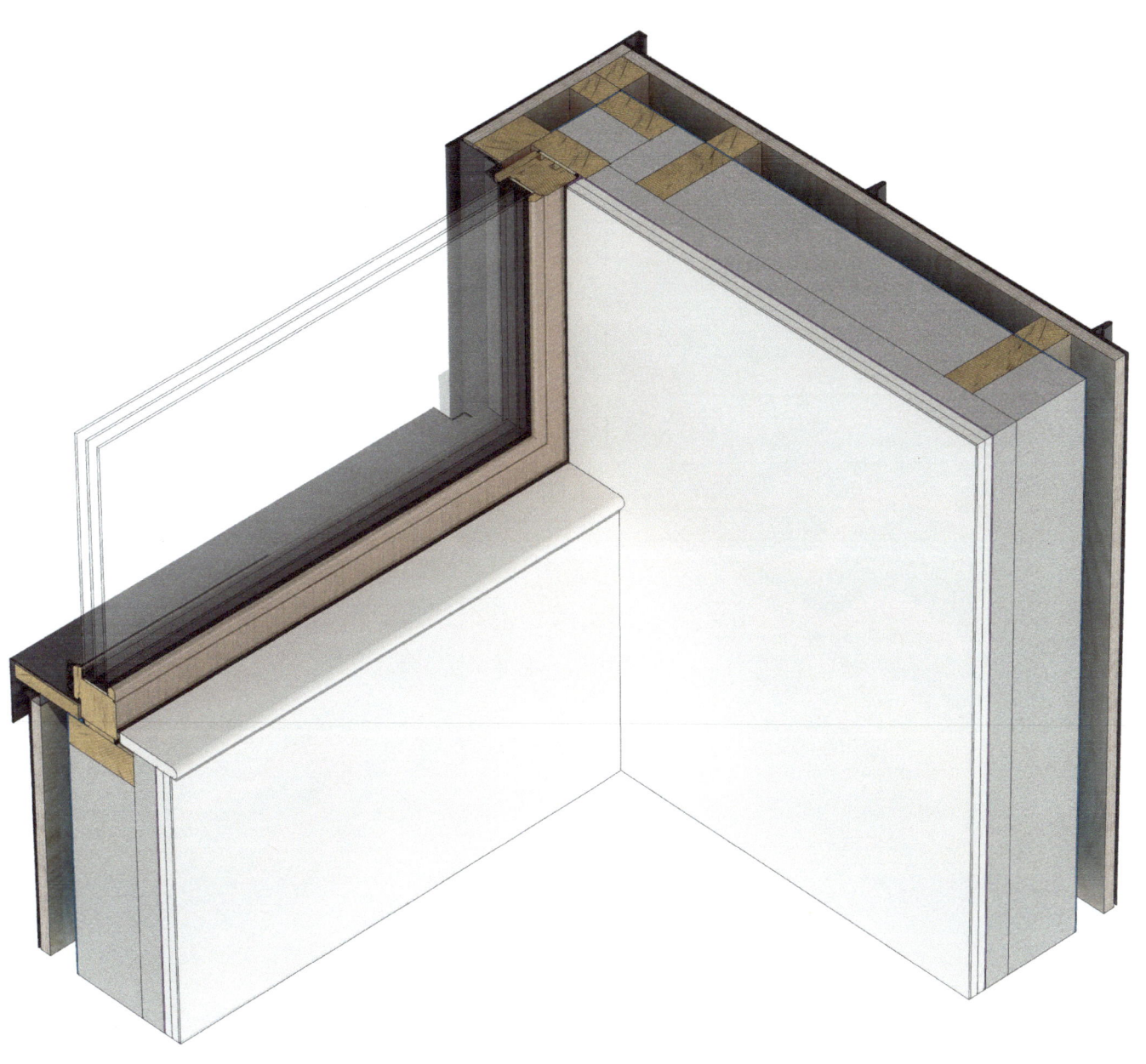

3D Detail LC-38 - Standing seam zinc dormer cheek to flush window plan detail - fixed window

LC-39A
STANDING SEAM VERTICAL ZINC DORMER CORNER DETAIL A

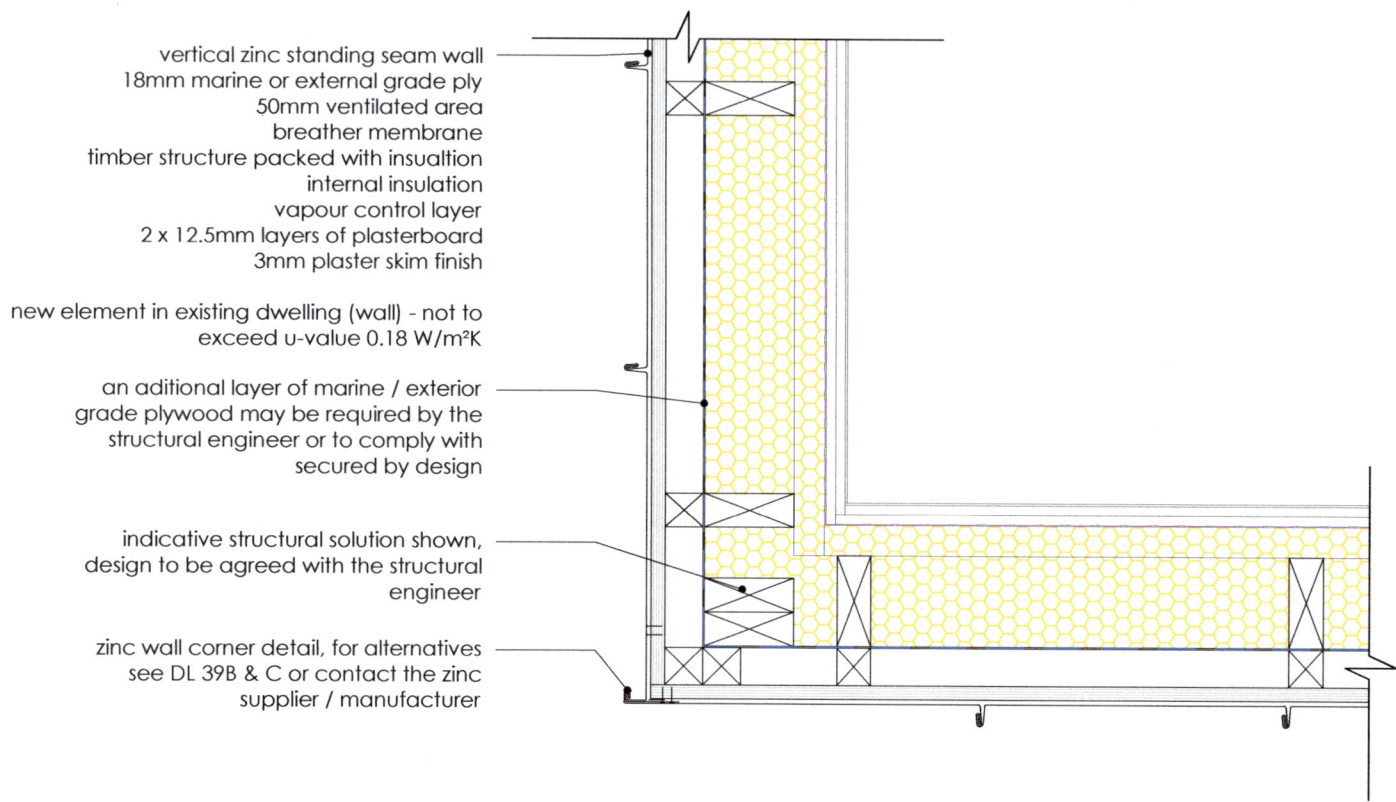

- vertical zinc standing seam wall
- 18mm marine or external grade ply
- 50mm ventilated area
- breather membrane
- timber structure packed with insualtion
- internal insulation
- vapour control layer
- 2 x 12.5mm layers of plasterboard
- 3mm plaster skim finish

new element in existing dwelling (wall) - not to exceed u-value 0.18 W/m²K

an aditional layer of marine / exterior grade plywood may be required by the structural engineer or to comply with secured by design

indicative structural solution shown, design to be agreed with the structural engineer

zinc wall corner detail, for alternatives see DL 39B & C or contact the zinc supplier / manufacturer

2D Detail LC-39A - Standing seam vertical zinc dormer corner detail A

Drawing note: this is a standard ventilated zinc wall corner plan and flush fixed window detail, alternative zinc setting out includes horizontal standing seam, interlocking panels, overlapping panels, flat lock panels, composite panels, wave profiles and zinc tiles. any new timber or steel columns will need to be carefully designed & detailed by a structural engineer to take account of imposed & super-imposed (live & dead) loads from snow / wind, roof & floor.

3D Detail LC-39A - Standing seam vertical zinc dormer corner detail A

LC-39B

STANDING SEAM VERTICAL ZINC DORMER CORNER DETAIL B

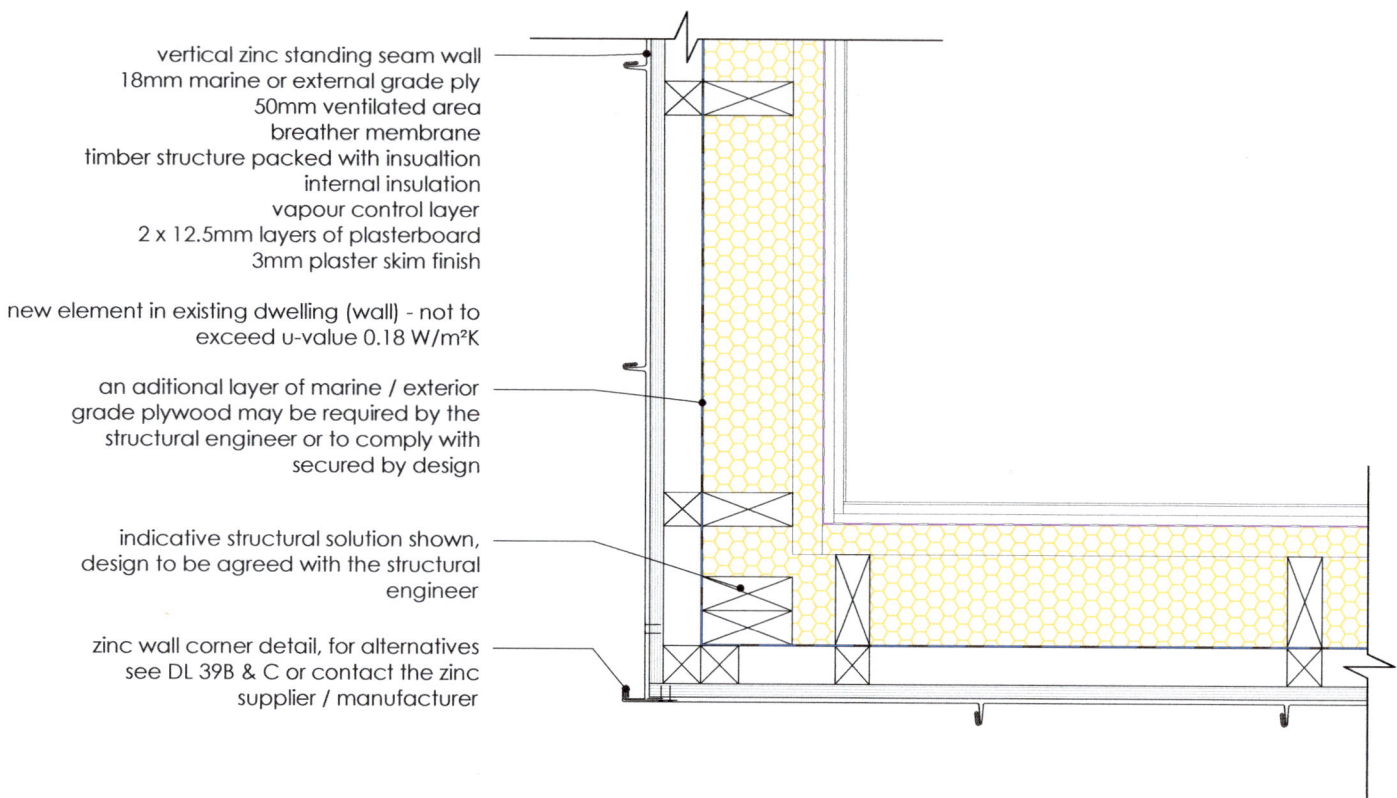

2D Detail LC-39B - Standing seam vertical zinc dormer corner detail B

Drawing note: this is a standard ventilated zinc wall corner plan and flush fixed window detail, alternative zinc setting out includes horizontal standing seam, interlocking panels, overlapping panels, flat lock panels, composite panels, wave profiles and zinc tiles.
any new timber or steel columns will need to be carefully designed & detailed by a structural engineer to take account of imposed & super-imposed (live & dead) loads from snow / wind, roof & floor.

3D Detail LC-39B - Standing seam vertical zinc dormer corner detail B

LC-39C

STANDING SEAM VERTICAL ZINC DORMER CORNER DETAIL C

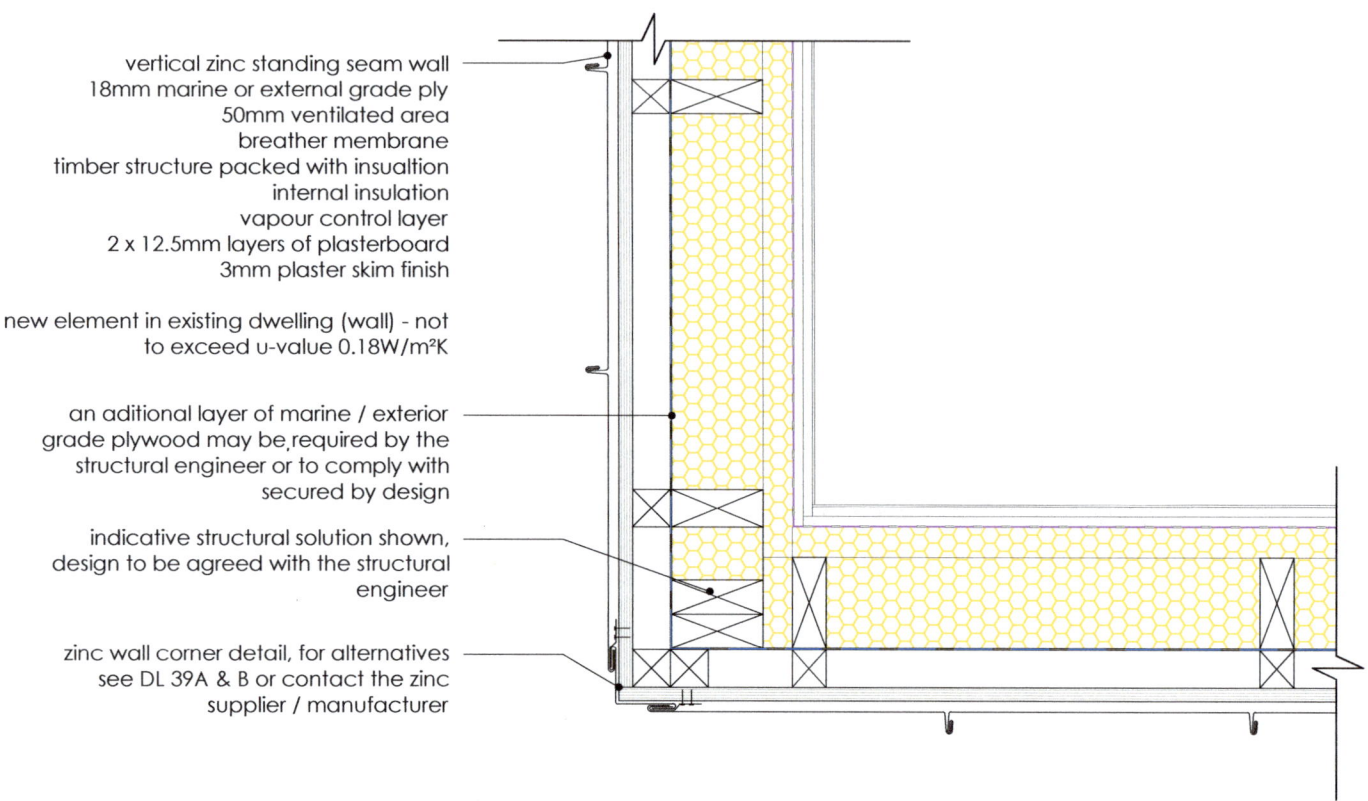

- vertical zinc standing seam wall
- 18mm marine or external grade ply
- 50mm ventilated area
- breather membrane
- timber structure packed with insualtion
- internal insulation
- vapour control layer
- 2 x 12.5mm layers of plasterboard
- 3mm plaster skim finish

new element in existing dwelling (wall) - not to exceed u-value 0.18W/m²K

an aditional layer of marine / exterior grade plywood may be required by the structural engineer or to comply with secured by design

indicative structural solution shown, design to be agreed with the structural engineer

zinc wall corner detail, for alternatives see DL 39A & B or contact the zinc supplier / manufacturer

2D Detail LC-39C - Standing seam vertical zinc dormer corner detail C

Drawing note: this is a standard ventilated zinc wall corner plan and flush fixed window detail, alternative zinc setting out includes horizontal standing seam, interlocking panels, overlapping panels, flat lock panels, composite panels, wave profiles and zinc tiles.
any new timber or steel columns will need to be carefully designed & detailed by a structural engineer to take account of imposed & super-imposed (live & dead) loads from snow / wind, roof & floor.

3D Detail LC-39C - Standing seam vertical zinc dormer corner detail C

Velux Details

This final set of details shows some of the options for rooflights in a loft conversion. The details include a standard rooflight for pitched roof, along with some more contemporary Velux rooflight configurations.

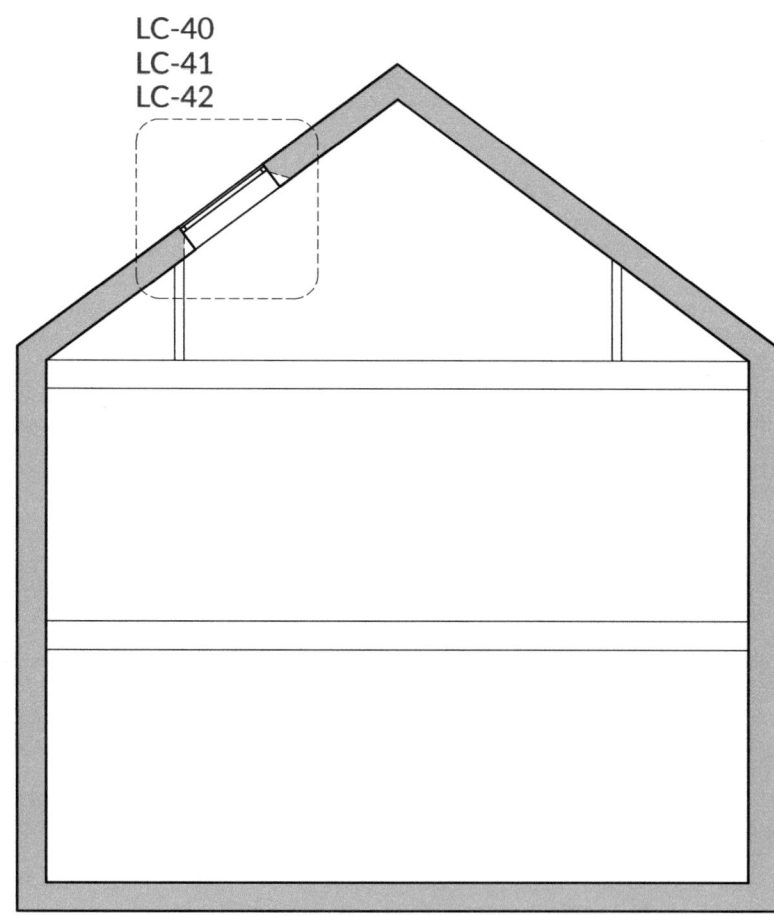

LC-40
LC-41
LC-42

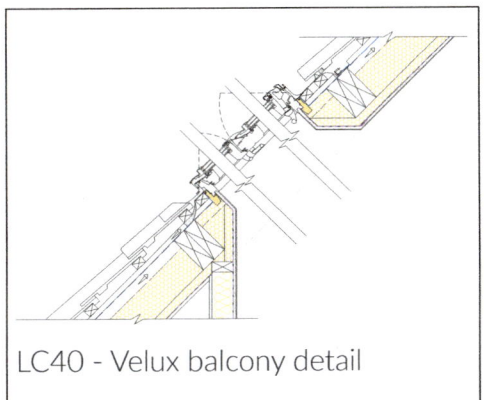
LC40 - Velux balcony detail

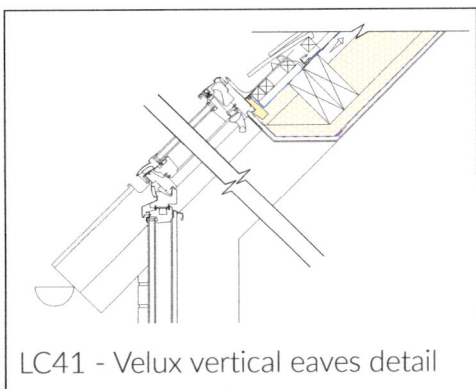
LC41 - Velux vertical eaves detail

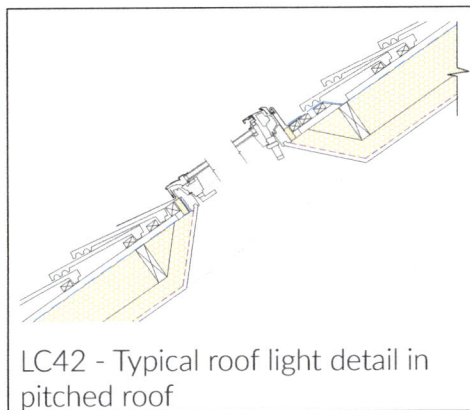
LC42 - Typical roof light detail in pitched roof

LC-40
VELUX BALCONY

"Warm" roof: as cold roof note below but without the need for ventilation space above the insulation - ensure insulation is pressed up tight to underside of rafters - both options shown on this drawing

"Cold" roof: high performance PIR insulation board fitted between rafters to maintain a 50mm min. air gap over insulation for ventilation purposes & underdrawn with a thicker amount of the same board with taped joints to provide a vapour control layer & air leakage barrier. staple independent VCL to underside "warm" side of insulation if not taping joints of vapour check plasterboard.
upgrade existing element (roof) - not to exceed u-value 0.15 W/m²K

existing roof tiling, battens & roofing felt left in-situ - rooflight opening trimmed out with doubled-up rafters both sides & at head / base.
ensure insulation to reveals to eliminate cold bridging

Note: cill level of any window to be used as a means of escape to be 1100mm max. above finished floor level to comply with Part B of the current Building Regulations

rooflight to be installed with standard flashing kit which will alter between different manufacturers

vertical height of stud wall typically 900-1200mm above finished floor level

2D Detail LC-40 - Velux balcony

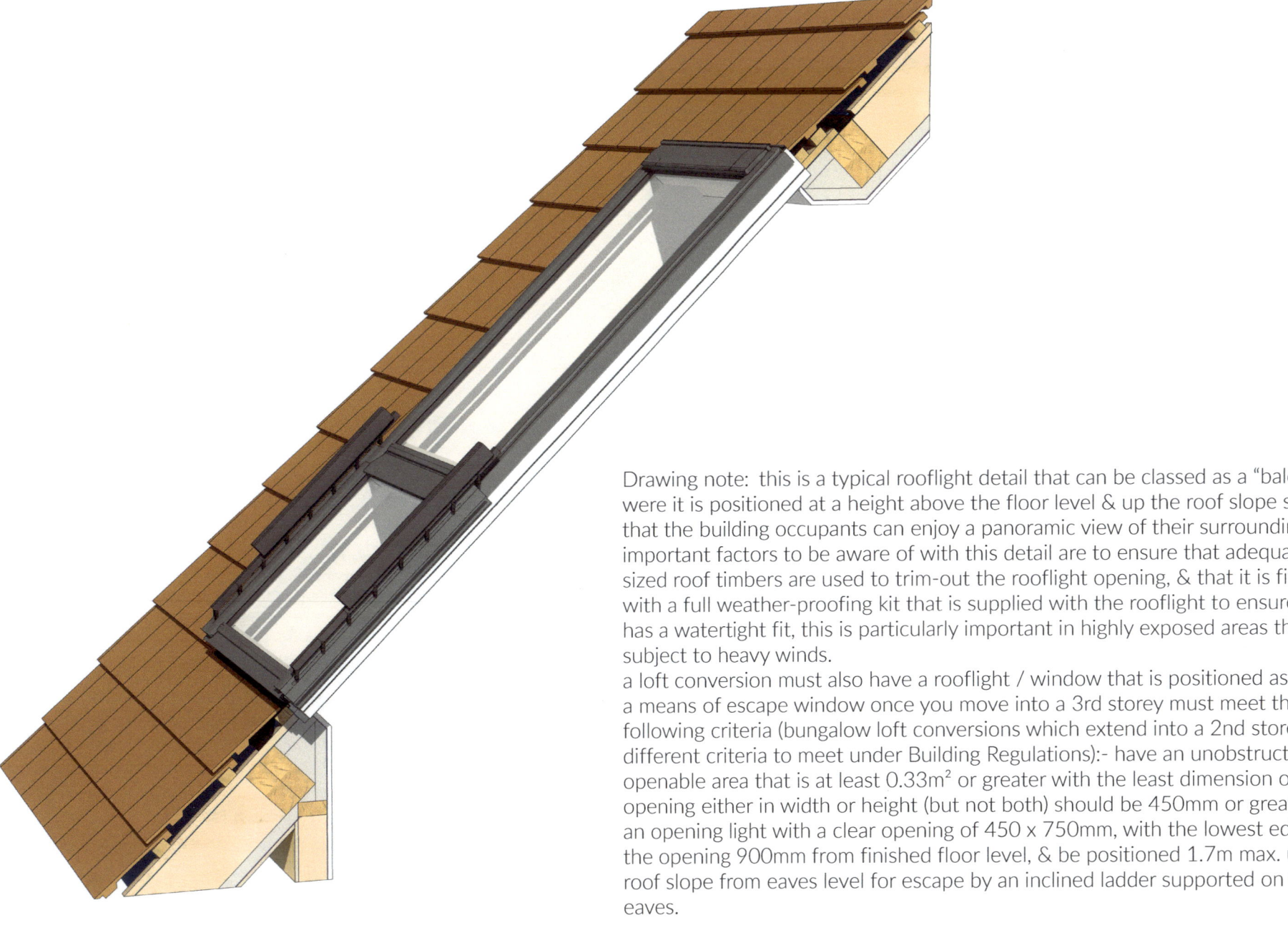

Drawing note: this is a typical rooflight detail that can be classed as a "balcony" were it is positioned at a height above the floor level & up the roof slope so that the building occupants can enjoy a panoramic view of their surroundings - important factors to be aware of with this detail are to ensure that adequately sized roof timbers are used to trim-out the rooflight opening, & that it is fitted with a full weather-proofing kit that is supplied with the rooflight to ensure it has a watertight fit, this is particularly important in highly exposed areas that are subject to heavy winds.
a loft conversion must also have a rooflight / window that is positioned as a means of escape window once you move into a 3rd storey must meet the following criteria (bungalow loft conversions which extend into a 2nd storey have different criteria to meet under Building Regulations):- have an unobstructed openable area that is at least 0.33m² or greater with the least dimension of the opening either in width or height (but not both) should be 450mm or greater, with an opening light with a clear opening of 450 x 750mm, with the lowest edge of the opening 900mm from finished floor level, & be positioned 1.7m max. up the roof slope from eaves level for escape by an inclined ladder supported on the eaves.

3D Detail LC-40 - Velux balcony

LC-41
VELUX VERTICAL EAVES WINDOW

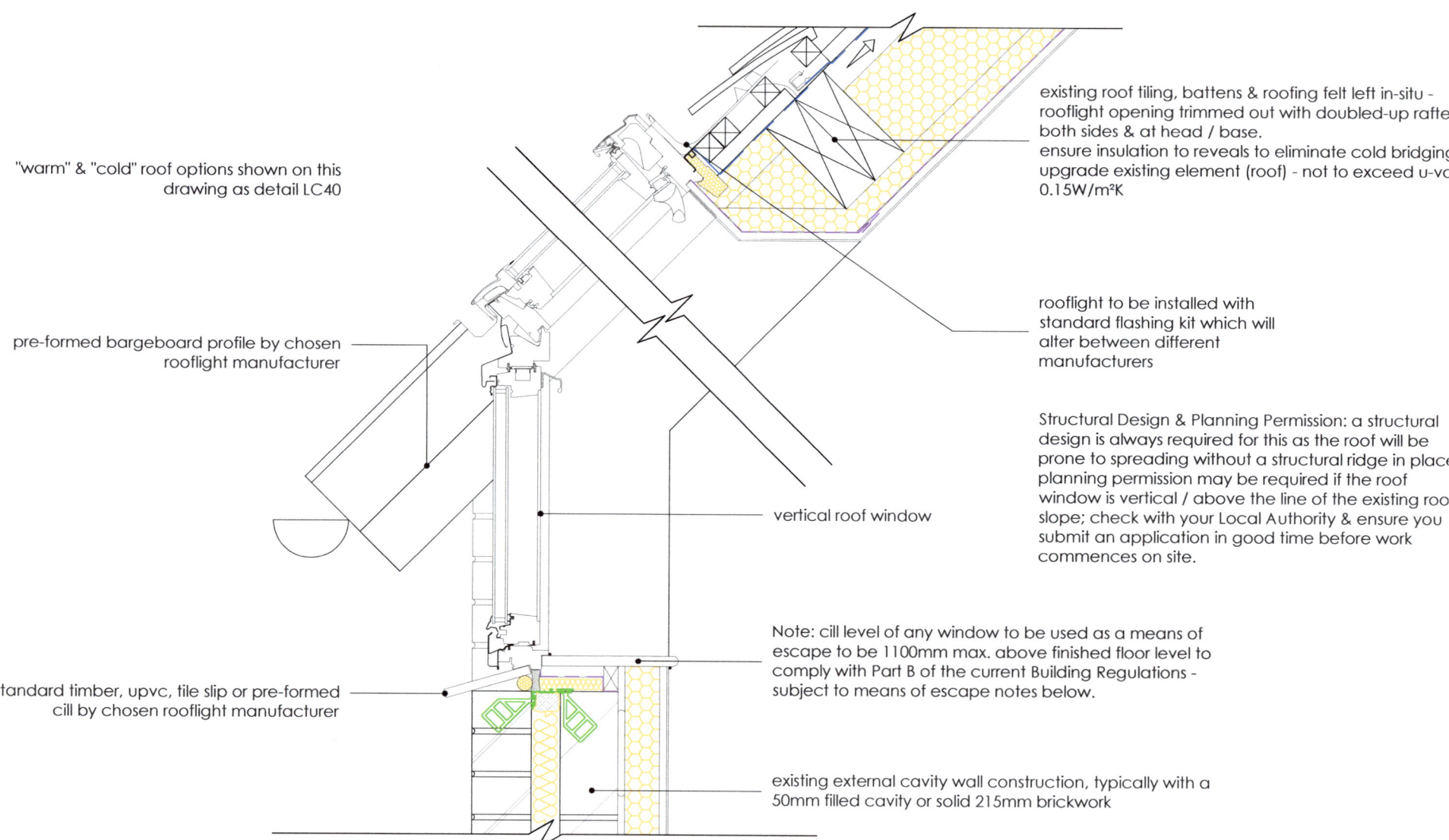

"warm" & "cold" roof options shown on this drawing as detail LC40

pre-formed bargeboard profile by chosen rooflight manufacturer

standard timber, upvc, tile slip or pre-formed cill by chosen rooflight manufacturer

existing roof tiling, battens & roofing felt left in-situ - rooflight opening trimmed out with doubled-up rafte both sides & at head / base.
ensure insulation to reveals to eliminate cold bridging upgrade existing element (roof) - not to exceed u-vc 0.15W/m²K

rooflight to be installed with standard flashing kit which will alter between different manufacturers

Structural Design & Planning Permission: a structural design is always required for this as the roof will be prone to spreading without a structural ridge in place planning permission may be required if the roof window is vertical / above the line of the existing roo slope; check with your Local Authority & ensure you submit an application in good time before work commences on site.

vertical roof window

Note: cill level of any window to be used as a means of escape to be 1100mm max. above finished floor level to comply with Part B of the current Building Regulations - subject to means of escape notes below.

existing external cavity wall construction, typically with a 50mm filled cavity or solid 215mm brickwork

2D Detail LC-41 - Velux vertical eaves window

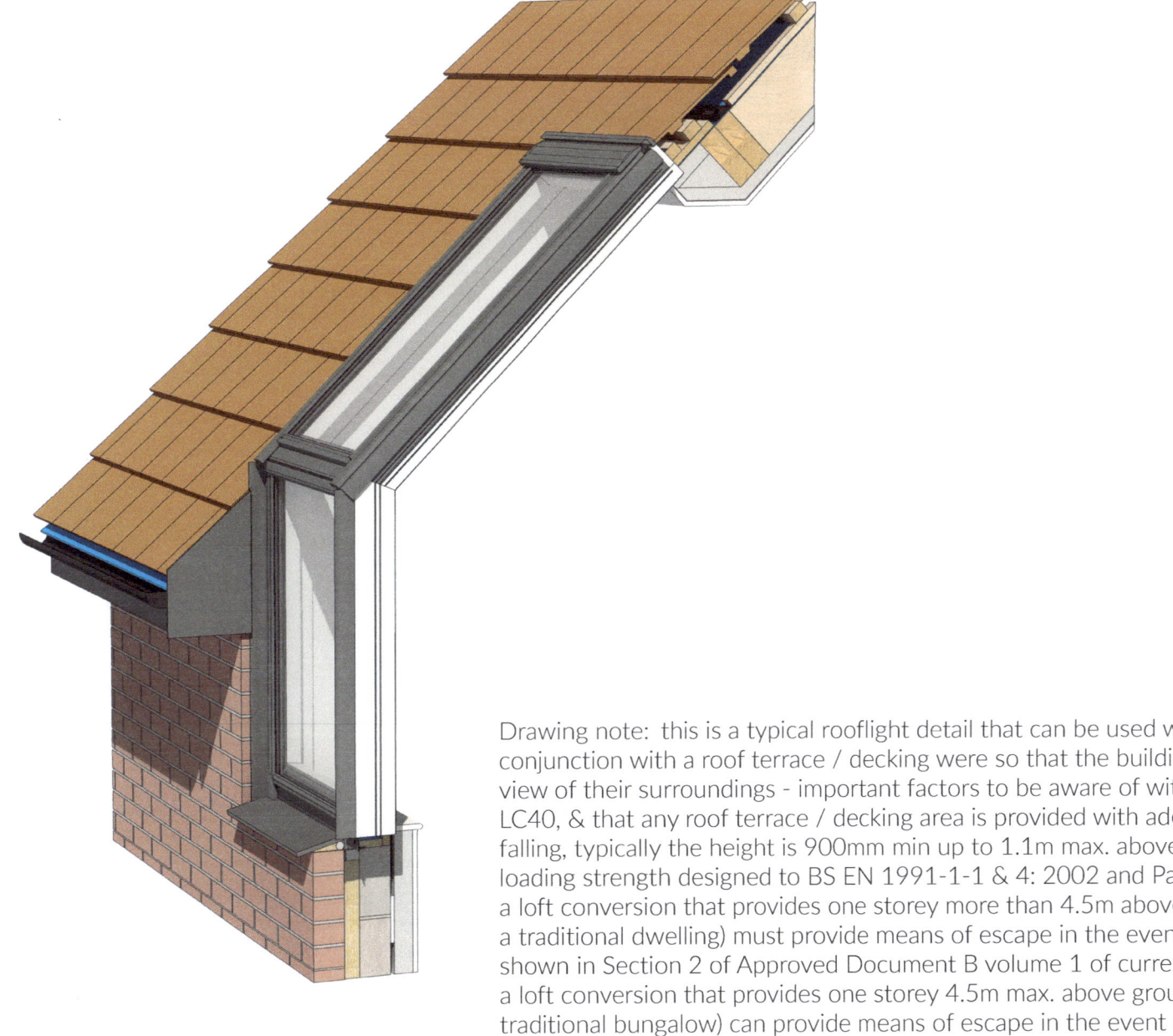

Drawing note: this is a typical rooflight detail that can be used with a vertical window (as shown) or in conjunction with a roof terrace / decking were so that the building occupants can enjoy a panoramic view of their surroundings - important factors to be aware of with this detail are as drawing number LC40, & that any roof terrace / decking area is provided with adequate balustrading to protect from falling, typically the height is 900mm min up to 1.1m max. above finished floor / deck level, with a loading strength designed to BS EN 1991-1-1 & 4: 2002 and Part B of the current Building Regulations.
a loft conversion that provides one storey more than 4.5m above ground level (typically a 3rd storey in a traditional dwelling) must provide means of escape in the event of a fire by a protected stairway as shown in Section 2 of Approved Document B volume 1 of current Building Regulations.
a loft conversion that provides one storey 4.5m max. above ground level (typically a 2nd storey in a traditional bungalow) can provide means of escape in the event of a fire by stairs & an emergency escape window or external door, or direct access to a protected stairs as shown in Section 2 of Approved Document B volume 1 of current Building Regulations.

3D Detail LC-41 - Velux vertical eaves window

LC-42
TYPICAL ROOF LIGHT IN PITCHED ROOF

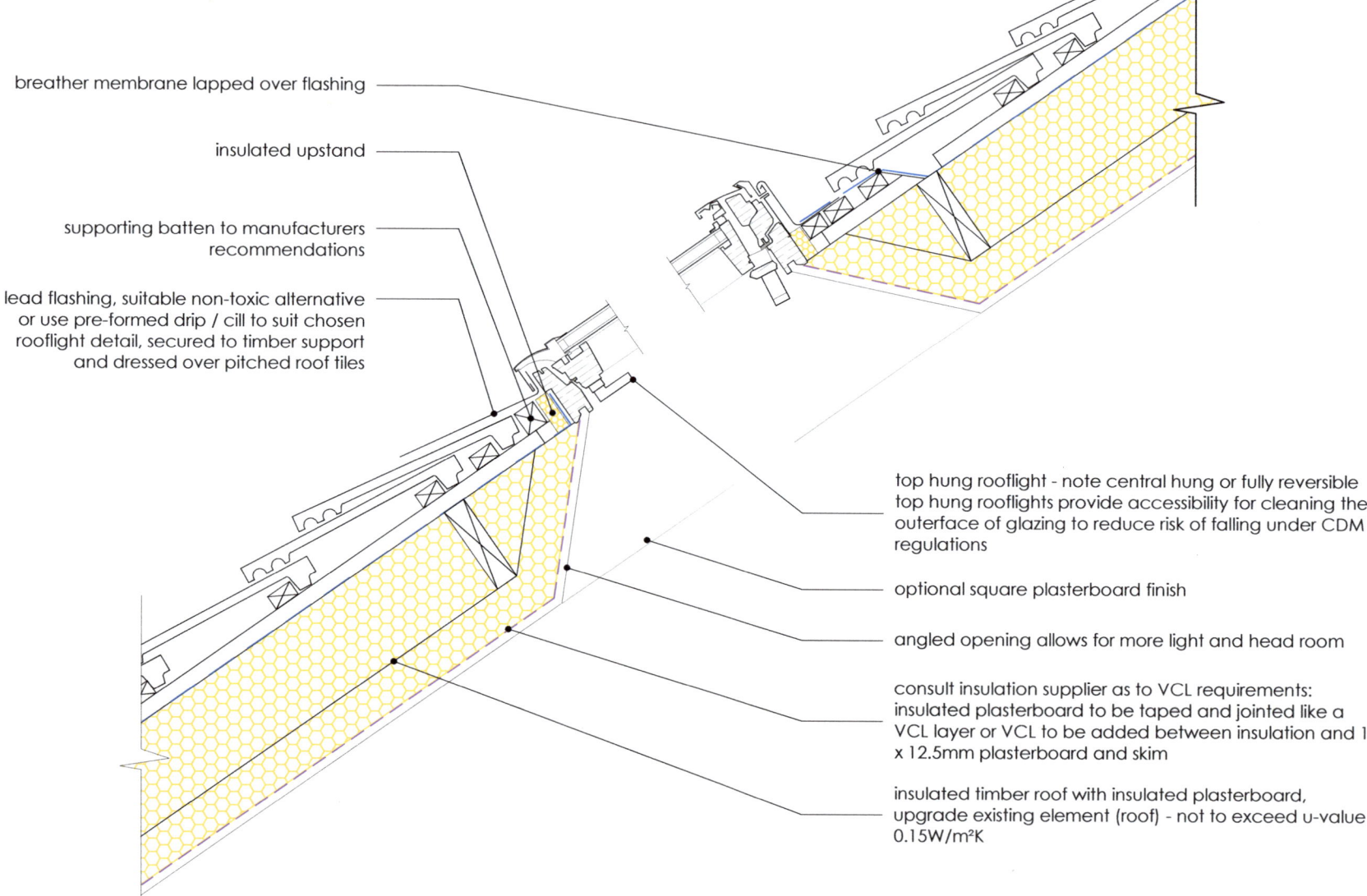

2D Detail LC-42 - Typical roof light in pitched roof

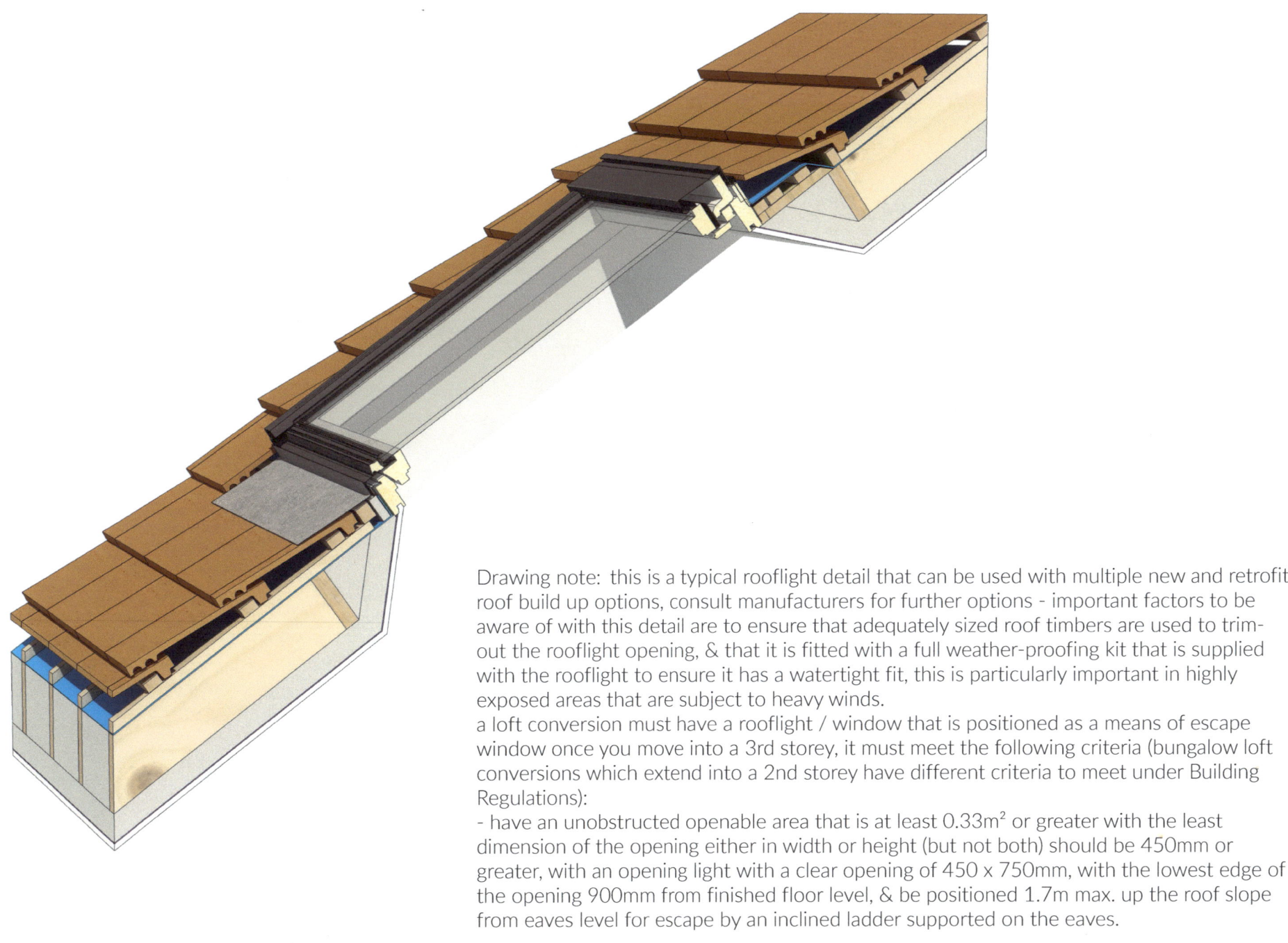

Drawing note: this is a typical rooflight detail that can be used with multiple new and retrofit roof build up options, consult manufacturers for further options - important factors to be aware of with this detail are to ensure that adequately sized roof timbers are used to trim-out the rooflight opening, & that it is fitted with a full weather-proofing kit that is supplied with the rooflight to ensure it has a watertight fit, this is particularly important in highly exposed areas that are subject to heavy winds.

a loft conversion must have a rooflight / window that is positioned as a means of escape window once you move into a 3rd storey, it must meet the following criteria (bungalow loft conversions which extend into a 2nd storey have different criteria to meet under Building Regulations):

- have an unobstructed openable area that is at least $0.33m^2$ or greater with the least dimension of the opening either in width or height (but not both) should be 450mm or greater, with an opening light with a clear opening of 450 x 750mm, with the lowest edge of the opening 900mm from finished floor level, & be positioned 1.7m max. up the roof slope from eaves level for escape by an inclined ladder supported on the eaves.

3D Detail LC-42 - Typical roof light in pitched roof

RESOURCES

BOOKS

Loft Conversion Handbook - by Construction Products Association and RIBA Publishing

Loft Conversion Manual by Ian Alistair Rock

Metric Handbook: Planning and Design Data 6th Edition by Pamela Buxton

Traditional Details: For Building Restoration, Renovation, and Rehabilitation by Charles George Ramsey

WEBSITES

Planning and Regulations

Planning Portal - www.planningportal.co.uk

Planning Portal Interactive Guide - www.interactive.planningportal.co.uk/mini-guide/loft-conversion/0

Planning Portal Volume Calculator - www.planningportal.co.uk/info/200211/volume_calculator

Building Regulations - www.gov.uk/government/collections/approved-documents

Local Authority Building Control - www.labc.co.uk

Many local authorities provide their own guidance to loft conversions - be sure to check out your local authority website for further information.

Other Useful Websites

Party Wall Act Guidance - www.gov.uk/guidance/party-wall-etc-act-1996-guidance

Approved Party Wall Inspectors - www.fpws.org.uk

TRADA Span Tables - www.trada.co.uk/ad-hoc/span-tables/

England Listed Buildings - www.historicengland.org.uk/listing/the-list/

Scotland Listed Buildings - www.historicenvironment.scot/advice-and-support/listing-scheduling-and-designations/listed-buildings/search-for-a-listed-building/

Wales Listed Buildings - www.cadw.gov.wales/advice-support/cof-cymru/search-cadw-records

Northern Ireland Listed Buildings - www.nidirect.gov.uk/articles/finding-listed-building

Measured Survey Guide - www.firstinarchitecture.co.uk/measured-survey-how-to-measure-a-building/

Detail Library - www.detail-library.co.uk

2D Detail Index

2D Detail LC-01 - Underdraw detail / landing trimmer	32
2D Detail LC-02 - Floor detail showing new joists alongside existing	34
2D Detail LC-03 - Floor detail showing support under stud walls	36
2D Detail LC-04 - Eaves detail - cold roof	38
2D Detail LC-05 - Eaves detail - warm roof	40
2D Detail LC-06 - Alternative flush eaves detail - ventilated	42
2D Detail LC-07 - Alternative flush eaves detail - warm roof	44
2D Detail LC-08 - Gable end wall upgrade detail	46
2D Detail LC-09 - Party wall upgrade detail	48
2D Detail LC-10 - Dormer window head detail	52
2D Detail LC-11 - Dormer window cill detail	54
2D Detail LC-12 - Dormer window jamb detail	56
2D Detail LC-13A - Dormer window pitched roof eaves detail with gutter	58
2D Detail LC-13B - Dormer window pitched roof eaves detail with flashing	60
2D Detail LC-13C - Dormer window pitched roof eaves detail with mansard	62
2D Detail LC-14A - Dormer wall sole plate aligned with inside face of ext wall	66
2D Detail LC-14B - Dormer window sole plate with French doors and Juliet balcony	68
2D Detail LC-15 - French door and Juliet balcony plan detail	70
2D Detail LC-16A - Rear dormer wall sole plate 'insert' into existing roof structure	72
2D Detail LC-16B - Rear dormer wall sole plate 'insert' into existing roof structure with window	74
2D Detail LC-17 - Flat roof eaves detail - warm roof	76
2D Detail LC-18 - Dormer - flat roof / ridge abutment	78
2D Detail LC-19 - Dormer - flat roof /edge abutment	80
2D Detail LC-20 - Standing seam zinc dormer detail - window jamb	84
2D Detail LC-21 - Standing seam zinc dormer detail - window head	86
2D Detail LC-22 - Standing seam zinc dormer eaves detail - fall to forward gutter	88
2D Detail LC-23 - Standing seam zinc dormer eaves detail - fall back to existing roof	90
2D Detail LC-24 - Standing seam zinc detail - window cill	92
2D Detail LC-25 - Standing seam zinc base detail - to existing roof	94
2D Detail LC-26 - Standing seam zinc base detail - to existing wall	96
2D Detail LC-27 - Standing seam zinc dormer abutment detail - to party wall	98
2D Detail LC-28 - Forward sloping dormer - ridge abutment to existing roof	100
2D Detail LC-29 - Rear sloping dormer - ridge abutment and valley gutter to existing roof	102

2D Detail LC-30 - Zinc dormer - side junction to existing roof — 104
2D Detail LC-31 - Standing seam angled zinc dormer detail - fixed window jamb — 108
2D Detail LC-32 - Standing seam angled zinc dormer detail - opening window jamb — 110
2D Detail LC-33 - Standing seam angled zinc dormer detail - fixed window head — 112
2D Detail LC-34 - Standing seam angled zinc window detail - to existing roof — 114
2D Detail LC-35 - Standing seam zinc dormer detail - ridge vent — 116
2D Detail LC-36 - Standing seam zinc dormer detail - eaves and connection to existing roof — 118
2D Detail LC-37 - Standing seam zinc dormer cheek to window plan detail - fixed window — 120
2D Detail LC-38 - Standing seam zinc dormer cheek to flush window plan detail - fixed window — 122
2D Detail LC-39A - Standing seam vertical zinc dormer corner detail A — 124
2D Detail LC-39B - Standing seam vertical zinc dormer corner detail B — 126
2D Detail LC-39C - Standing seam vertical zinc dormer corner detail C — 128
2D Detail LC-40 - Velux balcony — 132
2D Detail LC-41 - Velux vertical eaves window — 134
2D Detail LC-42 - Typical roof light in pitched roof — 136

3D Detail Index

3D Detail LC-01 - Underdraw detail / landing trimmer — 33
3D Detail LC-02 - Floor detail showing new joists alongside existing — 35
3D Detail LC-03 - Floor detail showing support under stud walls — 37
3D Detail LC-04 - Eaves detail - cold roof — 39
3D Detail LC-05 - Eaves detail - warm roof — 41
3D Detail LC-06 - Alternative flush eaves detail - ventilated — 43
3D Detail LC-07 - Alternative flush eaves detail - warm roof — 45
3D Detail LC-08 - Gable end wall upgrade detail — 47
3D Detail LC-09 - Party wall upgrade detail — 49
3D Detail LC-10 - Dormer window head detail — 53
3D Detail LC-11 - Dormer window cill detail — 55
3D Detail LC-12 - Dormer window jamb detail — 57
3D Detail LC-13A - Dormer window pitched roof eaves detail with gutter — 59
3D Detail LC-13B - Dormer window pitched roof eaves detail with flashing — 61
3D Detail LC-13C - Dormer window pitched roof eaves detail with mansard — 63
3D Detail LC-14A - Dormer wall sole plate aligned with inside face of ext wall — 67
3D Detail LC-14B - Dormer window sole plate with French doors and Juliet balcony — 69
3D Detail LC-15 - French door and Juliet balcony plan detail — 71
3D Detail LC-16A - Rear dormer wall plate 'insert' into existing roof structure — 73
3D Detail LC-16B - Rear dormer wall plate 'insert' into existing roof structure with window — 75
3D Detail LC-17 - Flat roof eaves detail - warm roof — 77
3D Detail LC-18 - Dormer - flat roof / ridge abutment — 79
3D Detail LC-19 - Dormer - flat roof / edge abutment — 81
3D Detail LC-20 - Standing seam zinc dormer detail - window jamb — 85
3D Detail LC-21 - Standing seam zinc dormer detail - window head — 87
3D Detail LC-22 - Standing seam zinc dormer eaves detail - fall to forward gutter — 89
3D Detail LC-23 - Standing seam zinc dormer eaves detail - fall back to existing roof — 91
3D Detail LC-24 - Standing seam zinc detail - window cill — 93
3D Detail LC-25 - Standing seam zinc base detail - to existing roof — 95
3D Detail LC-26 - Standing seam zinc base detail - to existing wall — 97
3D Detail LC-27 - Standing seam zinc dormer abutment detail - to party wall — 99
3D Detail LC-28 - Forward sloping dormer - ridge abutment to existing roof — 101

3D Detail LC-29 - Rear sloping dormer - ridge abutment and valley gutter to existing roof — 103
3D Detail LC-30 - Zinc dormer - side junction to existing roof — 105
3D Detail LC-31 - Standing seam angled zinc dormer detail - fixed window jamb — 109
3D Detail LC-32 - Standing seam angled zinc dormer detail - opening window jamb — 111
3D Detail LC-33 - Standing seam angled zinc dormer detail - fixed window head — 113
3D Detail LC-34 - Standing seam angled zinc window detail - to existing roof — 115
3D Detail LC-35 - Standing seam zinc dormer detail - ridge vent — 117
3D Detail LC-36 - Standing seam zinc dormer detail - eaves and connection to existing roof — 119
3D Detail LC-37 - Standing seam zinc dormer cheek to window plan detail - fixed window — 121
3D Detail LC-38 - Standing seam zinc dormer cheek to flush window plan detail - fixed window — 123
3D Detail LC-39A - Standing seam vertical zinc dormer corner detail A — 125
3D Detail LC-39B - Standing seam vertical zinc dormer corner detail B — 127
3D Detail LC-39C - Standing seam vertical zinc dormer corner detail C — 129
3D Detail LC-40 - Velux balcony — 133
3D Detail LC-41 - Velux vertical eaves window — 135
3D Detail LC-42 - Typical roof light in pitched roof — 137

www.ingramcontent.com/pod-product-compliance
Lightning Source LLC
Chambersburg PA
CBHW042106090526
44590CB00004B/111